Consolidated Financial
A Step-by-step A

Consolidated Financial Statements: A Step-by-step Approach

Paul Mahony

Published by
Chartered Accountants Ireland
Chartered Accountants House
47–49 Pearse Street
Dublin 2
www.charteredaccountants.ie

ISBN: 978-1-907214-92-9

Typeset by Datapage
Printed by Turners Printing Company

Contents

Preface

The preparation and the presentation of consolidated financial statements have long been a cause of difficulty for students preparing for examinations in accountancy, both those of the accountancy bodies, such as Chartered Accountants Ireland, as well as those studying for third-level qualifications involving financial or corporate reporting.

With 30 years' experience as a lecturer in corporate reporting, I set out to write a step-by-step guide that would remove the mystery from 'consolidation'. I wanted to design a user-friendly text for students and lecturers alike.

This textbook covers:

1. The regulatory, legal and economic requirements for consolidated financial statements.
2. The preparation and presentation of a consolidated statement of financial position (SoFP) incorporating a subsidiary, an associate, a joint venture and a trade (simple) investment and including 'complications', such as intragroup balances, unrealised profits on intragroup transactions and intragroup dividends (IASs 1, 27, 28, 31 and IFRS 3).
3. The preparation and presentation of a consolidated statement of comprehensive income (SoCI) and a consolidated statement of changes in equity (SoCE), again incorporating a subsidiary, an associate, a joint venture and a trade (simple) investment, and including 'complications' (IASs 1, 27, 28, 31 and IFRS 3).
4. IFRS 3 *Business Combinations*, which has as its objective "to improve the relevance, reliability and comparability of the information that a reporting entity provides in its financial statements about a business combination and its effects".
5. The treatment of a foreign operation in consolidated financial statements (IAS 21).
6. The preparation and presentation of a consolidated statement of cash flows (IAS 7).
7. The disposal of a subsidiary or shares in a subsidiary by a parent (IAS 27).

I believe that the approach in this book is unique in that, for every example and question involving the preparation of a consolidated SoFP, workings are presented using both:

- the traditional **T account method** (which is my preferred method); and
- the **columnar method**, which is now used by many lecturers.

As stated in the text, both methods result in identical consolidated statements of financial position.

I have always advised students to study alternative texts as another author's approach and focus can only assist the learning process. In this regard, I can confidently refer you to the relevant chapters of *International Financial Accounting and Reporting* (3rd Edition) by Ciaran Connolly (Chartered Accountants Ireland, 2011).

When you are finished studying ***Consolidated Financial Statements: A Step-by-step Approach***, I am confident that you will be more than adequately prepared to sit your examinations in 'consolidation' and that I will have realised my goal of making the subject more approachable and understandable. 'Consolidation' is my favourite topic and I hope you will feel the same.

(***Note:*** This text adopts the principles and practices of the relevant IAS/IFRS extant at the time of writing.)

Paul Mahony, FCA, FCPA, MBS

Abbreviations

The following abbreviations are used throughout this text in order to help with presentation and clarity:

A Ltd	associate
COC	cost of control
IAS	international accounting standard(s)
IFRS	international financial reporting standard (s)
JV	joint venture
S Ltd	subsidiary/subsidiary company
SoCE	statement of changes in equity
SoCF	statement of cash flows
SoCI	statement of comprehensive income
SoFP	statement of financial position
NCI	non-controlling interests
OCI	other comprehensive income
P Ltd	parent/parent company
TCI	total comprehensive income

Chapter 1

Why Consolidate Financial Statements?

Learning Objectives

After reading this chapter you should be able to:

- explain why companies engage in business combinations;
- identify the legal and regulatory requirements to prepare consolidated financial statements; and
- demonstrate an understanding of the need for consolidated financial statements.

Introduction

Terms such as 'takeovers', 'acquisitions', 'mergers' and 'amalgamations' have traditionally been used to describe situations where two or more businesses come together. The term '**business combinations**' is now the most appropriate term to summarise all the above.

A business combination is deemed to occur where the assets acquired and the liabilities assumed constitute a business. If the assets acquired are not a business, the transaction is deemed to be an asset acquisition (IFRS 3 *Business Combinations*).

Business combinations occur for many reasons such as synergies, economies of scale, taxation advantages, risk diversification, increased efficiencies, elimination of competition, etc., and can be achieved by two common methods:

1. **Acquisition of Net Assets** This is where *all* of the **assets** of the acquired company (entity) are purchased and its **liabilities** assumed, i.e. the net assets are acquired (a national supermarket chain might use this method, for example, to acquire a local franchise in order to increase market share);
2. **Acquisition of Shares** This where the **shares** of the acquired company are purchased.

These two methods are quite different in substance and therefore give rise to **different accounting treatments** (post-acquisition) in the accounts of the acquiring company.

Now, let us take two companies, Apple Ltd and Banana Ltd, to illustrate the alternative approaches to business combinations.

Method 1: Acquisition of Net Assets

Apple Ltd can carry out the acquisition with one of two approaches:

(a) Apple Ltd acquires the net assets of Banana Ltd. Banana Ltd goes out of existence and subsequently the statement of financial position of Apple Ltd contains the combined net assets of both companies.
(b) A new company Banap Ltd could be formed to acquire the net assets of both Apple Ltd and Banana Ltd. In this case, both of the previous companies would be liquidated and the statement of financial position of Banap Ltd would then show the combined net assets.

> ***Key Note***: The significant feature of the above examples is that a group is *not* formed in either case and, therefore, the requirement to prepare consolidated financial statements does *not* arise.

Method 2: Acquisition of Shares

Apple Ltd could acquire the share capital of Banana using one of two approaches:
(a) Apple Ltd could acquire all the issued share capital of Banana Ltd. Apple Ltd would now be a *parent* and Banana Ltd its *subsidiary*. Both companies would continue to exist and would prepare their individual financial statements after the business combination.
(b) A new company Banap Ltd could be formed to acquire all the issued share capital of both Apple Ltd and Banana Ltd. After the acquisition there would be three companies in existence: Banap Ltd would be the parent; and both Apple Ltd and Banana Ltd would be its subsidiaries.

> ***Key Note***: Each of these examples gives rise to the formation of a **group**, as the holding company (parent) now owns all of the share capital of the subsidiary companies. **There is now both a legal and regulatory requirement, as well as an economic need, to prepare consolidated financial statements.**

IFRS 3 *Business Combinations*

IFRS 3 *Business Combinations* defines a **'business'** as "an integrated set of activities and assets that is capable of being conducted and managed for the purpose of providing a return in the form of dividends, lower costs or other economic benefits directly to investors or other owners, members or participants."

A '**business combination**' is defined as "a transaction or other event in which an acquirer obtains control of one or more businesses."

A business consists of inputs, e.g. non-current assets, intellectual property, employees, etc., and processes applied to those inputs, e.g. strategic management processes, operational processes, etc., that have an ability to create outputs that can generally be either sold or exchanged and provide a return. The nature of the elements of a business varies by industry and by the structure of an entity's operations. An established business may have many different types of inputs, processes and outputs, while a new business often has few inputs and processes and only one or two outputs. Though nearly all businesses have liabilities, this need not necessarily be the case.

IFRS 3 (the subject of **Chapter 9**) determines that all business combinations within its scope should be accounted for using the **acquisition method**, which looks at a business combination from the perspective of the acquirer. Fair values are a key aspect of the acquisition method of accounting. The standard also deals with the calculation and treatment of goodwill.

Definition of a 'Group'

IAS 27 defines a **'group'** as "a parent and all its subsidiaries" (IAS 27, paragraph 4).

Requirements to Prepare Consolidated Financial Statements

Both international accounting standards (IFRS/IAS) and Irish/EU company law require the presentation of consolidated financial statements when a group exists. As stated above, a **group** is deemed to exist where a parent company owns one or more subsidiaries.

The International Accounting Standards Framework

IAS 27, *Consolidated and Separate Financial Statements* states the following (at para 9 and 12):

1. a parent entity must present consolidated financial statements in which it consolidates its investments in subsidiaries, *and*
2. consolidated financial statements must include all subsidiaries of the parent.

Note, however, that IAS 27, paragraph 10, permits **exemptions** from this requirement *principally* when:

(a) the parent is itself a wholly-owned subsidiary;
(b) the parent's debt or equity instruments are not traded in a public market;
(c) the parent did not file nor is in the process of filing its financial statements with securities commission or other regulatory organisation for the purpose of issuing any class of instruments in the public market; and
(d) the ultimate or any intermediate of the parent produces consolidated financial statements available for public use that comply with IFRS.

The Legal Framework

In addition to preparing their own accounts, parent undertakings are required to prepare consolidated group accounts and to lay them before their annual general meetings (AGMs) at the same time as their own annual accounts.

In Ireland, the requirement to prepare group accounts is contained in regulation 5 of the European Communities (Companies: Group Accounts) Regulations 1992 (S.I. No. 201 of 1992) (the 'GAR 1992'), which states that:

> "At the end of its financial year a parent undertaking shall prepare group accounts in accordance with these Regulations and such accounts shall be laid before the annual general meeting at the same time as the undertaking's annual accounts are so laid."

Note, however, **exemption** from this requirement is contained in regulation 7 of the GAR 1992 where the parent is a private company and certain financial and size constraints are not exceeded.

The Economic Need to Prepare Consolidated Financial Statements

Even if there were no legal or regulatory requirements to prepare group financial statements, business and economic needs would demand them. In essence, both the international accountancy standards and company law recognise these needs. This is because the financial statements of a parent alone would not give a complete account of the parent's economic activities or financial position as its statement of financial position merely reflects the cost of its investment in the subsidiary. The various users of a parent's financial statements (particularly the shareholders) would require further information about, for example, the:

- financial results for the period in question;
- financial position at the reporting date;
- cash flows for the period; and
- changes in financial position;

of the group as a whole.

Consolidated financial statements provide such information because they contain information about the results and financial position of a group **as if it were a single entity**.

> ***Key Note***: The concept behind the concluding phrase in this chapter, '**as if it were a single entity**', is extremely important, as you will realise when you study **Chapters 3** and **4**.

In this chapter, we have identified the statutory and regulatory requirements for the presentation of consolidated financial statements as well as the economic and business needs for these.

Once an investing company acquires an interest, i.e. makes an investment, in another entity, this will bring about accounting requirements. In the next chapter, we will discuss the different levels of investment that a parent can make and the consequential accounting treatment appropriate to each type of investment.

Summary

- Business combinations can be achieved either by one company acquiring the net assets of another or by acquiring the shares of the acquired entity.
- If a company acquires a controlling interest in the shares of another, a *group* is formed.
- The formation of a group brings accounting responsibilities both under IAS and company law to present consolidated financial statements.
- The requirements to present consolidated financial statements are in essence recognising the economic needs of the shareholders and other stakeholders of the parent to receive information about the parent's investment in a subsidiary or subsidiaries.

Questions

Question 1.1

Describe the ways in which a business combination can be achieved.

Solution

A business combination can be achieved by either:
(a) the investing company acquiring the net assets of another entity; or
(b) the investing company acquiring the shares of another entity.

Question 1.2

When is a group formed?

Solution

A group is formed when a parent acquires a subsidiary or subsidiaries.

Question 1.3

Explain the IAS/IFRS consequences of the formation of a group.

Solution

IAS 27 and Irish company law both require a parent with a subsidiary or subsidiaries to prepare and present consolidated financial statements. All subsidiaries must be consolidated under the requirements of IAS 27.

Question 1.4

Explain the need for consolidated financial statements.

Solution

The need for consolidated financial statements arises from the fact that financial statements of the parent alone would not give an adequate account of its economic activities or financial position. Consolidated financial statements are prepared so as to present the results and financial position of a group as if it were a single entity.

Chapter 2

Accounting for Investments

Learning Objectives

After reading this chapter you should be able to:

- Understand **four** levels of investment that an investing entity can make;
- State the degree of influence that the investor gets over the policies of the investee in each case; and
- Set out the accounting treatment for each type of investment.

Introduction

This chapter will provide you with the first crucial steps on the road to understanding and applying the principles and techniques for the preparation of consolidated financial statements. Indeed, this chapter is a roadmap for the rest of this book.

Beware! When sitting examinations in financial accounting and reporting, you must be able to clearly identify the nature of each investment undertaken by an investing company in order to be able to apply the correct international accounting standard. If you cannot do this, you will lose a significant amount of the marks allocated to the question.

When an investing company decides to purchase an investment in another entity using the acquisition of shares method (see **Chapter 1**), the percentage of share capital acquired is likely to determine:

(a) the level of influence that the investor can exercise over the policies of the investee; and
(b) the accounting treatment which applies to the investment under international accounting standards (IAS/IFRS), in the financial statements of the investor.

Investments in other entities can give rise to influence over the **operating and financial policies** of the investee, ranging from control to limited influence.

The proportion of voting shares purchased in another entity is likely to be the principle determining factor in the amount of influence the investor may have. The 'operating and financial policies' of an entity usually include the following:

- dividend policy (of course, this will be crucial for the investor to control);
- raising of finance;
- strategic direction;
- approval of business plans and budgets;
- approving capital expenditure.

In this chapter, we will examine **four levels of voting shares** recognised by IFRS that an investing company could acquire in another entity and the associated degree of influence acquired in each case.

The size of the holding acquired by an investing company ('P Ltd') in another company is usually the determining factor in the application of IFRS. There are four important types of investment interest:
1. Subsidiary
2. Associate
3. Joint Venture
4. Trade (or Simple) Investment

These are summarised as follows:

1. Subsidiary

Accounting Standards: IAS 27 *Consolidated and Separate Financial Statements*
IFRS 3 *Business Combinations*

Keyword: 'Control'

Definition of a 'Subsidiary'

IAS 27 ***Consolidated and Separate Financial Statements*** defines a subsidiary as "an entity, including an unincorporated entity such as a partnership, that is controlled by another entity (known as the parent)". Control is presumed to exist when the parent owns more than 50% of the voting power of an entity (see **Example 2.1**).

Definition of a 'Control'

'Control' is defined by IAS 27 as "the power to govern the financial and operating policies of an entity so as to **obtain benefits** from its activities". However, under IAS 27, paragraph 13, control may *also* exist where the investing company does not acquire more than 50% of the voting rights of the subsidiary but when there is:
(a) power over more than 50% of the voting rights by virtue of an agreement with other investors (for example, a shareholder owning 45% of the voting rights might have an agreement with another investor owning 8%);
(b) power to govern the financial and operating policies under statute or an agreement;

(c) power to appoint or remove the majority of the members of the board of directors and control of the entity is by that board (see **Example 2.2**); or
(d) power to cast the majority of votes at meetings of the board of directors and control of the entity is by that board.

Examples of Different Types of Subsidiaries

Example 2.1: De Facto Control of Subsidiary
Where 'P Ltd' acquires more than 50% of the Voting Rights of an Entity ('S Ltd')

On 1 July 2010, Park Ltd acquired 240,000 of the ordinary shares of Stop Ltd. At that date Stop Ltd had 300,000 ordinary shares in issue. Park Ltd has acquired an 80% holding.

Park Ltd (the parent), acquires a *subsidiary* (Stop Ltd) because it has acquired more than **50%** of the voting shares. A group has been formed. It is presumed that Park Ltd has **control** over the operating and financial policies of Stop Ltd so as to obtain benefits from its activities. Significantly, this includes control over the dividend policy of Stop Ltd.

Example 2.2: Control of Board of Directors
Where 'P Ltd' acquires 50% of the Voting Rights of an Entity ('S Ltd')

Pepper Ltd acquired **50%** of the ordinary shares of Salt Ltd on 1 March 2011. Salt Ltd has 10 directors, five of whom are appointed by Pepper Ltd, one of whom is always chairman with a casting vote. Pepper Ltd has **control over the board of directors and therefore over the policies of Salt Ltd**. Salt Ltd is a *subsidiary* of Pepper Ltd.

Accounting Treatment for Subsidiaries

A subsidiary is accounted for using **full consolidation** (see **Chapter 3**, "The Consolidated Statement of Financial Position" (SoFP) and **Chapter 7**, "The Statement of Comprehensive Income and the Statement of Changes in Equity" (SoCI/SoCE), where full consolidation is comprehensively demonstrated). Full consolidation is a method of accounting that produces a statement of financial position (SoFP) similar to the SoFP that would be produced if the parent had acquired the net assets of the subsidiary rather than a majority of its voting shares (as discussed as '**Method 1**' in **Chapter 1**).

2. Associate

Accounting Standard: IAS 28 *Investments in Associates*

Keywords: 'Significant Influence'

Definition of Associate

IAS 28 *Investments in Associates* defines an **associate** as an "entity, including an unincorporated entity such as a partnership, over which the investor has **significant influence** and that is neither a subsidiary nor an interest in a joint venture".

Definition of Significant Influence

Significant influence is the "power to participate in the financial and operating policy decisions of the investee but is **not** control or joint control over those policies".

Example 2.3: Acquisition of an Associate
Where 'P Ltd' acquires between 20% and 50% of the voting power of an entity ('A Ltd')

On 1 January 2011 Pear Ltd, who has a subsidiary Sloe Ltd, acquired 80,000 of the 200,000 ordinary shares in issue by Apple Ltd. Pear Ltd has now acquired an *associate* (because it has purchased between 20% and 50% of the voting shares). The leverage is reduced from control in the case of a subsidiary (see **Subsidiary** above) to **significant influence** over an associate, meaning the power **to participate** in the operating and financial policies (including dividend policy) of Apple, but not to control them.

Note: The aquisition of between 20% and 50% of an entity *usually* gives rise to an investment in an associate unless this can this be rebutted, meaning that it can be shown that significant influence does not exist.

Accounting Treatment for Associates

An associate is accounted for in consolidated financial statements using the **equity method** (see **Chapter 5** (SoFP) and **Chapter** 7 (SoCI/SoCE)). Under this method the investment in A Ltd is initially recorded at cost and adjusted thereafter by the post-acquisition change in the investor's share of the net assets of the investee. In simple terms, the *value* of the investment in the associate in the consolidated SoFP is 'topped up' each year by the group's share of the profit of the associate.

3. Joint Venture

ACCOUNTING STANDARD: IAS 31 *Interests in Joint Ventures*

KEYWORDS: 'Joint Control'

Definition of Joint Venture

IAS 31 *Interests in Joint Ventures* defines a **joint venture** as a "contractual arrangement whereby two or more parties undertake an economic activity that is subject to **joint control**" (para 3).

Definition of 'Joint Control'

Joint control is the "contractually agreed sharing of control over an economic activity, and exists only when the strategic financial and operating decisions relating to the activity require the unanimous consent of the parties sharing control (the venturers)" (para 3).

EXAMPLE 2.4: ACQUISITION OF AN INTEREST IN A JOINT VENTURE
Where a Parent (P Ltd') acquires an interest in another entity so that P Ltd and another venturer jointly control that entity

Paint Ltd has two subsidiaries. On 1 March 2011 Paint Ltd and Cement Ltd, companies that are not related, acquire 50% each of the ordinary shares of Grass Ltd and will jointly control its activities as well as sharing equally in dividends and assets in any liquidation.

Accounting Treatment for Joint Ventures

A joint venture (which is an entity) is accounted for in consolidated financial statements using **proportionate consolidation** (see **Chapter 6** (SoFP) **and Chapter** 7 (SoCI/SoCE)), which involves consolidating the group's share of its assets, liabilities, income and expenses. **Equity accounting** (see **Chapter 5**) is also permitted but not encouraged by IAS 31 because proportional consolidation better reflects "the substance and economic reality of a venturer's interest in a jointly controlled entity" (IAS 31, para. 40).

4. Trade (or Simple) Investment

Definition of Trade (or Simple) Investment

A trade (or simple) investment arises where an investor acquires less than 20% of the voting rights of the investee and the investment cannot be deemed to give rise to significant influence.

ACCOUNTING STANDARD: IAS 39 *Financial Instruments Recognition and Measurement*[1]
IFRS 9 *Financial Instruments*

KEYWORDS: 'Little or No Influence'

EXAMPLE 2.5: ACQUISITION OF A TRADE INVESTMENT
Where P Ltd acquires less than 20% of the shares of an entity

On 1 May 2011 Pot Ltd, which has two subsidiaries, acquired 15% of the ordinary shares of Kettle Ltd as part of its investment strategy.

This is termed a *trade* (or *simple*) investment, which probably gives Pot Ltd **little or no influence** over the operating and financial policies of the investee Kettle Ltd.

Accounting Treatment for Trade Investments

The investment is recorded at **fair value**. Such an investment is the subject of IAS 39/ IFRS 9, details of which are outside the scope of this text. However, it is important to note that the investment is carried to the consolidated SoFP and any dividends received/ receivable will be credited to the consolidated statement of comprehensive income (SoCI).

Conclusion

The contents of this chapter will enable you to differentiate between:
1. investments in subsidiaries
2. investments in associates
3. investments in joint ventures; and
4. trade investments.

You should now be able to relate each type of investment to the appropriate international accounting standard and the correct accounting treatment. **Chapters 3 to 8** will now comprehensively explain how to consolidate a group which consists of a parent, a subsidiary, an associate and a joint venture, as well as how to account for a trade investment.

Recommended Reading

The author advises students to read alternative texts, as the opinions and methods of others can only help to develop a greater understanding of all topics. To this end and in

[1] See Chapter 25, "Financial Instruments" of *International Financial Accounting and Reporting* by Ciaran Connolly (3rd Edition, Chartered Accountants Ireland, 2011) ('***Connolly***').

the context of this chapter, it is recommended that you also read Chapter 26, "Business Combinations and Consolidated Financial Statements", of *International Financial Accounting and Reporting* (3rd Edition) by Ciaran Connolly.

Summary

A parent acquires:

1. A **subsidiary**, if the parent purchases a majority of the voting shares of the investee or gains control. The parent can **control** the operating and financial policies of the subsidiary. **Full consolidation** is the required accounting treatment for a subsidiary in consolidated financial statements.
2. An **associate**, if between 20% and 50% of the voting shares are purchased. In this case, the parent can exercise **significant influence** (unless rebutted) over the policies of the investee and the investment is accounted for in consolidated financial statements using the **equity method**.
3. A **joint venture**, if the investor and another entity outside the group jointly own and **jointly control** another entity. Jointly controlled entities are accounted for using **proportionate consolidation.**
4. A **trade** or **simple investment**, if less than 20% of the voting shares of the investee are purchased (unless significant influence can be proven). The investment is accounted for under IAS 39/IFRS 9. The parent accounts for dividends received/receivable from the investee.

Questions

Question 2.1

The following is the summarised statement of financial position of Red Ltd as at 31 August 2011:

	€000
Sundry net assets	5,700
Ordinary share capital (€1)	2,000
Share premium	1,000
Retained earnings	2,700
	5,700

Requirement:

1. Explain the relationship between Black Ltd and Red Ltd in each of the following cases:
   (a) Black Ltd acquires 800,000 of the ordinary shares of Red Ltd.
   (b) Black Ltd acquires 1,500,000 of the ordinary shares of Red Ltd.

(c) Black Ltd acquires 200,000 of the ordinary shares of Red Ltd.
(d) Black Ltd and Cloud Ltd each acquire 1,000,000 of the ordinary shares of Red Ltd and will exercise joint control over its affairs.

2. Give both:
   (a) The level of influence which Black Ltd can exercise over the policies of Red Ltd as a consequence of each of the four investments in question 1; and
   (b) The accounting treatment for each investment.

Solution

1. (a) Black Ltd acquired a 40% holding in the ordinary shares of Red Ltd (800,000/2,000,000), therefore, Red Ltd is an associate of Black Ltd.
   (b) Black Ltd acquired 1,500,000/2,000,000 or 75% of the voting shares of Red Ltd. Red Ltd would be a subsidiary of Black Ltd.
   (c) This investment would be regarded as a simple or trade investment as Black Ltd acquired 10% of the ordinary shares of Red Ltd.
   (d) Red Ltd would be a joint venture of Black Ltd and Cloud Ltd.
2. (a)
   (i) Black Ltd would be able to exercise **significant influence** over the policies of Red Ltd.
   (ii) Black Ltd could **contro**l the policies of Red Ltd.
   (iii) Black Ltd would have **little or no influence** over the policies of Red Ltd.
   (iv) Black Ltd and Cloud Ltd could exercise **joint control** over the policies of Red Ltd.

   (b)
   (i) Equity accounting.
   (ii) Full consolidation.
   (iii) Account for the investment under IAS 39 and dividends received/receivable.
   (iv) Proportionate consolidation.

Chapter 3

The Consolidated Statement of Financial Position: Accounting for Subsidiaries

Learning Objectives

After reading this chapter you should be able to:

- Understand how a wholly-owned subsidiary is accounted for in the consolidated SoFP;
- Explain the concept of **non-controlling interests** and their effect on the consolidated SoFP;
- Describe a methodology for the preparation of a consolidated SoFP;
- Demonstrate an understanding of the consolidation procedures; and
- Complete questions which support the above theory and practice.

Introduction

In order to understand consolidated financial statements, it is generally considered to be more beneficial to first study the preparation of a consolidated statement of financial position (SoFP), as the application of double entry facilitates the understanding of the processes and adjustments involved.

This chapter outlines the preparation of a **basic** consolidated statement of financial position (formerly known as a consolidated balance sheet) of a parent and subsidiary. Associates, joint ventures and trade investments will be examined in **Chapters 5** and **6**.

Both a parent and its subsidiary prepare their own individual financial statements, i.e. each entity prepares a separate set of accounts reflecting the activity of that entity for a defined period (usually a year) and its SoFP at a specified date. As stated in **Chapter 1**, the requirements to prepare consolidated financial statements are specified by both international accounting standards and company law. The directors of the parent are responsible for the preparation of these consolidated financial statements. Group companies must use uniform accounting policies for reporting like transactions and other events in similar circumstances. For example, valuation of inventories at the lower of cost and net realisable value (IAS 2 *Inventories*).[1] All group entities should prepare their own financial statements to the same reporting date. However, when the end of the reporting period

[1] See Chapter 11, "Inventories", of *International Financial Accounting and Reporting* by Ciaran Connolly (3rd Edition, Chartered Accountants Ireland, 2011) ('***Connolly***').

of the parent is different from that of a subsidiary, the subsidiary must prepare additional financial statements as of the same date as the financial statement of the parent, unless it is impracticable to do so (IAS 27, para 22).

The Cornerstone of Full Consolidation

Where a parent entity has an investment in the share capital of a subsidiary, the non-current asset section of the financial statements of the parent will include an asset termed 'Investment in S Ltd'. However, this will not give the users of those financial statements information about the assets and liabilities of that subsidiary and how they contribute to the net asset of the group as a whole. Consolidated financial statements, on the other hand, present information about a group **as if it were a single entity**. In the consolidated statement of financial position, the investment in S Ltd is replaced by its assets and liabilities. This is the cornerstone of full consolidation, and it bears repeating:

> ***Key Note:*** When accounting for a subsidiary (S Ltd) in the consolidated SoFP, the investment in S Ltd is **replaced** by **all** its assets and liabilities (net assets). See **Examples 3.1** and **3.2** below.

Goodwill

In consolidated financial statements, goodwill can be derived from two sources:

1. Goodwill attributable to the parent
   This arises where the cost of the investment in a subsidiary exceeds the group's share of the net assets (capital and reserves) at the date of acquisition. If the reverse applies, there is a gain from a bargain purchase. Only this element of goodwill is dealt with in **Chapters 3–8** inclusive and in the accompanying examples and questions.
2. Goodwill attributable to the non-controlling interests
   This element of goodwill has recently been introduced by IFRS 3 *Business Combinations*. It will be explained in **Chapter 9** with relevant examples and will be tested in some questions from Chapter 9 onwards

In accounting terms, goodwill attributable to a parent is the excess of what a parent pays for its investment in a subsidiary over what it gets for that investment, i.e. the acquirer's share of the fair value of the share capital and reserves (*net assets*) acquired at the **acquisition date**. Goodwill is recorded as an intangible non-current asset in the consolidated SoFP and only written down when its value becomes impaired.[2]

Where the amount paid for the investment is *less* than the acquirer's share of the value of the share capital and reserves purchased at the acquisition date, this is classified by IFRS 3 as a '**a gain from a bargain purchase**', which must be recognised in profit or loss in the consolidated statement of comprehensive income (SoCI).

[2] See ***Connolly***, Chapter 10, "Impairment".

This chapter shows you how to calculate both goodwill and a gain from a bargain purchase, and how to treat these items in the consolidated workings. In **Chapter 9** we will deal with the more complex aspects of goodwill, with which it is expected you will be more comfortable once you have become familiar with the basics of preparing consolidated financial statements.

Calculation of Goodwill (Attributable to a Parent)

The cost of control account comprises:

1. the debit entry for the cost of the investment in S Ltd (what the parent paid);
2. credit entries for the group share of the share capital and reserves of S Ltd at the date of acquisition (what the parent got for its investment).

> ***Key Note***: This, in pro-forma, is a blueprint for **every** calculation of goodwill attributable to P Ltd (or gain from a bargain purchase) in a subsidiary.

PRO-FORMA: COST OF CONTROL

Cost of Control

Debit	**Credit**
Investment in S Ltd	Group's share of share capital of S Ltd and each reserve at the date of acquisition.

Note: S Ltd may have a number of different reserves at acquisition date, e.g. share premium, revaluation reserve, retained earnings, etc. As stated, cost of control is credited with the group's share of **each reserve at the date of acquisition**.

Introducing Full Consolidation, including Goodwill

Preparing a Consolidated SoFP – The T Account Method

Using the T account method, the following steps are common to every consolidated SoFP preparation:

1. Calculate the group structure, which is always based on the number of shares acquired.
2. Open a T account for each heading in the statements of financial position of P Ltd and S Ltd and enter the balances.
3. Open a cost of control account. An account for non-controlling interests (NCI) will also be used in cases where the parent has not acquired a 100% interest in the subsidiary.
4. Apportion the share capital and each reserve of S Ltd using the group structure.
5. Close all T accounts and extract the consolidated SoFP.

Author's Note: Though I prefer the T account method when preparing a consolidated statement of financial position, other methodologies are also used. Consequently, each consolidated SoFP example and question will be followed by a solution using both the T accounts method and also the 'columnar' method, which is also frequently employed. It must be stressed that all methods should produce an **identical** consolidated SoFP.

The following example incorporates full consolidation, which involves replacing the investment in S Ltd by all of its assets and liabilities in the consolidated SoFP and calculating and treating goodwill.

Example 3.1: Consolidating a Wholly-owned Subsidiary

P Ltd and S Ltd
Statements of Financial Position
as at 30 June 2011

	P Ltd €000	**S Ltd €000**
Assets		
Non-current assets:		
Property, plant and equipment	2,800	1,900
Investment in S Ltd	1,300	---
Current assets	850	460
Total assets	**4,950**	**2,360**
Equity and liabilities		
Equity		
Ordinary share capital (€1)	1,000	400
Retained earnings	2,600	1,200
Total equity	3,600	1,600
Non-current liabilities	900	500
Current liabilities	450	260
Total equity and liabilities	**4,950**	**2,360**

Note: P Ltd acquired 400,000 ordinary shares in S Ltd on 1 January 2010 when the retained earnings of S Ltd were €800,000.

Solution Guidelines

1. The key date for the cost of control is the date of acquisition, i.e. 1 January 2010.
2. Share capital plus reserves of a company are represented by net assets – the terms are interchangeable.
3. Only the post-acquisition profits of S Ltd are consolidated with the profits of P Ltd. The group's share of pre-acquisition profits of S Ltd are capitalised or frozen at the date of acquisition.
4. Group structure:
   Group $\frac{400{,}000}{400{,}000} = 100\%$
5. All assets and liabilities of S Ltd are consolidated.

Solution

Workings (T account method)

Property, Plant and Equipment

Debit		**Credit**	
P	2,800		
S	1,900	SoFP	4,700
	4,700		4,700

Investment in S

Debit		**Credit**	
P	1,300	Cost of control	1,300

Current Assets

Debit		**Credit**	
P	850		
S	460	SoFP	1,310
	1,310		1,310

Ordinary Shares

Debit		**Credit**	
Cost of control (100% × 400)	400	P	1,000
SoFP	1,000	S	400
	1,400		1,400

Retained Earnings

Debit		**Credit**	
Cost of control (100% × 800)	800	P	2,600
SoFP	3,000	S	1,200
	3,800		3,800

***Note*:** The consolidated retained earnings, i.e. €3,000 can be defined as the retained earnings of P Ltd at the reporting date **plus** the group's share of the **post-acquisition** retained earnings of S Ltd.

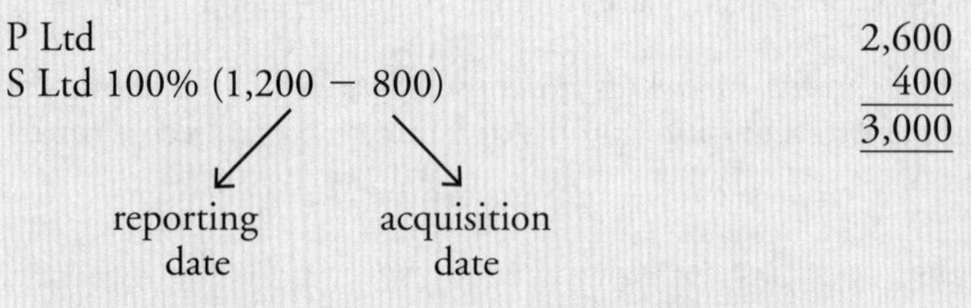

Non-Current Liabilities

Debit		**Credit**	
		P	900
SoFP	1,400	S	500
	1,400		1,400

Current Liabilities

Debit		**Credit**	
		P	450
SoFP	710	S	260
	710		710

Cost of Control

Debit		**Credit**	
Investment in S Ltd	1,300	Ordinary shares S Ltd	400
		Retained earnings S Ltd	800
		SoFP – goodwill	100
	1,300		1,300

WORKINGS (Columnar Method)

	P Ltd €000	**S Ltd €000**	**Adjustment €000**	**Consol. SoFP €000**
Property, Plant & Equipment	2,800	1,900	0	4,700
Investment in S Ltd	1,300	0	(1,300)	0
Goodwill (W1)	0	0	100	100
Current assets	850	460	0	1,310
	4,950	2,360	(1,200)	6,110
Ordinary shares	1,000	400	(400)	1,000
Retained earnings (W2)	2,600	1,200	(800)	3,000

Non-current liabilities	900	500	0	1,400
Current liabilities	450	260	0	710
	4,950	2,360	(1,200)	6,110

(W1) Goodwill

Cost of investment		1,300
S Ltd at Acquisition date:		
Share capital	400	
Retained earnings	800	
	1,200	
Group's share 100%		1,200
Goodwill		100

(W2) Retained earnings

P Ltd at reporting date		2,600
S Ltd at reporting date	1,200	
At acquisition date	800	
Post-acquisition × 100%	400	400
		3,000

Consolidated Statement of Financial Position
as at 30 June 2011

Assets	**€000**
Non-current assets	
Property, plant and equipment	4,700
Goodwill	100
Current assets	1,310
Total assets	**6,110**
Equity and liabilities	
Equity	
Ordinary share capital	1,000
Retained earnings	3,000
Total equity	4,000
Non-current liabilities	1,400
Current liabilities	710
Total equity and liabilities	**6,110**

Introducing Non-controlling Interests

Where a parent does not acquire 100% of the equity shares of a subsidiary, **non-controlling interests (NCI)** arise. These are the balance of the shares in the subsidiary (S Ltd) owned by shareholders outside the group.

Definition of Non-controlling Interests

'Non-controlling interests' is "the equity in a subsidiary not attributable, directly or indirectly, to a parent" (IAS 27 *Consolidated and Separate Financial Statements*, para 4).

Accounting for Non-controlling Interests

The consolidated SoFP should show separately the aggregate of share capital and each reserve of S Ltd attributable to NCI at the **reporting period end**. This represents the aggregate share of the net assets of S Ltd at that date. This amount should be presented within 'equity', separately from the parent shareholders' equity, in the statement of financial position as follows:

PRO-FORMA: CONSOLIDATED SOFP (EXTRACT) INCLUDING NON-CONTROLLING INTERESTS

CONSOLIDATED STATEMENT OF FINANCIAL POSITION
as at 31 May 2011

	31 May 2011	31 May 2010
Equity	**€**	**€**
Share capital	X	X
Share premium	X	X
Retained earnings	X	X
Total shareholders' equity	X	X
Non-controlling interests (NCI)	X	X
Total equity	X	X

The non-controlling interest is calculated using a T account as follows:

PRO-FORMA: NON-CONTROLLING INTEREST ACCOUNT

Non-Controlling Interest

Debit	**Credit**
Consolidated SoFP	NCI % of share capital of S Ltd and each reserve at the reporting date

Note: does not contain any element of goodwill.

The treatment of non-controlling interests (NCI) is outlined in **Example 3.2**, which also involves full consolidation and goodwill.

Example 3.2: Consolidating a Subsidiary with Non-controlling Interests

Preparation of a Consolidated SoFP where P Ltd owns less than 100% of the voting shares of S Ltd

Statements of financial position
as at 30 June 2011

	Pompey Ltd €000	Saints Ltd €000
Assets		
Non-current assets		
Property, plant and equipment	8,500	4,300
Investment in S Ltd	2,450	–
Current assets	2,700	1,400
Total assets	**13,650**	**5,700**
Equity and liabilities		
Equity		
Ordinary share capital (€1)	5,000	2,000
Retained earnings	4,950	1,900
Total equity	9,950	3,900
Non-current liabilities	1,800	700
Current liabilities	1,900	1,100
Total equity and liabilities	**13,650**	**5,700**

Pompey Ltd acquired 1,500,000 shares in Saints Ltd on 1 November 2009 when the retained earnings of S Ltd were €1,200,000.

Solution

Group Structure

Group 1,500,000/2,000,000	=	75%
Non-controlling Interest (NCI)	=	25%

Note: The group structure is always based on the number of shares acquired.

Solution Guidelines

1. Although the group owns only 75% of Saints Ltd in this case, **all** the assets and liabilities of Saints Ltd are still consolidated with those of Pompey Ltd.
2. Non-controlling interests are credited with their share of the share capital and reserves (net assets) of Saints Ltd **at the reporting date**.

3. In the consolidated SoFP, the non-controlling interest figure is shown under equity but *after* the shareholder's equity. Non-controlling interest is not a liability of a group because it does not constitute a liability under IAS 37 *Provisions, Contingent Liabilities and Contingent Assets,* as there is not a present obligation arising from past events, the settlement of which would result in an outflow of economic benefits.[3]

WORKINGS (T account Method)

Property, Plant and Equipment

Debit		**Credit**	
P	8,500		
S	4,300	SoFP	12,800
	12,800		12,800

Investment in S Ltd

Debit		**Credit**	
P	2,450	Cost of control	2,450

Current Assets

Debit		**Credit**	
P	2,700		
S	1,400	SoFP	4,100
	4,100		4,100

Ordinary Shares

Debit		**Credit**	
Cost of control (75% × 2,000)	1,500	P	5,000
		S	2,000
NCI (25% × 2,000)	500		
SoFP	5,000		–
	7,000		7,000

Note: The ordinary share capital of Saints Ltd is apportioned 75% : 25% and transferred to cost of control and non-controlling interests respectively. The ordinary share capital of the group is Pompey Ltd's share capital.

[3] See ***Connolly***, Chapter 14, "Provisions, Contingent Liabilities and Contingent Assets".

Retained Earnings

Debit		**Credit**	
Cost of control	900	P	4,950
(75% × 1,200) (*see note*)		S	1,900
NCI (25% × 1,900) (*see note*)	475		
SoFP	5,475		
	6,850		6,850

Note: The group's share (75%) of the retained earnings of Saints Ltd at the **date of acquisition** (€1,200) is transferred to cost of control. The NCI's share (25%) of the retained earnings of Saints Ltd at the **reporting date** (€1,900) is transferred to their account.

Non-Current Liabilities

Debit		**Credit**	
		P	1,800
SoFP	2,500	S	700
	2,500		2,500

Current Liabilities

Debit		**Credit**	
		P	1,900
SoFP	3,000	S	1,100
	3,000		3,000

Cost of Control

Debit		**Credit**	
		Ordinary shares S	1,500
Investment in S	2,450	Retained earnings S	900
		SoFP: Goodwill	50
	2,450		2,450

Non-Controlling Interests

Debit		**Credit**	
		Ordinary shares S	500
SoFP	975	Retained earnings S	475
	975		975

Workings (Columnar Method)

	Pompey	**Saints**	**Adjustment**	**Consol. SoFP**
	€000	**€000**	**€000**	**€000**
Property, plant & equipment	8,500	4,300	0	12,800
Investment in S Ltd	2,450	0	(2,450)	0
Goodwill (*W1*)	0	0	50	50
Current assets	2,700	1,400	0	4,100
	13,650	**5,700**	**(2,400)**	**16,950**
Ordinary share capital	5,000	2,000	(2,000)	5,000
Retained earnings (*W2*)	4,950	1,900	(1,375)	5,475
Non-controlling interests (*W3*)	0	0	975	975
Non-current liabilities	1,800	700	0	2,500
Current liabilities	1,900	1,100	0	3,000
	13,650	**5,700**	**(2,400)**	**16,950**

(W1) Goodwill	**€000**	**€000**
Cost of investment		2,450
S at date of acquisition:		
Ordinary share capital	2,000	
Retained earnings	1,200	
	3,200	
Group's share = 75%		2,400
Goodwill		50

(W2) Retained earnings		
P at reporting date		4,950
S:		
At reporting date	1,900	
At acquisition date	1,200	
Post-acquisition	700	
Group's share: 75%		525
		5,475

(W3) Non-controlling interests		
S at reporting date:		
Ordinary share capital	2,000	
Retained earnings	1,900	
	3,900	
NCI share: 25%		975

P Limited
CONSOLIDATED STATEMENT OF FINANCIAL POSITION
as at 30 June 2011

Assets	**€000**
Non-current assets	
Property, plant and equipment	12,800
Goodwill	50
Current assets	4,100
Total assets	**16,950**
Equity and liabilities	
Equity	
Ordinary share capital	5,000
Retained earnings	5,475
Total shareholders' equity	10,475
Non-controlling interests	975
Total equity	11,450
Non-current liabilities	2,500
Current liabilities	3,000
Total equity and liabilities	**16,950**

SUMMARY

1. All the assets and liabilities of a subsidiary are consolidated with those of the parent. This applies whether the parent acquires 100%, 90%, 70%, etc., of the voting shares of a subsidiary.
2. Goodwill (attributable to a parent) is calculated by comparing the cost of the investment in S Ltd with the group's share of the share capital and each reserve (as represented by net assets) of S Ltd at the **date of acquisition**. If the cost of the investment is greater, the goodwill should be treated as an intangible asset in the consolidated SoFP and only written down if its value becomes impaired. If the cost of the investment is less, a gain from a bargain purchase arises. This gain should be taken immediately to the consolidated statement of comprehensive income (SoCI).

3. When a parent acquires less than 100% of the voting shares of a subsidiary, the balance of the shares are owned by the **non-controlling interests (NCI)**.
4. The consolidated SoFP should disclose under equity the non-controlling interests in the share capital of S Ltd and each reserve (net assests) at **the reporting date**.
5. Consolidated retained earnings can be defined as the retained earnings of P Ltd at the reporting date plus the group's share of the **post-acquisition** retained earnings of S Ltd at the same date.

IFRS 5 Discontinued Operations

When a subsidiary is acquired with the intention of resale, it gets special treatment in the **consolidated SoFP**. The subsidiary is consolidated in the normal way in the workings. However, in the consolidated SoFP its total assets and liabilities are shown separately as follows:

Assets held for sale	€000
Liabilities held for sale	€000
And in the SoCI:	
Profit/loss on discontinued operation	€000

See below **Appendix 1**, Question D.

Conclusion

You should now be in a position to prepare a consolidated SoFP involving calculating non-controlling interests and goodwill, and present the SoFP in a form suitable for publication in accordance with IAS 1 *Presentation of Financial Statements.*[4]

Recommended Reading

As previously stated, you are encouraged to read alternative texts, as the opinions and methods of others can only help to develop a greater understanding of all topics. To this end and in the context of this chapter, it is recommended that you also read Chapter 26, "Business Combinations and Consolidated Financial Statements", of *International Financial Accounting and Reporting* (3rd Edition) by Ciaran Connolly.

[4] See also ***Connolly***, Chapter 2 "Presentation of Financial Statements".

Questions

Question 3.1

Explain the difference between goodwill (attributable to a parent) and a gain from a bargain purchase.

Solution

Goodwill arises when the cost of an investment in a subsidiary exceeds the group's share of the share capital and reserves of the subsidiary at the **date of acquisition**. A gain from a bargain purchase arises when the investment cost is less than the group's share of the share capital and reserves of the subsidiary at acquisition date. Share capital and reserves are represented by net assets.

Question 3.2

What are the components of the following figures in the consolidated statement of financial position?
(a) retained earnings
(b) non-controlling interests.

Solution

(a) Consolidated retained earnings comprise the retained earnings of the parent at the **reporting date** plus the group's share of the post-acquisition retained earnings of the subsidiary to that date.
(b) Non-controlling interests comprise their share of the share capital and each reserve of the subsidiary at the **reporting date**.

Question 3.3

The following are the summarised statements of financial position of Red Ltd and Blue Ltd at 30 June 2011:

	Red Ltd	Blue Ltd
	€000	€000
Sundry net assets	8,400	5,700
Investment in Blue Ltd	3,680	–
	12,080	5,700
Ordinary share capital	5,000	3,000
Retained earnings	7,080	2,700
	12,080	5,700

Red Ltd acquired 2,400,000 ordinary shares in Blue Ltd on 1 December 2009 when the retained earnings of Blue Ltd were €1,500,000.

Requirement Calculate the following, which would appear in the consolidated statement of financial position of the Red Ltd group as at 30 June 2011:
(a) Goodwill
(b) Retained earnings
(c) Non-controlling interests.

Solution to Question 3.3

Cost of Control

Debit		**Credit**	
Investment in Blue Ltd	3,680	Ordinary shares Blue Ltd	2,400
		Retained earnings Blue Ltd	1,200
		Goodwill	80
	3,680		3,680

Retained Earnings

Debit		**Credit**	
Cost of control	1,200	Red	7,080
(80% × 1,500)		Blue	2,700
NCI (20% × 2,700)	540		
SoFP	8,040		
–	9,780		9,780

Non-controlling Interests

Debit		**Credit**	
		Ordinary shares Blue	600
SoFP	1,140	Retained earnings Blue	540
	1,140		1,140

> ***Note*:** The following questions, **Questions 3.4** and **3.5**, are longer, review-type questions, which underpin the content of **Chapter 3** and involve dealing with more than one reserve in the SoFP of the subsidiary. Each solution contains:
> 1. The T account method workings
> 2. The columnar method workings; and
> 3. The consolidated SoFP

Question 3.4

The following are the statements of financial position of Black Ltd and White Ltd as at 31 July 2011:

	Black Ltd €000	White Ltd €000
Assets		
Non-current assets		
Property, plant and equipment	7,600	3,040
Investment in White Ltd	1,280	
Current assets	2,280	920
Total assets	**11,160**	**3,960**
Equity and liabilities		
Equity		
Ordinary share capital	4,000	1,000
Share premium	1,000	200
Retained earnings	3,620	1,630
Total equity	8,620	2,830
Non-current liabilities	1,300	500
Current liabilities	1,240	630
Total equity and liabilities	**11,160**	**3,960**

Black Ltd acquired 600,000 ordinary shares in White Ltd on 1 November 2009 when White Ltd had the following reserves:

	€000
Share premium	200
Retained earnings	800

Requirement Prepare the consolidated statement of financial position of the Black Ltd group as at 31 July 2011.

Solution to Question 3.4

Group structure:

Group	600,000/1,000,000	=	60%
Non-controlling Interest (NCI)		=	40%

Workings (T account Method)

Property, Plant and Equipment

Debit		**Credit**	
Black	7,600		
White	3,040	SoFP	10,640
	10,640		10,640

Investment in White Ltd

Debit		Credit	
Black	1,280	Cost of control	1,280

Current Assets

Debit		Credit	
Black	2,280		
White	920	SoFP	3,200
	3,200		3,200

Ordinary Shares

Debit		Credit	
Cost of control (60%)	600		
NCI (40%)	400	Black	4,000
SoFP	4,000	White	1,000
	5,000		5,000

Share Premium

Debit		Credit	
Cost of control (60% × 200)	120	Black	1,000
NCI (40% × 200)	80		
SoFP	1,000	White	200
	1,200		1,200

Retained Earnings

Debit		Credit	
Cost of control (60% × 800)	480	Black	3,620
NCI (40% × 1630)	652		
SoFP	4,118	White	1,630
	5,250		5,250

Non-current Liabilities

Debit		Credit	
		Black	1,300
SoFP	1,800	White	500
	1,800		1,800

Current Liabilities

Debit		Credit	
		Black	1,240
SoFP	1,870	White	630
	1,870		1,870

Cost of Control

Debit		Credit	
		Ordinary shares	600
		Share premium	120
Investment in White Ltd	1,280	Retained earnings	480
		Goodwill	80
	1,280		1,280

Non-controlling Interests

Debit		Credit	
		Ordinary shares	400
		Share premium	80
SoFP	1,132	Retained earnings	652
	1,132		1,132

WORKINGS (Columnar Method)

	Black €000	White €000	Adjustment €000	Consol. SoFP €000
Property, plant and equipment	7,600	3,040	0	10,640
Investment in White	1,280	0	(1,280)	0
Goodwill *(W1)*	0	0	80	80
Current assets	2,280	920	0	3,200
Total Assets	**11,160**	**3,960**	**(1,200)**	**13,920**
Ordinary shares	4,000	1,000	(1,000)	4,000
Share premium *(W2)*	1,000	200	(200)	1,000
Retained earnings *(W3)*	3,620	1,630	(1,132)	4,118
Non-controlling interests *(W4)*	0	0	1,132	1,132
Non-current liabilities	1,300	500	0	1,800
Current liabilities	1,240	630	0	1,870
Total equity and liabilities	**11,160**	**3,960**	**(1,200)**	**13,920**

(W1) Goodwill	**€000**	**€000**
Cost of investment		1,280
White Ltd at acquisition date:		
Ordinary shares	1,000	
Share premium	200	
Retained earnings	800	
	2,000	
Group Share: 60%		1,200
SoFP		80

(W2) Share premium	**€000**	**€000**
Black Ltd at reporting date		1,000
White Ltd at reporting date	200	
at acquisition date	200	
Post-acquisition		0
Consolidated SoFP		1,000

(W3) Retained earnings

Black Ltd at reporting date		3,620
White Ltd: At reporting date	1,630	
At acquisition date	(800)	
Post-acquisition	830	
Group Share: 60%		498
SoFP		4,118

(W4) Non-controlling interests

White Ltd at reporting date:		
Ordinary shares	1,000	
Share premium	200	
Retained earnings	1,630	
	2,830	
NCI share: 40%		1,132

Black Ltd
CONSOLIDATED STATEMENT OF FINANCIAL POSITION
as at 31 July 2011

Assets	**€000**
Non-current assets	
Property, plant and equipment	10,640
Goodwill	80
Current Assets	3,200
Total assets	**13,920**
Equity and liabilities	
Equity	
Ordinary share capital	4,000
Share premium	1,000
Retained earnings	4,118
Total shareholders' equity	9,118
Non-controlling interests	1,132
Total equity	10,250
Non-current liabilities	1,800
Current liabilities	1,870
Total equity and liabilities	**13,920**

Question 3.5

Planet Plc acquired 80,000 of the ordinary shares in Sun Ltd at a cost of €160,000 on 1 May 2010. The following are the statements of financial position as at 30 April 2011:

	Planet Plc	Sun Ltd
	€000	€000
Assets		
Non-Current Assets		
Property, plant and equipment	218	140
Investment in Sun Ltd	160	-
	378	140
Current Assets		
Inventories	111	65
Trade receivables	30	15
Cash	19	2
	160	82
Total assets	**538**	**222**
Equity and liabilities		
Equity		
Ordinary shares (€1)	300	100
Share premium	20	10
General reserve	68	15
Retained earnings	50	35
Total equity	438	160
Current liabilities		
Trade payables	50	32
Taxation	50	30
	100	62
Total equity and liabilities	**538**	**222**

The following additional information is available:

At 1 May 2010 the balances on the reserves of Sun Ltd were as follows:

	€000
Share premium	10
General reserve	20
Retained earnings	30

Requirement Prepare a consolidated statement of financial position of Planet Plc and its subsidiary Sun Ltd as at 30 April 2011.

Solution to Question 3.5

Group structure:

Group	80,000/100,000	= 80%
Non-controlling interest (NCI)		= 20%

WORKINGS (T account Method)

Property, Plant and Equipment

Debit		**Credit**	
Planet	218		
Sun	140	SoFP	358
	358		358

Investment in Sun Ltd

Debit		**Credit**	
Planet	160	Cost of Control	160

Inventories

Debit		**Credit**	
Planet	111		
Sun	65	SoFP	176
	176		176

Trade Receivables

Debit		**Credit**	
Planet	30		
Sun	15	SoFP	45
	45		45

Cash

Debit		**Credit**	
Planet	19		
Sun	2	SoFP	21
	21		21

Ordinary Shares

Debit		**Credit**	
Cost of control (80% × 100)	80	Planet	300
NCI (20% of 100)	20	Sun	100
SoFP	300		
	400		400

Share Premium

Debit		Credit	
Cost of control (80% × 10)	8	Planet	20
NCI (20% of 10)	2	Sun	10
SoFP	20		
	30		30

General Reserve

Debit		Credit	
Cost of control (80% × 20)	16	Planet	68
NCI (20% of 15)	3	Sun	15
SoFP	64		
	83		83

Retained Earnings

Debit		Credit	
Cost of control (80% × 30)	24	Planet	50
NCI (20% × 35)	7	Sun	35
SoFP	54		
	85		85

Trade Payables

Debit		Credit	
		Planet	50
SoFP	82	Sun	32
	82		82

Taxation

Debit		Credit	
		Planet	50
SoFP	80	Sun	30
	80		80

Cost of Control

Debit		Credit	
Investment in Sun Ltd	160	Ordinary Shares	80
		Share Premium	8
		General Reserve	16
		Retained Earnings	24
		SoFP – Goodwill	32
	160		160

Non-controlling Interest (NCI)

Debit		**Credit**	
SoFP	32	Ordinary Shares	20
		Share Premium	2
		General Reserve	3
		Retained Earnings	7
	32		32

WORKINGS (Columnar Method)

	Planet Plc. €000	**Sun Ltd €000**	**Adjustment €000**	**Consol. SoFP €000**
Property, plant and equipment	218	140	0	358
Goodwill (*W1*)	0	0	32	32
Investment in Sun Ltd	160	0	(160)	0
Inventories	111	65	0	176
Trade receivables	30	15	0	45
Cash	19	2	0	21
Total assets	**538**	**222**	**(128)**	**632**
Ordinary shares	300	100	(100)	300
Share premium *(W2)*	20	10	(10)	20
General reserve *(W3)*	68	15	(19)	64
Retained earnings *(W4)*	50	35	(31)	54
Non-controlling interests *(W5)*	0	0	32	32
Trade payables	50	32	0	82
Taxation	50	30	0	80
Total equity and liabilities	**538**	**222**	**(128)**	**632**

(W1) Goodwill	**€000**	**€000**
Cost of investment		160
Sun Ltd at acquisition date:		
Ordinary shares	100	
Share premium	10	
General reserve	20	
Retained earnings	30	
	160	
Group Share: 80%		128
Goodwill		32

(W2) Share premium	€000	€000
Planet Ltd at reporting date		20
Sun Ltd at reporting date	10	
At acquisition date	10	
Post-acquisition	nil	
Consolidated SoFP		20

(W3) General reserve

Planet Ltd at reporting date		68
Sun Ltd at reporting date	15	
at acquisition date	(20)	
Post-acquisition	(5)	
Group Share: 80%		(4)
Consolidated SoFP		64

(W4) Retained earnings

Planet Ltd at reporting date		50
Sun Ltd at reporting date	35	
At acquisition date	30	
Post-acquisition	5	
Group Share: 80%		4
Consolidated SoFP		54

(W5) Non-controlling interests

Sun Ltd at reporting date:		
Ordinary shares	100	
Share premium	10	
General reserve	15	
Retained earnings	35	
	160	
NCI share: 20%		32

Planet Plc
CONSOLIDATED STATEMENT OF FINANCIAL POSITION
as at 30 April 2011

Assets	**€000**
Non-current Assets	
Property, plant and equipment	358
Goodwill	32
	390

Current Assets	
Inventories	176
Receivables	45
Cash	21
	242
Total assets	**632**
Equity and liabilities	
Equity	
Ordinary shares	300
Share premium	20
General reserve	64
Retained earnings	54
Total shareholders' equity	438
Non-controlling interest	32
Total equity	470
Current Liabilities	
Trade payables	82
Taxation	80
	162
Total equity and liabilities	**632**

Chapter 4

The Consolidated Statement of Financial Position: Complications

Learning Objectives

After reading this chapter you should be able to:
- demonstrate an understanding of the various complications;
- make adjustments to account for each complication; and
- undertake questions on the preparation of a consolidated statement of financial position of a parent and subsidiary, which includes a combination of complications.

Introduction

Beware! At the end of **Chapter 3** you were in a position to prepare and present a basic consolidated SoFP. However, you should avoid the temptation to become complacent as in this chapter we will introduce accounting issues that will make the preparation of the consolidated SoFP more complex and intricate.

As stated, the basics of preparing a consolidated SoFP are explained in **Chapter 3**. These basics would remain the same irrespective of how many subsidiaries are acquired, i.e.:

1. Consolidate all the assets and liabilities of **each subsidiary** with those of the parent.
2. Debit cost of control with the investment in the subsidiary.
3. Credit cost of control with the group's share of the share capital of the subsidiary and each of its reserves at the **date of acquisition**.
4. Credit non-controlling interest with their share of the share capital and each reserve of the subsidiary at **the period end**.
5. Share capital and reserves are represented by net assets.

However, in the world of business, group entities trade with one another and subsidiaries pay dividends to parents. Frequently, there are amounts owing by one group entity to another at the reporting date. Such events give rise to a set of adjustments which will be termed 'complications'. **Every examination question on consolidated financial statements contains a combination of complications so their understanding is essential.**

The key factor in considering these complications is that consolidated financial statements present information about a group **as if it were a single entity** (see **Chapter 1**). Therefore, for example, if the parent (P Ltd) owes the subsidiary (S Ltd) €20,000 at the period end for goods purchased, it is correct for P Ltd to show this amount as a payable and for S Ltd to include a corresponding amount as a receivable in their **individual** financial statements. However, there is a problem in preparing a set of consolidated financial statements in this case. Under full consolidation, the net assets of S Ltd would be combined with those of P Ltd. **If this were done without adjustment, both the assets and liabilities of the group would be overstated.** In the consolidated workings, therefore, the receivables of S Ltd need to be reduced by €20,000, as do the payables of P Ltd. The relevant T accounts would then show the following adjusting entries:

Receivables

Debit		**Credit**	
		Journal Adjustment	20,000

Payables

Debit		**Credit**	
Journal Adjustment	20,000		

> ***Key Note***: having now pointed to the fact that complications do arise, the term '**full consolidation**' is defined throughout the remainder of this text as: combining the assets and liabilities of P Ltd and S Ltd **after adjustment for the effects of any complications.**

The Complications

A number of adjustments or 'complications' frequently arise when individual group member SoFPs are consolidated to create the consolidated statement of financial position (SoFP). The main complications can be characterised as follows:

1. Unrealised inventory profit
2. Unrealised profit on sale of tangible non-current assets
3. Revaluation of a subsidiary's net assets at acquisition date
4. Proposed preference dividends by a subsidiary
5. Proposed ordinary dividends
6. Dividends paid out of pre-acquisition profits of a subsidiary
7. Intragroup balances
8. Impairment of goodwill (attributable to a parent)
9. Preference shares in issue by a subsidiary

> ***Key Note:*** Before dealing with the accounting treatment for each of the complications, it is important to understand that any adjustment that affects the reserves of the subsidiary will also affect the calculation of non-controlling interests (NCI). As stated in Chapter 3, *non-controlling interests* is their share of the share capital and

each reserve of the subsidiary at the reporting date. This is defined throughout the remainder of this text as their share of the share capital and each reserve of the subsidiary after adjusting for the complications.

Complication 1 – Unrealised Inventory Profits

IAS 2 *Inventories* states that inventories should be valued at the lower of cost and net realisable value. When one group company sells goods to another at a profit and some/all of those goods are in the inventory of the buying company (at cost to them) at the reporting date, an element of unrealised profit is included in the closing inventory of the **group**.

Example 4.1: Treatment of Unrealised Inventory Profit

P Ltd owns 80% of the share capital of S Ltd. P Ltd buys goods for €100 and sells them to S Ltd for €150. At the reporting date, S Ltd still has these goods in inventory. In the **individual** SoFP of S Ltd, these goods are valued at cost €150 in accordance with IAS 2 and this is correct. Now consider the consolidated SoFP. If the inventory of S Ltd were consolidated (without adjustment) with the inventory of P Ltd the result would be that the group bought these goods for €100 and valued its inventory at €150 which contravenes IAS 2. There is unrealised profit from a group perspective of €50.

Accounting Treatment

Eliminate all the unrealised profit	**€**	**€**
Dr. Retained Earnings (selling Company P Ltd)	50	
Cr. Inventory		50

However, if S Ltd was the selling company and the unrealised profit arose in the inventory of P Ltd, then the adjustment would affect the non-controlling interests because S Ltd's retained earnings at the reporting date are now reduced by €50 (see also below, **Question 4.7**).

Complication 2 – Unrealised Profit on Sale of Tangible Non-current Assets

This complication arises when one group company sells a non-current asset to another at a profit, and the asset is in the statement of financial position of the buying company at the period end. When looking at the group as a single entity, both the profits (from the sale of the asset) and non-current assets are overstated. IAS 16 *Property, Plant and Equipment* states that an asset should be carried at:

1. **Cost**, less accumulated depreciation and impairment; **OR**
2. **Revaluation,** being its fair value at the date of revaluation less subsequent depreciation and impairment.[1]

Example 4.2: Treatment of Unrealised Profit on Sale of Non-current Assets

P Ltd bought an item of property, plant and equipment (PPE) on 1 August 2008 at a cost of €300,000 and is depreciating it at 10% straight line. On 1 August 2010 P Ltd sold the asset to S Ltd for €280,000 who is currently depreciating over the remaining years. A consolidated SoFP is prepared as at 31 July 2011.

1 August 2010	
Carrying value of asset (€300,000 − 2 years' depreciation)	€240,000
Sale proceeds	€280,000
Profit on disposal	€40,000

If the consolidated SoFP as at 31 July 2011 was prepared without adjustment both the profits and the property, plant and equipment (PPE) figures would be overstated by €40,000.

Accounting Treatment

Eliminate unrealised profit in the selling company's accounts:

Dr.	Retained Earnings (P Ltd)	€40,000	
Cr.	PPE		€40,000

This transaction is further complicated by the fact that the asset in question is subject to depreciation. At present, **the depreciation is overstated from a group perspective** calculated as follows:

Year ended 31 July 2011:		
Depreciation per S Ltd financial statements €280,000 @ 12.5%	=	€35,000
Depreciation if asset not sold at a profit €300,000 @ 10%	=	€30,000
Over-provision		€5,000

Write back the over-provision of depreciation in the buying company

Dr.	PPE	€5,000	
Cr.	Retained Earnings (S Ltd)		€5,000

Remember: The depreciation adjustment changes the retained earnings of S Ltd, therefore, the calculation of non-controlling interests must take this into account. (See also below, **Question 4.8.**)

[1] See also ***Connolly***, Chapter 6, "Property, Plant and Equipment".

Complication 3 – Revaluation of a Subsidiary's Net Assets at Acquisition Date

When a parent (P Ltd) acquires a subsidiary (S Ltd) the purchase consideration is based on the **fair value** of the subsidiary's net assets and not the carrying values, which are frequently significantly different, particularly in the case of tangible assets such as property.

IFRS 3 *Business Combinations* defines 'fair value' as "the amount for which an asset could be exchanged, or a liability settled, between knowledgeable, willing parties in an arm's length transaction".

IFRS 3 also requires that all the assets and liabilities of a subsidiary (S Ltd) be revalued (with same exceptions) for consolidation purposes to **fair value** at the date of acquisition. However, there is no obligation on S Ltd to reflect the revaluation in its own financial statements. If S Ltd has recorded the revaluation in its own financial statements no adjustment is necessary. If not, adjustments are necessary in the consolidation workings. If the assets are increased in value the surplus is split between cost of control and non-controlling interests, using the group structure.

If any of the revalued assets are subject to depreciation, another entry must be made to account for the cumulative additional depreciation on the revaluation surplus. The practical implications of Complication 3 are all illustrated in **Example 4.3**.

Example 4.3: Revaluation of Net Assets of Subsidiary

The following is the summarised statement of financial position of a subsidiary (S Ltd) on 1 June 2009:

	€000
Property, plant and equipment	4,400
Current assets	1,300
Total assets	**5,700**
Ordinary share capital	2,000
Retained earnings	1,800
Non-current liabilities	1,000
Current liabilities	900
Total equity and liabilities	**5,700**

P Ltd acquired 60% of the ordinary shares of S Ltd on the 1 June 2009. At the date of acquisition the fair value of the property, plant and equipment (PPE) exceeded the carrying value by €300,000 while those assets had an average remaining useful life of five years. S Ltd did not record the revaluation.

In the consolidated workings as at 31 May 2011 (the reporting date) the following adjustments would be necessary:

ACCOUNTING TREATMENT

		€000	€000
1.	**Account for surplus**		
	Dr. PPE	300	
	Cr. Cost of Control (60%)		180
	Cr. Non-Controlling interests (40%)		120
2.	**Account for cumulative additional depreciation**		
	Dr. Retained Earnings (S Ltd)	120	
	Cr. Accumulated Depreciation – PPE		120

With the cumulative additional depreciation, i.e. €300,000 × 2/5

Remember: there is an effect on non-controlling interests because the retained earnings of S Ltd at the **reporting date** are reduced.
(See also below, **Question 4.8.)**

Complication 4 – Proposed Preference Dividends by a Subsidiary

Complication 4(a) This arises where a subsidiary (S Ltd) has proposed a preference dividend at the reporting date **and the parent (P Ltd) has taken credit for its share.**

If a subsidiary proposes a dividend, part of which is payable to P Ltd, the **intragroup figure must be eliminated** in the consolidated workings, otherwise both the assets and liabilities of the group would be overstated. The remainder of the dividend is payable to non-controlling interests which is a liability of the group and is shown under current liabilities in the consolidated SoFP.

EXAMPLE 4.4: TREATMENT OF PROPOSED PREFERENCE DIVIDENDS BY A SUBSIDIARY

P Ltd owns 80% of the preference shares of S Ltd.

Extract from statements of financial position as at 31 August 2011:

	P Ltd	**S Ltd**
Assets	**€**	**€**
Dividends receivable	40,000	
Liabilities		
Proposed dividends		50,000

The proposed dividend €50,000 is payable as follows:
€40,000 to P Ltd
€10,000 to NCI

Accounting Treatment

Cancel the intragroup dividend	**€**	**€**
Dr. Proposed dividends	40,000	
Cr. Dividends receivable with intragroup dividend		40,000

Dividends Receivable

Debit		**Credit**	
P	40,000	Journal	40,000

Proposed Dividends

Debit		**Credit**	
Journal	40,000	S	50,000
SoFP (NCI)	10,000		
	50,000		50,000

Note: The proposed dividends due of €10,000 are disclosed under current liabilities as due to non-controlling interests.

Complication 4(b) Where S Ltd has proposed a preference dividend **and P Ltd has not taken credit** for its share.

Example 4.5: Treatment of Proposed Preference Dividends included in a Subsidiary only

P Ltd owns 80% of the preference shares of S Ltd.

Extract: Statements of Financial Position
at 30 August 2011

	P Ltd	**S Ltd**
Proposed dividend		€50,000

The proposed dividend is again payable as follows:
€40,000 to P Ltd – this is intragroup.
€10,000 to NCI – this is a group liability.

ACCOUNTING TREATMENT

In this instance the intragroup dividend cannot as yet be cancelled because P Ltd has not taken credit for its share, therefore:

1. **Bring in dividend receivable into P's accounts**

Dr. Dividends receivable	€40,000	
Cr. Retained earnings (P Ltd)		€40,000

And then

2. **Cancel the intragroup dividend**

Dr. Proposed dividends	€40,000	
Cr. Dividends receivable		€40,000

Dividends Receivable – P Ltd

Debit		**Credit**	
Journal 1	40,000	Journal 2	40,000

Proposed Dividends – S Ltd

Debit		**Credit**	
Journal 2	40,000	S	50,000
SoFP – NCI	10,000		
	50,000		50,000

Note: Disclose €10,000 under current liabilities as due to non-controlling interests.

Complication 5 – Proposed Ordinary Dividends

Under IAS 10 *Events after the Reporting Period*, proposed ordinary dividends at the reporting date do not normally constitute a liability as there is **no obligation** to transfer economic benefits until the dividend is formally approved by the shareholders at the annual general meeting. However, some exam questions contain ordinary dividends proposed by S Ltd, which **are approved** before the year end and accounted for. If this is the case, the treatment in the consolidated workings would be the same as in the case of the preference dividends as per Complication 4 above, i.e.:

(a) Where S Ltd has proposed an ordinary dividend and P Ltd **has** taken credit for its share;

or

(b) Where S Ltd has proposed an ordinary dividend and P Ltd **has not** taken credit for its share.

***Note*:** any dividends in the SoFP of the parent do not give rise to adjustments. They are liabilities of the group, and are shown in the consolidated SoFP as current liabilities, assuming they have been approved.

Complication 6 – Dividends Paid out of Pre-Acquisition Profits of a Subsidiary

Occasionally, a subsidiary pays a dividend to a parent out of profits in existence at the date of acquisition. Company law has, since 1963, regulated that such dividends cannot be treated as distributable by the parent. Accordingly, in the preparation of consolidated accounts, the parent traditionally reduced the cost of its investment in the subsidiary by the dividend received.

IAS 27 *Consolidated and Separate Financial Statements* has effectively removed the complication in abolishing the distinction between pre-acquisition and post-acquisition dividends. Formerly, dividends received by a parent (P Ltd) from pre-acquisition profits of a subsidiary (S Ltd) were deducted from the cost of its investment in S Ltd because the dividend was deemed to be a **refund** of part of the investment. Though IAS 27, paragraph 38A, states that an entity shall recognise a dividend from a subsidiary in profit or loss in its separate financial statements. This is at variance with current company law.

Example 4.6(A) addresses this issue in accordance with IFRS, while **Example 4.6(B)** follows the principles of company law requirements.

IAS/IFRS As explained above, a parent (P Ltd) would include such a dividend paid out of pre-acquisition profits in its statement of comprehensive income and goodwill would be calculated as if the dividend were paid out of post-acquisition profits.

Example 4.6(A): IAS/IFRS Treatment of Dividends paid out of Pre-Acquisition Profits

On 1 August 2010, P Ltd acquired 80% of the share capital of S Ltd when the issued capital of S Ltd was €500,000 and the retained earnings €800,000. The cost of investment was €1,090,000. During December 2010, S Ltd paid a dividend of €50,000 out of the profits in existence at the date of acquisition.

Under IAS/IFRS, P Ltd should take the dividend it receives (€40,000) to its statement of comprehensive income. It has **no effect on the calculation of goodwill.**

Workings (T account Method)

Cost of Control

Debit	**€000**	**Credit**	**€000**
Investment in S Ltd	1,090	Ordinary Shares S Ltd (80%)	400
		Retained earnings S Ltd (80% × 800)	640
		Goodwill	50
	1,090		1,090

WORKINGS (Columnar Method)

	€000	€000
Cost of investment		1,090
S Ltd at date of acquisition:		
Ordinary shares	500	
Retained earnings	800	
	1,300	
Group's share 80%		1,040
Goodwill		50

Company Law When a parent (P Ltd) receives a dividend out of pre-acquisition profits of a subsidiary (S Ltd), the dividend cannot be taken to profit or loss in the financial statements of the parent. Instead, the dividend received by P Ltd is deemed to be a **partial return** of its investment. In this case the amount of goodwill is unaffected but some of the figures used in its calculation are changed.

ACCOUNTING TREATMENT

1. Credit investment in S Ltd with the **actual** dividend received.
2. Reduce the retained earnings of S Ltd at the date of acquisition by **total** dividend paid by S Ltd.

EXAMPLE 4.6(B): COMPANY LAW TREATMENT OF DIVIDENDS PAID OUT OF PRE-ACQUISITION PROFITS

(Using the same example as under IAS/ IFRS above)

WORKINGS (T account Method)

Cost of Control

Debit	**€000**	**Credit**	**€000**
Investment in S Ltd *(W1)*	1,050	Ordinary Shares S Ltd (80%)	400
		Retained earnings S Ltd *(W2)*	600
		Goodwill	50
	1,050		1,050

Both the Investment in S Ltd and the Retained Earnings of S Ltd are reduced by the amount of the dividend paid out of pre-acquisition profits.

(W1) (1,090 – 40) *(W2)* 80% (800 – 50)

Workings (Columnar Method)

	€000	€000
Cost of investment	1,090	
Less pre-acq. dividend received	40	1,050
S Ltd at acquisition date		
Ordinary shares	500	
Retained earnings	800	
Pre-acquisition dividend paid	(50)	
	1,250	
Group's share 80%		1,000
Goodwill		50

Complication 7 – Intragroup Balances

When looking at a group as a **single entity**, it follows that all intragroup balances should be eliminated, otherwise both the assets and liabilities of a group would be overstated.

Example 4.7: Treatment of Intragroup Balances

In their respective statements of financial position as at 30 June 2011, P Ltd shows an amount of €50,000 owing to S Ltd while S Ltd has a corresponding receivable due from P Ltd.

Accounting Treatment

Cancel intragroup balances

	€000	€000
Dr. Trade payables	50	
Cr. Trade receivables		50

Sometimes group companies operate through current accounts. If this were the case, the adjustment would be:

Dr. Current a/c with S Ltd	50	
Cr. Current a/c with P Ltd		50

Intragroup balances can only be eliminated if they are **in agreement**. The balances could differ for two reasons:

1. Cash in transit
2. Goods in transit

When accounting for items in transit between a parent and a subsidiary, the adjustments are made in the financial statements of the **parent**.

Example 4.8: Adjustments for Items in Transit

At 31 August 2011 the SoFP of P Ltd showed the following receivable:
Current account with S Ltd: €100,000.

On the same date P Ltd was included as a payable in the SoFP of S Ltd:
Current account with P Ltd: €60,000

During late August, the following occurred:
(a) P Ltd sent goods to S Ltd at invoice value €30,000 at a mark-up of 25%. S Ltd did not receive the goods until 6 September 2011.
(b) S Ltd sent a cheque for €10,000 to P Ltd on 31 August 2011.

Solution

Journal 1 *Account for the cash in transit*

Dr.	Cash	€10,000	
Cr.	Current a/c with S Ltd		€10,000

Journal 2 *Account for the goods in transit*

Dr.	Inventory (cost price)	€24,000	
Dr.	Retained Earnings (P Ltd) (profit)	€6,000	
Cr.	Current a/c with S Ltd (total)		€30,000

The current account balances are now in agreement.

Journal 3 *Eliminate the intragroup balances*

Dr.	Current a/c with P Ltd	€60,000	
Cr.	Current a/c with S Ltd		€60,000

In T account Format

Current Account with S Ltd

Debit		**Credit**	
P	€100,000	Journal 1	€10,000
		Journal 2	€30,000
		Journal 3	€60,000
	€100,000		€100,000

Current Account with P Ltd

Debit		**Credit**	
Journal 3	€60,000	S	€60,000

Complication 8 – Impairment of Goodwill (Attributable to a Parent)

IAS 36 *Impairment of Assets* states that assets should be carried at no more than their recoverable amount. IAS 36 defines an 'impairment loss' as "the amount by which the carrying amount of an asset or a cash generating unit exceeds its recoverable amount". An asset is carried at more than its recoverable amount if its carrying value exceeds the amount to be recovered through use or sale of the asset. In simple terms, impairment occurs when the value of an asset is reduced by an amount that is greater than the normal reduction through depreciation or amortisation. If this is the case, the asset is impaired and the entity must recognise the impairment loss. Under IAS 36, goodwill acquired in a business combination must be tested for impairment **annually**.

Example 4.9: Treatment of Impairment of Goodwill

On 1 May 2009, P Ltd acquired 90% of the ordinary shares of S Ltd at a cost of €1,680,000. On that date the issued share capital of S Ltd was €1,000,000 and its retained earnings €800,000.

The goodwill was impaired as follows:
Year ended 30 April 2010 €20,000
Year ended 30 April 2011 €15,000

Workings 30/4/2011 (T account Method)

Dr.	Retained earnings (P Ltd)	€35,000	
Cr.	Cost of control		€35,000

Cost of Control

Debit	**€000**	**Credit**	**€000**
Investment in S Ltd	1,680	Ordinary shares (90% × 1 million)	900
		Retained earnings (800 × 90%)	720
		Journal – Goodwill impairment	35
		SoFP – Goodwill	25
	1,680		1,680

Workings (Columnar Method)

	€000	**€000**
Cost of investment		1,680
S Ltd at acquisition date		
Ordinary shares	1,000	
Retained earnings	800	
	1,800	

Group's share 90%	1,620
Goodwill on acquisition	60
Cumulative impairment to 30 April 2011	35
Consolidated SoFP as at 30 April 2011	25

Complication 9 – Preference Shares in Issue by a Subsidiary

Sometimes a parent acquires preference shares of a subsidiary along with the acquisition of ordinary shares. Preference shares usually carry a fixed rate of dividend which is expressed as a percentage of the nominal value. The holders of preference shares are paid before distributions are made to the ordinary shareholders and there is also preference to a distribution of assets in a winding up.

Example 4.10: Treatment of Preference shares in a Subsidiary

S Ltd
Summarised Statement of Financial Position
as at 30 June 2011

	€000
Sundry net assets	4,630
Ordinary shares (€1)	1,000
10% Cumulative Preference shares (€1)	1,000
Retained earnings	2,630
	4,630

P Ltd acquired 80% of the ordinary shares of S Ltd on 1 July 2010 when the retained earnings of S Ltd were €2 million. The cost of the investment was €2.5 million. On the same date, it purchased 30% of the preference shares of S Ltd at a cost of €320,000.

Workings (T account Method)

(a) The acquisition of the preference shares in S Ltd is dealt with in the cost of control account as follows:

		€000	**€000**
Dr.	Cost of control with cost of investment	320	
Cr.	Cost of Investment in S Ltd		320
Dr.	Preference Shares S Ltd	300	
Cr.	Cost of control with nominal value acquired		300

The difference is included as part of the goodwill.

(b) The nominal value of the preference shares owned by non-controlling interests is credited to their account as follows:

Dr.	Preference Shares S Ltd	700	
Cr	Non-controlling Interests		700

Preference Shares

Debit		**Credit**	
Cost of control (30%)	300		
Non-controlling interests (70%)	700	S	1,000
	1,000		1,000

Cost of Control

Debit		**Credit**	
Investment in S Ltd (Ord. Shares)	2,500	Ordinary Shares (80%)	800
Investment in S Ltd (Pref. Shares)	320	Preference Shares (30%)	300
		Retained Earnings (2,000 × 80%)	1,600
		Goodwill	120
	2,820		2,820

Non-controlling Interests

Debit		**Credit**	
		Ordinary shares (20%)	200
		Preference shares (70%)	700
SoFP	1,426	Retained earnings (2,630 × 20%)	526
	1,426		1,426

Workings (Columnar Method)

	€000	€000
Goodwill		
Cost of investment		2,820
S Ltd at **acquisition date:**		
Ordinary shares	1,000	
Retained earnings	2,000	
	3,000	
Group's share 80%		(2,400)
Preference shares	1,000	
Group's share 30%		(300)
Goodwill		120
Non-controlling interests		
S Ltd at **reporting date**		
Ordinary shares	1,000	

Retained earnings	2,630	
	3,630	
NCI share 20%		726
Preference shares	1,000	
NCI share 70%		700
Total NCI		1,426

Conclusion

It must be emphasised that when the above complications are individually considered the adjustments are easily understood. In examination questions, however, combinations of these complications and how they affect consolidation are invariably tested. It is highly advisable that you are completely familiar with the existence and treatment of each and all of these complications. Questions 4.7 and 4.8 below have been devised to this end and you would be wise to attempt them and study their solutions.

SUMMARY

1. Consolidated financial statements are prepared as if the group were a single entity.
2. Complications arise in the preparation of consolidated financial statements when group entities trade with each other, subsidiaries pay dividends to parents or there are amounts owing from one group entity to another at a reporting date.
3. Intragroup balances and dividends must be eliminated in full.
4. Profits and losses resulting from transactions between group entities that are recognised in assets such as inventory and property, plant and equipment must be eliminated.
5. Goodwill that arises on the acquisition of a subsidiary must be tested for impairment annually and written down to its recoverable amount if impairment occurs.
6. The assets and liabilities of a subsidiary must be re-valued to fair value for consolidation purposes on acquisition by a parent. A depreciation adjustment will also be necessary if a depreciable asset is increased or decreased in value.

QUESTIONS

Question 4.1

(a) What is meant by unrealised profit on inventory?

(b) During August 2011, S Ltd sold goods to P Ltd at invoice value €250,000 on which S Ltd earned a mark-up of 25%. At the reporting date, 31 August 2011, P Ltd had one half of these goods in inventory. Show the necessary journal entry in the consolidated workings for the year ended 31 August 2011.

Solution

(a) Unrealised inventory profit arises when one group entity sells goods to another at a profit and some or all of those goods are in the inventory of the buyer at the reporting date. If the unrealised profit were not accounted for, both the profits and inventories of the group would be overstated.

(b) Calculation of unrealised profit:

€250,000 × 1/5 × ½ = €25,000

	€	€
Dr. Retained earnings S Ltd	25,000	
Cr. Inventory		25,000

Question 4.2

(a) On 1 July 2009 P Ltd sold an item of plant to S Ltd for €280,000. P Ltd purchased the asset for €400,000 on 1 July 2006 and is depreciating it at 12.5% straight line. Record the journal entries to deal with this transaction in the consolidated workings as at 30 June 2011.

(b) Explain the accounting treatment.

Solution to Question 4.2

(a)

	€
Cost of asset 1 July 2006	400,000
Depreciation 30 June 2007	(50,000)
30 June 2008	(50,000)
30 June 2009	(50,000)
Carrying value 30 June 2009	250,000
Sale proceeds	280,000
Profit on sale	30,000

Accounting Entry

Eliminate the profit

	€	€
Dr. Retained earnings P Ltd	30,000	
Cr. Property, plant and equipment		30,000

The buying entity S Ltd now depreciates the asset on cost €280,000 over the remaining useful life of five years, i.e. €56,000 per annum.

			€
Depreciation per S Ltd 30 June 2010 and 2011:			
€280,000 @ 20% (1/5) × 2 years	2 × €56,000	=	112,000

Depreciation if asset were not sold:			
€400,000 @ 12.5% × 2 years	2 × 50,000	=	100,000
Over charge (Group)			12,000

Accounting entry

Dr. Property, plant and equipment	12,000	
Cr. Retained earnings S Ltd		12,000

(b) The sale of an asset at a profit by one group entity to another gives rise to unrealised profit which, if not eliminated on consolidation, would give rise to an overstatement of both group assets and profits. Furthermore, if the asset in question is subject to depreciation, an adjustment is necessary which will correct both the carrying value of the asset and the group profit in the consolidated financial statements.

Question 4.3

(a) P Ltd acquired 70% of the ordinary shares of S Ltd on 1 November 2009. At that date the fair values of the net assets of S Ltd were the same as their carrying values with the exception of property, plant and equipment which showed a surplus of €400,000. At the date of acquisition the average remaining useful lives of the property, plant and equipment was five years. Show the journal entries to reflect the revaluation in the consolidated workings as at 31 July 2011.
(b) Explain any assumptions you made.

Solution to Question 4.3

		€	€
(a)	(i) Dr. Property, plant and equipment	400,000	
	Cr. Cost of control (70%)		280,000
	Cr. Non-controlling interests (30%)		120,000
	(ii) Dr. Retained earnings S Ltd	160,000	
	Cr. Property, plant and equipment (€400,000 × 2/5)		160,000

(b) The solution assumes that the subsidiary had not recorded the revaluation surplus in its own financial statements.

Question 4.4

(a) What is meant by the term 'dividends out of pre-acquisition profits of S Ltd?
(b) Do such dividends affect the calculation of goodwill under IAS/IFRS?

Solution

(a) A dividend out of pre-acquisition profits occurs when a subsidiary makes a distribution to its parent out of the profits in existence on the date the parent acquired the subsidiary.

(h) IAS 27 requires a parent to take all dividends from a subsidiary to the statement of comprehensive income as part of profit or loss. Consequently, such an event would not have an effect on the calculation of goodwill in the consolidated financial statements.

Question 4.5

What is the accounting treatment for inter-company balances at a group reporting date and why is such treatment necessary?

Solution

All inter-company balances at a reporting date should be eliminated in the preparation of a consolidated statement of financial position. The aim of a consolidated statement of financial position is to show the financial position of a group as if it were a single entity. Failure to eliminate inter-company balances would result in an overstatement of both the assets and liabilities of a group.

Question 4.6

Explain the implication of impairment of goodwill on the consolidated statement of financial position.

Solution

Goodwill (attributable to a parent) becomes impaired when its recoverable amount is less than the carrying amount. Impairment has the following implications for the consolidated SoFP:

1. the carrying amount of goodwill is reduced to its recoverable amount; and
2. the retained earnings of P Ltd and therefore the consolidated retained earnings are reduced by the amount of the impairment.

> ***Note:*** The following questions, Questions 4.7 and 4.8, are longer, review-type questions. The solutions to both questions require many journal entries to account for the complications.
>
> Each solution contains:
> 1. the journal adjustments
> 2. the T account method workings
> 3. the columnar method workings; and
> 4. the consolidated SoFP.

Question 4.7

Pit Plc acquired 80% of the ordinary share capital of Stop Ltd for €150,000 and 50% of the issued 10% cumulative preference shares for €10,000, both purchases being effected on 1 May 2010. There have been no changes in the issued share capital of S Ltd since that date. The following balances are taken from the books of the two companies at 30 April 2011:

	Pit Plc €000	Stop Ltd €000
Assets		
Non-current assets		
Property, plant and equipment	218	160
Investment in Stop	160	–
	378	160
Current assets		
Inventories	111	65
Trade receivables	30	15
Cash	19	2
	160	82
Total assets	**538**	**242**
Equity and liabilities		
Equity		
Ordinary shares (€1)	300	100
10% Cumulative Pref. Shares (€1)	–	20
Share premium	20	10
General reserve	68	15
Retained earnings	50	35
Total equity	438	180
Current Liabilities		
Trade payables	50	30
Taxation	50	30
Proposed dividends		2
	100	62
Total equity and liabilities	**538**	**242**

The following additional information is available:

1. Inventories of Pit Plc include goods purchased from Stop Ltd for €20,000. Stop Ltd charged out these goods at cost plus 25%.
2. Proposed dividend of Stop Ltd represents a full year's preference dividend. No interim dividends were paid during the year by either company.
3. Payables of Pit Plc include €6,000 payable to Stop Ltd in respect of goods purchased. Receivables of Stop Ltd include €10,000 due from Pit Plc. The parent company sent a cheque for €4,000 to its subsidiary on 29 April 2011 which was not received by Stop Ltd until May 2011.
4. At 1 May 2010 the balances on the reserves of Stop Ltd were as follows:

	€000
Share premium	10
General reserve	20
Retained earnings	30

5. Goodwill is impaired during the year ended 30 April 2011 in the amount of €2,200.

Requirement Prepare a consolidated statement of financial position for Pit Plc and its subsidiary Stop Ltd at 30 April 2011.

Solution to Question 4.7

Journal Entries

			€000	€000
1.	Dr.	Retained earnings (S Ltd)	4	
	Cr.	Inventory		4
		(being unrealised profit €20,000 × 1/5 – the margin must be applied not the mark up)		
2.	Dr.	Dividends receivable	1	
	Cr.	Retained earnings (P Ltd)		1
		(being share of preference dividend receivable from S Ltd)		
3.	Dr.	Proposed dividends	1	
	Cr.	Dividends receivable		1
		(Cancellation of inter-company dividend)		
4.	Dr.	Cash (P Ltd)	4	
	Cr.	Trade payables		4
		(being cash in transit brought back into P Ltd's accounts)		
5.	Dr.	Trade payables	10	
	Cr.	Trade receivables		10
		(cancellation of intragroup debt)		
6.	Dr.	Retained earnings (P Ltd)	2.2	
	Cr.	Cost of control		2.2
		(cumulative impairment of goodwill to reporting date)		

Workings (T account Method)

Property, Plant and Equipment

Debit		**Credit**	
P	218		
S	160	SoFP	378
	378		378

Investment in S

Debit		Credit	
P	160	Cost of Control	160

Inventories

Debit		Credit	
P	111	Journal 1	4
S	65	SoFP	172
	176		176

Trade Receivables

Debit		Credit	
P	30	Journal 5	10
S	15	SoFP	35
	45		45

Cash

Debit		Credit	
P	19		
S	2		
Journal 4	4	SoFP	25
	25		25

Ordinary Shares

Debit		Credit	
Cost of Control (80%)	80	P	300
NCI (20%)	20	S	100
SoFP	300		
	400		400

Preference Shares

Debit		Credit	
Cost of Control (50%)	10	S	20
NCI (50%)	10		-
	20		20

Share Premium

Debit		Credit	
Cost of Control (80% × 10,000)	8	P	20
NCI (20% × 10,000)	2	S	10
SoFP	20		
	30		30

General Reserve

Debit		Credit	
Cost of Control (80% × 20,000)	16	P	68
NCI (20% × 15,000)	3	S	15
SoFP	64		
	83		83

Retained Earnings

Debit		Credit	
Journal 1 (S)	4	P	50
Journal 6 (P)	2.2	S	35
Cost of Control (80% × 30k)	24	Journal. 2 (P)	1
NCI: 20% × (35 − 4)	6.2		
SoFP	49.6		
	86.0		86.0

(*Note:* S Ltd retained earnings at the reporting date must take account of the unrealised inventory profit.)

Trade Payables

Debit		Credit	
Journal 5	10	P	50
SoFP	74	S	30
		Journal 4	4
	84		84

Taxation

Debit		Credit	
SoFP	80	P	50
		S	30
	80		80

Dividends Proposed

Debit		Credit	
Journal 3	1	S	2
SoFP	1		
	2		2

Dividends Receivable

Debit		Credit	
Journal 2	1	Journal 3	1

Cost of Control

Debit		**Credit**	
Investment in S	160	Journal 6	2.2
		Ordinary shares	80
		Pref. shares	10
		Share prem.	8
		Gen. reserve	16
		Ret. earnings	24
		SoFP: Goodwill	19.8
	160		160

Non-controlling Interests

Debit		**Credit**	
SoFP	41.2	Ordinary shares	20
		Preference shares	10
		Share premium	2
		Gen. reserve	3
		Ret. Earnings	6.2
	41.2		41.2

WORKINGS (Columnar Method)

	Pit €000	**Stop €000**	**Adjustments €000**	**Consol. SoFP €000**
Property, plant and equipment	218	160	0	378
Goodwill *(W1)*	0	0	19.8	19.8
Investment in Stop	160	0	(160)	0
Inventories	111	65	(4)	172
Trade receivables	30	15	(10)	35
Dividends receivable			1(1)	0
Cash	19	2	4	25
Total assets	**538**	**242**	**(150.2)**	**629.8**
Ordinary Shares	300	100	(100)	300
Preference Shares	0	20	(20)	0
Share premium *(W2)*	20	10	(10)	20
General reserve (*W3*)	68	15	(19)	64
Retained earnings (*W4*)	50	35	(35.4)	49.6
Non-controlling interests (*W5*)	0	0	41.2	41.2
Trade payables	50	30	4,(10)	74

Taxation	50	30	0	80
Proposed dividend	0	2	(1)	1
Total equity and liabilities	**538**	**242**	**(150.2)**	**629.8**

(W1) Goodwill:	**€000**		**€000**
Cost of investment			160
Stop at acq. date:			
Ordinary share capital	100		
Share premium	10		
General reserve	20		
Retained earnings	30		
	160		
Group Share (80%)			(128)
Preference shares (20 × 50%)			(10)
Goodwill			22
Impairment			2.2
Consolidated SoFP			19.8
(W2) Share premium:			
Pit at reporting date			20
Stop at reporting date	10		
at acquisition date	(10)		
Post-acquisition	nil		-
Consolidated SoFP			20
(W3) General reserve			
Pit at reporting date			68
Stop at reporting date	15		
at acquisition date	(20)		
Post-acquisition	(5)	× 80%	(4)
Consolidated SoFP			64
W4 Retained earnings			
Pit at reporting date			50
Journal 2 – dividend receivable			1
Journal 6 – goodwill impairment			(2.2)
Stop at reporting date	35		
Journal 1 – unrealised inventory profit	(4)		
	31		
Pre-acquisition	30		
Post-acquisition	1	× 80%	0.8
Consolidated SoFP			49.6

(W5) Non-controlling interests

Stop Ltd at reporting date@		
Ordinary shares	100	
Share premium	10	
General reserve	15	
Retained earnings	35	
Journal 1	(4)	
	156	
NCI × 20%		31.2
Preference shares (20 × 50%)		10
Consolidated SoFP		41.2

Pit Plc
CONSOLIDATED STATEMENT OF FINANCIAL POSITION
as at 30 April 2011

Assets	**€000**
Non-current assets	
Property, plant and equipment	378.0
Goodwill	19.8
	397.8
Current assets	
Inventory	172.0
Trade receivables	35.0
Cash	25.0
	232.0
Total assets	**629.8**
Equity and liabilities	
Equity	300.0
Share premium	20.0
General reserve	64.0
Retained earnings	49.6
Total shareholders' equity	433.6
Non-controlling interests	41.2
Total equity	474.8
Current liabilities	
Trade payables	74.0
Taxation	80.0
Proposed preference dividend	1.0
	155.0
Total equity and liabilities	**629.8**

Question 4.8

STATEMENT OF FINANCIAL POSITION
as at 31 August 2011

	Push Ltd €000	Shove Ltd €000
Assets		
Non-current assets		
Property, plant and equipment	110	350
Loans	220	–
Investments in Shove	255	–
	585	350
Current assets		
Inventory	300	190
Trade receivables	270	90
Cash	160	50
	730	330
Total assets	**1,315**	**680**
Equity and liabilities		
Equity		
Ordinary shares (€1)	840	200
Retained profits	265	140
Total equity	1,105	340
Non-current liabilities		
Long-term loans	–	170
Current liabilities		
Trade payables	210	170
Total equity and liabilities	**1,315**	**680**

Additional information:

1. Push Ltd acquired 150,000 shares in Shove Ltd for €255,000 on 1 October 2009, at which date Shove Ltd had a balance on retained earnings of €60,000. Shove Ltd subsequently declared and paid a dividend of €20,000 out of pre-acquisition profits.
2. At the date of acquisition the property, plant and equipment of Shove Ltd had a fair value which exceeded the carrying value by €100,000. At that date the remaining useful life of the property, plant and equipment was five years.
3. Included in Push Ltd's loans is one of €130,000 to Shove Ltd.
4. Push Ltd supplied goods to the value of €125,000 for which it has not yet been paid. These goods cost Push Ltd €100,000 and Shove Ltd still had 4/5ths of them in inventory at 31 August 2011.

5. On 1 September 2010, Push Ltd supplied machinery to Shove Ltd at a price of €198,000. The machine had cost €180,000 one year earlier. It is group policy to depreciate machinery over 10 years.

Requirement Prepare the consolidated statement of financial position of the Push Ltd group as at 31 August 2011.

Solution to Question 4.8

(***Note:*** The dividend paid by Shove Ltd out of pre-acquisition profits has been treated in this solution in accordance with IAS/IFRS.)

Group Structure
Group 75%: 150,000/200,000
NCI: 25%

Journal Entries	€000	€000
1. Dr. Property, Plant & Equipment	100	
Cr. Cost of control		75
Cr. NCI		25
(With revaluation surplus)		
2. Dr. Retained Earnings (S Ltd)	40	
Cr. PPE		40
(With additional depreciation – 100,000 × 2/5)		
3. Dr. Long-term loans	130	
Cr. Loans		130
(With cancellation of inter-company loans)		
4. Dr. Trade payable	125	
Cr. Trade receivables		125
(With cancellation of inter-company debt)		
5. Dr. Retained earnings (P Ltd)	20	
Cr. Inventory		20
(With unrealised inventory profit 4/5 × 25,000)		
6. Dr. Retained earnings (P Ltd)	36	
Cr. Property, plant and equipment		36
(With unrealised profit €198k – (€180k × 90%)		
7. Dr. Property, plant and equipment	4	
Cr. Retained earnings (S Ltd)		4
(With write back of over-depreciation)		

Depreciation per S Ltd $\frac{198,000}{9 \text{ years}} = 22,000$

Depreciation on historic cost $\frac{180,000}{10} = 18,000$

SOLUTION NOTES

1. The dividend (€15,000) which Push Ltd received from the pre-acquisition profits of Shove Ltd has been correctly credited to its profits (IAS 27). The investment is carried in the SoFP of Push Ltd at €255,000 and the original cost of the investment was €255,000.
2. The retained earnings of Shove Ltd (€140,000) at the reporting date are adjusted by:
   (a) Additional depreciation on revaluation surplus (€40,000)
   (b) Over-depreciation on the asset bought from Push Ltd €4,000

   The revised amount €104,000 is used for the calculation of non-controlling interest.

WORKINGS (T account Method)

Property, Plant and Equipment

Debit		**Credit**	
P	110	Journal 2	40
S	350	Journal 6	36
Journal 1	100		
Journal 7	4	SoFP	488
	564		564

Loans

Debit		**Credit**	
P	220	Journal 3	130
		SoFP	90
	220		220

Investment in S

Debit		**Credit**	
P	255	Cost of control	255

Inventory

Debit		**Credit**	
P	300	Journal 5	20
S	190	SoFP	470
	490		490

Trade Receivables

Debit		**Credit**	
P	270	Journal 4	125
S	90	SoFP	235
	360		360

Cash

Debit		Credit	
P	160		
S	50	SoFP	210
	210		210

Trade Payables

Debit		Credit	
Journal 4	125	P	210
SoFP	255	S	170
	380		380

Long-term Loans

Debit		Credit	
Journal 3	130	P	–
SoFP	40	S	170
	170		170

Ordinary Shares

Debit		Credit	
Cost of Control (75%)	150	P	840
NCI (25%)	50	S	200
SoFP	840		
	1,040		1,040

Retained Earnings

Debit		Credit	
Journal 2 (S Ltd)	40	P	265
Journal 5 (P Ltd)	20	S	140
Journal 6 (P Ltd)	36	Journal 7 (S Ltd)	4
Cost of Control (75% × 60,000)	45	Cost of Control	15
NCI 25% (140 + 4 – 40)	26		
SoFP	257		
	424		424

Cost of Control

Debit		Credit	
Investment in S Ltd	255	Journal 1	75
Retained earnings – gain	15	Ordinary shares	150
		Ret. earnings	45
	270		270

A gain from a bargain purchase is transferred in full to retained earnings and included in arriving at profit for the year in the consolidated SoCI.

Non-controlling Interests

Debit		Credit	
		Journal 1	25
		Ord. shares	50
SoFP	101	Ret. earnings	26
	101		101

WORKINGS (Columnar Method)

	Push	Shove	Adjustments	Consol. SoFP
	€000	€000	€000	€000
Property, plant & equipment	110	350	100 (40) (36) 4	488
Loans	220		(130)	90
Goodwill *(W1)*				
Investment in Shove	255		(255)	
Inventory	300	190	(20)	470
Trade receivables	270	90	(125)	235
Cash	160	50		210
Total assets	**1,315**	**680**	**(502)**	**1,493**
Ordinary shares	840	200	(200)	840
Retained earnings *(W2)*	265	140	(148)	257
Non-controlling interests *(W3)*			101	101
Long-term loans		170	(130)	40
Trade payables	210	170	(125)	255
Total equity and liabilities	**1,315**	**680**	**(502)**	**1,493**

(W1) Goodwill	€000	€000
Cost of investment		255
Shove Ltd at acquisition date		
Ordinary shares	200	
Retained earnings	60	
Revaluation surplus	100	
	360	
Group's share – 75%		270
Gain from bargain purchase		15

(***Note:*** The gain from a bargain purchase is taken directly to the retained earnings of Push Ltd.)

(W2) Retained earnings

	€000	€000
Push Ltd at reporting date		265
Adjustments		
Journal 5: unrealised inventory profit		(20)
Journal 6: unrealised profit on sale of PPE		(36)
Gain from bargain purchase		15
		224
Shove Ltd at reporting date	140	
Adjustments		
Jnl 2 Additional depreciation	(60)	
Jnl 7 Depreciation write back	4	
	84	
Less: Balance at acquisition date	60	
Post-acquisition	24	
Group Share × 75%		13
Consolidated SoFP		257

(W3) Non-controlling interests

Shove Ltd at reporting date		
Ordinary shares	200	
Retained earnings	140	
Adjustments		
Jnl 1 Revaluation surplus	100	
Jnl 2 Additional depreciation	(40)	
Jnl 7 Depreciation write back	4	
	404	
NCI × 25%		101

Push Ltd
CONSOLIDATED STATEMENT OF FINANCIAL POSITION
as at 31 August 2011

Assets	**€000**
Non-current assets	
Property, plant and equipment	488
Loans	90
	578
Current assets	
Inventory	470
Trade receivables	235
Cash	210
	915
Total assets	**1,493**
Equity and liabilities	
Ordinary share capital	840
Retained earnings	257
Total shareholders' equity	1,097
Non-controlling interest	101
Total equity	1,198
Non-current liabilities	
Long term loans	40
Current liabilities	
Trade payables	255
Total equity and liabilities	**1,493**

Chapter 5

The Statement of Financial Position Accounting for Associates

Learning Objectives

After reading this chapter you should be able to:

- Define an associate;
- Explain the concept of significant influence;
- Explain the meaning of the equity method of accounting and its application to the consolidated SoFP; and
- Illustrate equity accounting through completion of relevant questions.

Introduction

Before discussing the group situation, it is important to note that equity accounting also applies when an investing company without subsidiaries acquires an associate. This chapter only deals with the effect of equity accounting on consolidated financial statements.

Your focus must now change from consolidating **all** the assets and liabilities of a subsidiary (**full consolidation**) to consolidating **none** of the assets and liabilities of an associate (**equity accounting**). As detailed in **Chapter 2**, a parent can only exercise significant influence over the financial and operating policies of an associate as it owns only between 20% and 50% of its voting shares. It is logical, therefore, that a different accounting treatment be given to an investment in an associate (A Ltd).

When consolidating a subsidiary (S Ltd) the investment in S Ltd is replaced in the consolidated SoFP by the net assets of S Ltd. In the case of an associate, the investment in A Ltd is carried to the consolidated SoFP (albeit at a valuation – see below) since the net assets of A Ltd are *not* consolidated. Thus, the treatments for subsidiaries and associates are effectively opposite in nature. (See also **Questions 5.6** and **5.7**.)

Prior to 1971, a long-term investment in another entity was treated either as: a trade investment; or an investment in a subsidiary. A trade investment was accounted for as a non-current asset (formerly, a *fixed asset*) and the investing company took credit in profit or loss for dividends received/receivable. However, it was considered that the interests of the shareholders of the investing company were not served by merely accounting for dividends received/receivable from an associate, as this would not measure accurately either the associate's performance or the share of the profit of the associate in which the investing company had a significant investment. The **equity method of accounting** was devised (through SSAP 1) to give such information and to reflect it in the financial statements of the investor.

Why a Parent would Acquire an Interest in an Associate

Many groups acquire interests in associates for such reasons as:
(a) attempting to ensure the supply of a vital raw material;
(b) securing a return on investment by way of a stream of dividends;
(c) gaining management expertise.

How Significant Influence is 'Evidenced'

Take an example of a shareholder in an associate company speaking to a director of its parent:

> "Can you tell me why your company is in a position to exercise significant influence over the affairs of my company?"

IAS 28 *Investments in Associates*, at paragraph 7, details the ways in which significant influence by an investor is evidenced, meaning that it can be shown that it exists:
"(a) representation on the board of directors or equivalent governing body of the investee;
(b) participation in policy-making processes, including participation in decisions about dividends or other distributions;
(c) material transactions between the investor and the investee;
(d) interchange of managerial personnel; or
(e) provision of essential technical information or expertise."

While any one of the above would be evidence of significant influence, representation on the board of directors of the investee is the strongest evidence. The investing company should be influential in the direction taken by the associate through participation in policy decisions such as strategy, dividends, capital expenditure, etc.

Accounting for Associates

Under the equity method of accounting (equity accounting) the investment in A Ltd is initially recorded at cost which is then increased or decreased each year by the investor's share of the profit or loss of A Ltd, and decreased by any impairment of premium/goodwill.[1] The resultant valuation is carried to the consolidated SoFP.

---

[1] 'A premium on acquisition' ('premium') is term normally used in practice when acquiring an interest in an associate, rather the term 'goodwill'.

Application of Equity Accounting

> ***Key Note:*** None of the individual assets and liabilities of an associate are consolidated. HOWEVER, the investment in an associate is carried to the consolidated SoFP at a valuation.

The carrying amount of an investment in a consolidated statement of financial position can be arrived at by using 1 of 2 methods of calculation, which are shown in **Example 5.1** below:

Example 5.1: Valuation of Carrying Amount of Investment in an Associate

P Ltd, which had two subsidiaries, purchased 40% of the ordinary shares of A Ltd on 1 August 2009 when A Ltd's issued ordinary share capital was €300,000 and its retained earnings €500,000. The cost of the investment was €340,000.

A Ltd
Draft Statement of Financial Position
as at 31 July 2011

	€
Sundry net assets	1,100,000
Ordinary share capital	300,000
Retained earnings	800,000
	1,100,000

The premium on acquisition (goodwill) of A Ltd was impaired during the year ended 31 July 2011 in the amount of €5,000.

Requirement Show the value of the investment in A Ltd in the consolidated statement of financial position of the P Ltd group as at 31 July 2011.

Solution

First, the **Premium on Acquisition (Goodwill)** must be calculated:

	€	€
Cost of investment		340,000
A Ltd at acquisition date:		
Ordinary share capital	300,000	
Retained earnings	500,000	
	800,000	
Group's share 40%		320,000
Premium on acquisition		20,000
Impairment		5,000
Remaining		15,000

Method 1

	€	€
Cost of investment		340,000
Plus		
Share of post-acquisition retained profits and reserves of A Ltd (to end of reporting period):		
Retained earnings at end of reporting period	800,000	
Less Retained earnings at acquisition date	(500,000)	
Post-acquisition retained earnings	300,000	
Group's Share: 40%		120,000
Less		
Any write-off of premium on acquisition (because of impairment)		(5,000)
Carrying amount of investment		455,000

(***Note:*** Method 1 is preferred in this text as it is more suited to the double-entry approach.)

Method 2

	€
Group's share of net asset of A Ltd (at reporting period) (40% × 1,100,000)	440,000
Plus	
Premium on acquisition not written off	15,000
Carrying amount of investment	455,000

(***Note:*** Premium (goodwill) is not amortised under IFRS 3 *Business Combinations* – it is tested for impairment annually and only written down if there is impairment (IAS 36) as in the case of a subsidiary (see **Chapters 3** and **4**.)

Accounting for an associate (using Method 1) can be achieved by means of **two journal entries** in the financial statements of the investing company, normally the parent (P Ltd), thus:

			€	€
1.	Dr.	Investment in A Ltd	120,000	
	Cr.	Retained earnings P Ltd		120,000

with the investor's share of the post-acquisition earnings and any other reserves of A Ltd to reporting date.

2.	Dr.	Retained earnings P Ltd	5,000	
	Cr.	Investment in A Ltd		5,000

with the cumulative impairment of premium to the reporting date.

Complications (when Accounting for an Associate)

Complication 1 – Unrealised Inventory Profit

Unrealised inventory profit can arise from transactions between a parent and an associate. An associate is *not* a group company but the **investors' share** of unrealised profit between P Ltd and A Ltd must be eliminated in the consolidated workings (see **Example 5.2**).

EXAMPLE 5.2: TREATMENT OF UNREALISED INVENTORY PROFIT

P Ltd has a subsidiary S Ltd and a 40%-owned associate (A Ltd), all of which have a reporting date of 31 August 2011.

P Ltd sells goods at a profit to A Ltd

During August 2011, P Ltd sold goods to A Ltd at invoice value €60,000 on which P Ltd made a gross profit of 20%. All of the goods were in the inventory of A Ltd at the reporting date.

ACCOUNTING TREATMENT

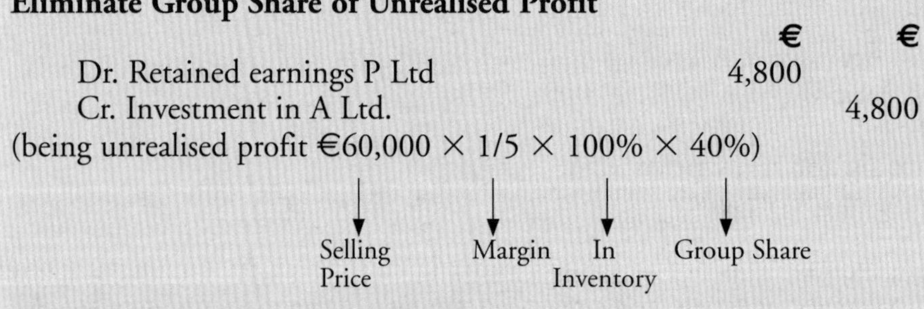

Eliminate Group Share of Unrealised Profit

	€	€
Dr. Retained earnings P Ltd	4,800	
Cr. Investment in A Ltd.		4,800

(being unrealised profit €60,000 × 1/5 × 100% × 40%)

A Ltd sells goods at a profit to P Ltd

During August 2011, A Ltd sells goods to P Ltd at invoice value €120,000 on which A Ltd made a mark-up of 50%. One half of the goods were in the inventory of P Ltd at the reporting date.

	€	€
Dr. Retained earnings P Ltd	8,000	
Cr. Inventory		8,000

(being unrealised profit €120,000 $\times \frac{1}{3} \times \frac{1}{2} \times$ 40%)

Complication 2 – Dividends

If an associate (A Ltd) has proposed a dividend before the period end, a portion of that dividend is naturally payable to the parent (P Ltd):

(a) if P Ltd has taken credit for its share of the dividend in its SoCI, **this figure should not be included in the consolidated SoCI;**
(b) the parent does, however, take credit in the consolidated SoCI for its share of the profits of A Ltd, **which includes its share of A Ltd's dividend**.

Complication 3 – Inter-company Balances

Inter-company balances between a parent (P Ltd) and an associate (A Ltd) at the reporting date **should not be eliminated. Any amounts in P Ltd's SoFP owing to/from A Ltd should be carried to the consolidated SoFP. A Ltd is not a group company.**

Share of Loss of Associate

The cost of the investment in an associate would be reduced each year by the investor's share of the losses of that associate. However, the total losses recognised cannot exceed the cost of the investment.

Conclusion

Beware! As none of the assets and liabilities of an associate (A Ltd) are consolidated, when preparing consolidated workings, do ***not*** include any balances from A Ltd.

Summary

1. IAS 28 defines an associate as "an entity, including an unincorporated entity such as a partnership, over which the investor has **significant influence** and that is neither a subsidiary nor an interest in a joint venture".
2. Significant influence normally arises when the investing entity or group acquires between 20% and 50% of the voting power of the investee. Conversely, if the investor holds less than 20% of the voting power of the investee, it is presumed that the investor does not have significant influence, unless such influence can be demonstrated.
3. The **equity method** of accounting is used for the treatment of an associate in consolidated financial statements.
4. None of the assets and liabilities of an associate are consolidated with those of a parent and subsidiary.
5. The investment in an associate is included in the consolidated statement of financial position at a valuation calculated as follows (Method 1):

	€
Cost of investment	X
Plus	
Group's share of the post-acquisition profits and any other reserves of A Ltd	X
Less	
Cumulative impairment of premium on acquisition to reporting date	(X)
	X

QUESTIONS

Question 5.1

What percentage of the voting rights of an investee must an investing entity or group purchase in order to acquire an associate?

Solution

If an investor holds between 20% and 50% of the voting power of an investee, it is presumed that the investor has significant influence over the investee and therefore an associate is acquired, unless this assumption can be rebutted.

Question 5.2

Explain the term 'significant influence' in the context of an investment in an associate.

Solution

Significant influence is the power to participate in the financial and operating policy decisions of the investee but not to control or jointly control them.

Question 5.3

What method is used to account for an associate in consolidated financial statements?

Solution

An investment in an associate is accounted for using the equity method.

Question 5.4

How is an investment in an associate accounted for in a consolidated statement of financial position?

Solution to Question 5.4

An investment in an associate is carried to the consolidated statement of financial position at a valuation, calculated in either of the following ways:

	€
Cost of investment	X
Group's share of post-acquisition profits and reserves of A Ltd	X
Less impairment of premium on acquisition	(X)
	X

Or

Group's share of net assets of A Ltd at reporting date	X
Premium not impaired	X
	X

Question 5.5

Explain the treatment of assets and liabilities of an associate in the consolidated statement of financial position.

Solution to Question 5.5

None of the assets and liabilities of an associate are consolidated with those of a parent and subsidiary.

> ***Note:*** Questions 5.6 and 5.7 are longer, review-type questions. They include an associate and also provide an opportunity to revise the principles of full consolidation of a subsidiary. Each of their solutions contains:
> 1. The T account method workings
> 2. The columnar method workings; and
> 3. The consolidated SoFP.

Question 5.6

The following are the summarised statements of financial position of Pearl Ltd, Sapphire Ltd and Amethyst Ltd as at 31 July 2011:

	Pearl Ltd €000	**Sapphire Ltd €000**	**Amethyst Ltd €000**
Assets			
Non-current assets			
Property, plant and equipment	12,830	7,690	5,130
Investment in Sapphire Ltd	5,040	–	–
Investment in Amethyst Ltd	1,390	–	–
Current assets	4,490	2,680	1,770
Total assets	**23,750**	**10,370**	**6,900**
Equity and liabilities			
Equity			
Ordinary share capital (€1)	10,000	5,000	4,000
Retained earnings	7,930	3,210	1,250
Non-current liabilities	2,000	1,200	900
Current liabilities	3,820	960	750
Total equity and liabilities	**23,750**	**10,370**	**6,900**

The following additional information is available:

1. Pearl Ltd acquired 3 million of the ordinary shares of Sapphire Ltd on 1 October 2009 when the retained earnings of Sapphire Ltd were €1,800,000.
2. Pearl Ltd acquired 30% of the ordinary shares of Amethyst Ltd on 1 March 2010 when the retained earnings of Amethyst Ltd were €500,000.
3. During July 2011 Amethyst Ltd sold goods to Pearl Ltd at invoice value €60,000 on which Amethyst Ltd earned a mark-up of 20%. Pearl Ltd had 60% of these goods in inventory at the reporting date and the invoice was not settled until 30 August 2011.
4. Premium on acquisition of Amethyst Ltd was impaired by €10,000 during the year ended 31 July 2011.

Requirement Prepare the consolidated statement of financial position of the Pearl Ltd group as at 31 July 2011.

Solution to Question 5.6

Group Structure

	Sapphire	**Amethyst**
Group	60%	30%
Non-Group interests	40%	

Journal Entries

	€000	**€000**
1. Dr. Retained earnings (Pearl)	1.8	
Cr. Inventories		1.8
(Unrealised profit €60,000 × 1/6 × 60% × 30%)		
2. Dr. Retained earnings (Pearl)	10	
Cr. Investment in Amethyst		10
(Impairment of premium)		
3. Dr. Investment in Amethyst	225	
Cr. Retained earnings (Pearl)		225

(Group's share of post-acquisition earnings of Amethyst: 30% × (1,250,000 − 500,000))

WORKINGS (T account Method)

Note: none of the assets and liabilities of Amethyst Ltd are consolidated.

Property, Plant and Equipment

Debit		**Credit**	
P	12,830		
S	7,690	SoFP	20,520
	20,520		20,520

Investment in Sapphire

Debit		**Credit**	
P	5,040	Cost of control	5,040

Investment in Amethyst

Debit		**Credit**	
P	1,390	Journal 2	10
Journal 3	225	SoFP	1,605
	1,615		1,615

Current Assets

Debit		**Credit**	
P	4,490	Journal 1	1.8
S	2,680	SoFP	7,168.2
	7,170		7,170

Ordinary Shares

Debit		**Credit**	
Cost of control 60%	3,000	P	10,000
NCI 40%	2,000	S	5,000
SoFP	10,000		
	15,000		15,000

Retained Earnings

Debit		**Credit**	
Journal 1 (P Ltd)	1.8	P	7,930
Journal 2 (P Ltd)	10	S	3,210
Cost of control (60%×€1,800)	1,080		
NCI (40% × €3,210)	1,284		
SoFP	8,989.2	Journal 3	225
	11,365		11,365

Non-current Liabilities

Debit		**Credit**	
		P	2,000
SoFP	3,200	S	1,200
	3,200		3,200

Current Liabilities

Debit		Credit	
		P	3,820
SoFP	4,780	S	960
	4,780		4,780

Cost of Control

Debit		Credit	
		Ordinary shares	3,000
		Retained earnings	1,080
Investment in S Ltd	5,040	SoFP: Goodwill	960
	5,040		5,040

Non-controlling Interests

Debit		Credit	
		Ordinary shares	2,000
SoFP	3,284	Retained earnings	1,284
	3,284		3,284

WORKINGS (Columnar Method)

	Pearl	Sapphire	Adjustments	Consol. SoFP
	€000	€000	€000	€000
Property. plant and equipment	12,830	7,690		20,520
Investment in Sapphire	5,040		(5,040)	—
Investment in Amethyst	1,390		225 (10)	1,605
Goodwill (W1)			960	960
Current assets	4,490	2,680	(1.8)	7,168.2
Total assets	**23,750**	**10,370**	**(3,866.8)**	**30,253.2**
Ordinary share capital	10,000	5,000	(5,000)	10,000
Retained earnings (*W2*)	7,930	3,210	(2,150.8)	8,989.2
Non-controlling interests (*W3*)			3284	3,284
Non-current liabilities	2,000	1,200		3,200
Current liabilities	3,820	960		4,780
Total equity and liabilities	**23,750**	**10,370**	**(3,866.8)**	**30,253.2**

(W1) Goodwill	**€000**	**€000**
Cost of investment		5,040
Saphire at acquisition date:		
Ordinary shares	5,000	
Retained earnings	1,800	
	6,800	
Group's share – 60%		4,080
SoFP		960

(W2) Retained earnings

Pearl at reporting date		7,930
Journal 1 (unrealised profit)		(1.8)
Journal 2 (premium impaired)		(10)
Journal 3 (share of post-acq. of A Ltd)		225
Sapphire: at reporting date	3,210	
at acquisition date	1,800	
post-acquisition	1,410	
Group's share: 60%		846
Consolidated SoFP		8,989.2

(W3) Non-controlling interests	€000	€000
Saphire at reporting date		
Ordinary shares	5,000	
Retained earnings	3,210	
	8,210	
× 40%		3,284

Pearl Ltd
STATEMENT OF FINANCIAL POSITION
as at 31 July 2011

	€000
Assets	
Non-current assets	
Property, plant and equipment	20,520
Goodwill	960
Investment in associate	1,605
Current assets	7,168.2
Total assets	**30,253.2**
Equity and liabilities	
Equity	
Ordinary share capital	10,000
Retained earnings	8,989.2
Total shareholders' equity	18,989.2
Non-controlling interests	3,284
Total equity	22,273.2
Non-current liabilities	3,200
Current liabilities	4,780
Total equity and liabilities	**30,253.2**

Question 5.7

The following are the Statements of Financial Position of Purple Plc, Silver Ltd and Amber Ltd. as at 30 June 2011:

	Purple Plc €000	Silver Ltd €000	Amber Ltd €000
Assets			
Non-current assets			
Property plant and equipment	10,350	9,520	16,200
Investment in Silver Ltd	5,450	–	–
Investment in Amber Ltd	4,950	–	–
	20,750	9,520	16,200
Current Assets			
Inventories	1,600	1,020	780
Trade Receivables	970	600	490
Cash	150	50	20
	2,720	1,670	1,290
Total assets	**23,470**	**11,190**	**17,490**
Equity and liabilities			
Equity			
Ordinary €1 shares	12,500	4,000	8,700
Share premium	1,000	800	1,500
Retained earnings	8,680	5,260	6,440
Total equity	22,180	10,060	16,640
Current liabilities			
Trade payables	1,290	1,130	850
Total equity and liabilities	**23,470**	**11,190**	**17,490**

The following additional information is available:

1. Purple Plc acquired 70% of the ordinary shares of Silver Ltd on 1 July 2008 when its reserves were:

	€000
Share premium account	800
Retained earnings	2,500

2. At 1 July 2008 the fair value of the property, plant and equipment of Silver Ltd. exceeded the book value by €100,000. This surplus has not been reflected in the financial statements of Silver Ltd. At that date the average remaining useful life of the assets was five years.
3. Purple Plc acquired 30% of the ordinary shares of Amber Ltd on 1 September 2008 when the reserves of Amber Ltd were:

	€000
Share Premium	1,500
Retained earnings	2,600

4. During March 2011 Silver Ltd sold goods to Purple Plc at invoice value €200,000 on which Silver Ltd made a gross profit of 20%. One half of these goods remained in the inventories of Purple Plc at 30 June 2011.
5. Impairment of goodwill/premium has occurred as follows:

Year ended 30 June 2011 –	on acquisition of Silver Ltd	€50,000
	on acquisition of Amber Ltd	€100,000

Requirement Prepare the consolidated statement of financial position of the Purple Plc group as at 30 June 2011.

Solution to Question 5.7

Journal Entries			**€000**	**€000**
1.	Dr.	PPE	100	
	Cr.	Cost of control (70%)		70
	Cr.	NCI (30%)		30
	(being increase in PPE at acquisition date from book value to fair value)			
2.	Dr.	Retained earnings (S Ltd)	60	
	Cr.	PPE		60
	(being cumulative depreciation on revaluation surplus 100,000 × 3/5)			
3.	Dr.	Retained earnings (S Ltd)	20	
	Cr.	Inventory		20
	(with unrealised profit on inventory: (€200,000 × 1/5 × 50%)			
4.	Dr.	Retained earnings (P Ltd)	50	
	Cr.	Cost of control		50
	(with cumulative impairment of goodwill on acquisition of Silver Ltd)			
		Accounting for the Associate		
5.	Dr.	Investment in Amber Ltd	1,152	
	Cr.	Share Premium (a)		nil
	Cr.	Retained Earnings (b)		1,152
	(a) Share Premium: 30% × (1,500 − 1,500)			
	(b) 30% (6,440 − 2,600)			
	(with 30% of the post-acquisition reserves of Amber Ltd)			
6.	Dr.	Retained Earnings P Ltd	100	
	Cr.	Investment in Amber Ltd		100
	(with cumulative impairment of premium on Amber Ltd)			

Workings (T Account Method)

Property, Plant and Equipment

Debit		**Credit**	
Journal 1	100	Journal 2	60
P	10,350		
S	9,520	SoFP	19,910
	19,970		19,970

Investment in Silver Ltd

Debit		Credit	
P	5,450	Cost of control	5,450

Investment in Amber Ltd

P	4,950	Journal 6	100
Journal 5	1,152	SoFP	6,002
	6,102		6,102

Inventories

Debit		Credit	
		Journal 3	20
P	1,600		
S	1,020	SoFP	2,600
	2,620		2,620

Trade Receivables

Debit		Credit	
P	970		
S	600	SoFP	1,570
	1,570		1,570

Trade Payables

Debit		Credit	
SoFP	2,420	P	1,290
		S	1,130
	2,420		2,420

Cash

Debit		Credit	
P	150	SoFP	200
S	50		
	200		200

Ordinary Shares

Debit		Credit	
Cost of control 70%	2,800	P	12,500
NCI 30%	1,200	S	4,000
SoFP	12,500		
	16,500		16,500

Share Premium

Debit		Credit	
Cost of Control (800 × 70%)	560	P	1,000
NCI (800 × 30%)	240	S	800
SoFP	1,000		
	1,800		1,800

Retained Earnings

Debit		Credit	
Journal 2 (S Ltd)	60	P	8,680
Journal 3 (S Ltd)	20	S	5,260
Journal 4 (P Ltd)	50	Journal 5 (P Ltd)	1,152
Journal 6 (P Ltd)	100		
Cost of Control (70% × 2,500)	1,750		
NCI 30% (5,260 – 60 – 20)	1,554		
SoFP	11,558		
	15,092		15,092

Cost of Control

Debit		Credit	
Investment in Silver	5,450	Journal 1	70
		Ordinary shares	2,800
		Share premium	560
		Retained earnings	1,750
		Journal 4	50
		SoFP – Goodwill	220
	5,450		5,450

Non-Controlling Interests

Debit		Credit	
SoFP	3,024	Journal 1	30
		Ordinary shares	1,200
		Share premium	240
		Retained earnings	1,554
	3,024		3,024

WORKINGS (Columnar Method)

	Purple	Silver	Adjustments	Consol. SoFP
	€000	€000	€000	€000
Property, plant and equipment	10,350	9,520	100 (60)	19,910
Investment in Silver	5,450		(5,450)	0
Investment in Amber	4,950		1,152 (100)	6,002
Goodwill *(W1)*			220	220
Inventories	1,600	1,020	(20)	2,600
Trade receivables	970	600		1,570
Cash	150	50		200
Total Assets	**23,470**	**11,190**	**(4,158)**	**30,502**
Ordinary shares	12,500	4,000	(4,000)	12,500
Share premium *(W2)*	1,000	800	(800)	1,000
Retained earnings *(W3)*	8,680	5,260	(2,382)	11,558
Non-controlling interests *(W4)*			3,024	3,024
Trade payables	1,290	1,130		2,420
Total Equity and Liabilities	**23,470**	**11,190**	**(4,158)**	**30,502**

(W1) Goodwill	€000	€000
Cost of investment		5,450
Silver at acquisition date:		
Ordinary shares	4,000	
Share premium	800	
Retained earnings	2,500	
Revaluation surplus	100	
	7,400	
Group's share – 70%		5,180
Goodwill		270
Impairment		50
SoFP		220

(W2) Share premium		
Purple at reporting date		1,000
Silver at reporting date	800	
at acquisition date	800	
post-acquisition	nil	
Group's share – 70%		nil
SoFP		1,000

(W3) Retained earnings	€000	€000
Purple at reporting date		8,680
Journal 4 Goodwill impairment		(50)
Journal 5 Share of Amber post-acq.		1,152
Journal 6 Premium impairment		(100)
		9,682
Silver at reporting date	5,260	
Journal 2 Depreciation	(60)	
Journal 3 Unrealised profit	(20)	
	5,180	
Silver at acquisition date	2,500	
Post-acquisition	2,680	
Group's share – 70%		1,876
		11,558
(W4) Non-controlling interests		
Silver at reporting date		
Ordinary shares	4,000	
Share premium	800	
Retained earnings	5,260	
Revaluation surplus	100	
Journal 2 Depreciation	(60)	
Journal 3 Unrealised profit	(20)	
	10,080	
NCI × 30%		3,024

Purple Plc
CONSOLIDATED STATEMENT OF FINANCIAL POSITION
as at 30 June 2011

Assets	**€000**
Non-current assets	
Property, plant and equipment	19,910
Goodwill	220
Investment in associate	6,002
	26,132
Non-current assets	
Inventory	2,600
Trade receivables	1,570
Cash	200
	4,370
Total assets	**30,502**

Equity and liabilities	
Equity	
Ordinary share capital	12,500
Share premium account	1,000
Retained earnings	11,558
Total shareholders' equity	25,058
Non-controlling interests	3,024
Total equity	28,082
Current liabilities	
Trade payables	2,420
Total equity and liabilities	**30,502**

Chapter 6

The Statement of Financial Position Accounting for Joint Ventures

Learning Objectives

After reading this chapter you should be able to:
- Define a joint venture;
- Explain the concept of joint control;
- Describe the accounting treatment for proportionate consolidation; and
- Account for a joint venture in a consolidated SoFP.

Introduction

Stop! Before we start in to this chapter, it is important now to recall:
1. how to treat a subsidiary in the consolidated SoFP: all its assets and liabilities are consolidated with those of the parent (P Ltd), whether or not there is non-controlling interests;
2. how to treat an associate in the consolidated SoFP: none of its assets and liabilities are consolidated with those of P Ltd and S Ltd.

In this chapter, we must deal with another type of investment, i.e. a joint venture (JV). IAS 31 applies equally to venturers who do not prepare group accounts and those who do. This chapter focuses on the latter. The way to account for a parent's interest in a JV is to consolidate the group's share of each asset and liability of the JV.

Key Feature of a Joint Venture

The key feature of a joint venture is **joint control**.

Forms of Joint Ventures

IAS 31 identifies **three broad types of joint venture**:
1. jointly controlled operations;
2. jointly controlled assets;
3. jointly controlled entities.

1. Jointly Controlled Operations

This involves the use of assets and other resources of the venturers rather than setting up a separate company, partnership or other entity.

> ***Key Note:*** An entity is not established. Therefore, no consolidation procedures are required, and so are not a topic for this text.[1]

2. Jointly Controlled Assets

Jointly controlled assets involve joint control and often joint ownership by the venturers of one or more assets contributing to or acquired for the joint venture.

> ***Key Note:*** An entity is not established. Therefore, no consolidation procedures are required, and so is not a topic for this text.[2]

3. Jointly Controlled Entities

A jointly controlled entity is a joint venture that involves the establishment of a company, partnership or other entity in which each venturer has an interest. The entity operates in the same way as other entities, except that a contractual arrangement between the venturers establishes joint control over the economic activity of the entity. The assets of the entity are jointly controlled and each venturer is entitled to a share of the profits.

> ***Key Note:*** A jointly controlled entity maintains its own accounting records and prepares its own financial statements and a venturer, who is a parent, must account for the joint venture in its consolidated financial statements.

The strategic decisions, e.g. distribution policy, capital expenditure, raising of finance, require the unanimous consent of the venturers. Decisions that arise in the day-to-day running of the joint venture's business may be taken by an operator or manager who acts within the financial and operating policies agreed by the venturers.

---

[1] See ***Connolly***, Chapter 30, "Joint Arrangements", Section 30.2.

[2] *Ibid.*

Accounting Treatment for Joint Ventures

(a) The Separate Accounts of a Venturer

IAS 31 states that, where a venturer prepares separate financial statements, an investment in a jointly controlled entity should be accounted for:

Either

1. At cost

Or

2. In accordance with IAS 39 *Financial Instruments: Recognition and Measurement.*[3]

(b) The Consolidated Financial Statements of a Venturer

A venturer recognises its interest in a jointly-controlled entity using either **proportionate consolidation** or the alternative **equity method** (see below, "**Use of Equity Method for Joint Ventures**"), as used for associates in accordance with IAS 28 *Investment in Associates* (see **Chapter 5**). Proportionate consolidation is at present the preferred method under the current version of IAS 31.

Proportionate Consolidation This is a method of accounting whereby a venturer's share of each of the assets, liabilities, income and expenses of a jointly controlled entity is combined line-by-line with similar items in the venturer's financial statements or reported as separate line items in the venturer's financial statements (IAS 31).

Proportionate consolidation should be discontinued from the date on which the venturer ceases to have joint control over a jointly-controlled entity, in which case equity accounting would probably become the appropriate accounting treatment (see **Example 4.1**).

Example 6.1: Changing from Proportionate Consolidation to Equity Accounting

A parent (P Ltd) owns 45% of a JV along with X Ltd, a company outside the group, who owns 55%. Joint control has been exercised for some time, therefore, proportionate consolidation was the appropriate accounting treatment. At the start of the current year, X Ltd began to assume control over strategic decisions because of its greater holding in the JV. The accounting treatment for the JV in the P Ltd group should now change to the equity method if the parent can now only exert significant influence.

Exception to Normal Consolidation of Joint Venture When an interest in a JV is classified as 'held for sale' it should be accounted for in accordance with IFRS 5 *Non-current Assets Held for Sale and Discontinued Operations.*

[3] IAS 39 is discussed in detail in ***Connolly***, Chapter 25 "Financial Instruments".

Accounting Entries for Proportionate Consolidation

The following entries are made in the consolidated workings:

1.
Dr. Assets (various)
Cr. Investment in JV
with the **group's share** of JV's assets.

2.
Dr. Investment in JV
Cr. Liabilities (various)
with the **group's share** of JV's liabilities.

3.
Dr. Investment in JV
Cr. Reserves
with the **group's share** of JV'S post-acquisition profits and reserves.

See **Example 6.2** below.

Disclosure of a Joint Venture in the Consolidated SoFP

IAS 31 allows two reporting formats to give effect to proportionate consolidation in the consolidated SoFP:

Method 1

The consolidated SoFP may include **separate line items** for the group's share of the assets and liabilities of the joint venture, e.g.:

		€	€
Property, plant and equipment:	Group	X	
	Share of JV	X	X

Method 2

Combine the share of the assets and liabilities of JV on the face of the SoFP with those of the group and supplement in the notes, e.g.:

	€
Property, plant and equipment (Total Group + Share of JV)	X

(***Key Note:*** This text uses Method 1 only.)

Example 6.2 deals with all the basic principles and practices of consolidating a JV (for the SoFP).

Example 6.2: Consolidating a Parent, a Subsidiary and Joint Venture

The following summarised statements of financial position have been prepared as at 31 August 2011:

	P Ltd €000	S Ltd €000	JV Ltd €000
Assets			
Non-current assets			
Property, plant and equipment	9,810	5,880	3,920
Investment in S Ltd	3,890		
Investment in JV Ltd	1,260		
Current assets	2,450	1,470	980
Total Assets	**17,410**	**7,350**	**4,900**
Equity and Liabilities			
Equity			
Ordinary share capital (€1)	10,000	3,000	1,000
Retained earnings	3,450	2,430	2,710
Total equity	13,450	5,430	3,710
Non-current liabilities	2,000	800	500
Current liabilities	1,960	1,120	690
Total Equity and Liabilities	**17,410**	**7,350**	**4,900**

The following additional information is available:

1. P Ltd acquired 2.7 million ordinary shares in subsidiary on 1 September 2009 when the retained earnings of subsidiary were €1,300,000.
2. P Ltd acquired 50% of joint venture on 1 March 2010 when the retained earnings of joint venture were €1,500,000.

Journal Entries

			€000	€000
1.	Dr.	Property, plant and equipment	1,960	
	Dr.	Current assets	490	
	Cr.	Investment in JV Ltd		2,450
	(Share of joint venture's assets)			
2.	Dr.	Investment in JV Ltd	595	
	Cr.	Non-current liabilities		250
	Cr.	Current liabilities		345
	(Share of joint venture's liabilities)			

3. Dr Investment in joint venture 605
   Cr Retained earnings (P) 605
   (Share of joint ventures post-acquisition profits 50% × (2,710 − 1,500))

WORKINGS (T account Method)

Property, Plant and Equipment

Debit		**Credit**	
P	9,810		
S	5,880		
Journal 1 share of JV	1,960	SoFP	17,650
	17,650		17,650

Investment in S Ltd

Debit		**Credit**	
P	3,890	Cost of control	3,890

Investment in JV Ltd

Debit		**Credit**	
P	1,260	Journal 1	2,450
Journal 2	595		
Journal 3	605	SoFP	10
	2,460		2,460

Current Assets

Debit		**Credit**	
P	2,450		
S	1,470		
Journal 1 – share of JV	490	SoFP	4,410
	4,410		4,410

Ordinary Shares

Debit		**Credit**	
Cost of control 90%	2,700	P	10,000
NCI 10%	300	S	3,000
SoFP	10,000		
	10,000		13,000

Retained Earnings

Debit		**Credit**	
Cost of control (90% × 1,300)	1,170	P	3,450
NCI (10% × 2,430)	243	S	2,430
SoFP	5,072	Journal 3 – share of JV	605
	6,485		6,485

Non-current Liabilities

Debit		Credit	
		P	2,000
		S	800
SoFP	3,050	Journal 2 – share of JV	250
	3,050		3,050

Current Liabilities

Debit		Credit	
		P	1,960
		S	1,120
SoFP	3,425	Journal 2 – share of JV	345
	3,425		3,425

Cost of Control

Debit		Credit	
Investment in S Ltd	3,890	Ordinary shares	2,700
		Retained earnings	1,170
		SoFP: goodwill	20
	3,890		3,890

Non-controlling Interests

Debit		Credit	
		Ordinary shares	300
SoFP	543	Retained earnings	243
	543		543

Workings (Columnar Method)

	P Ltd	S Ltd	Adjustment	Consol. SoFP
	€000	€000	€000	€000
Property, plant and equipment	9,810	5,880	1,960	17,650
Investment in S Ltd	3,890		(3,890)	–
Investment in JV Ltd	1,260		(2450) 595	10
			605	
Goodwill (*W1*)			20	20
Current assets	2,450	1,470	490	4,410
Total assets	**17,410**	**7,350**	**(2,670)**	**22,090**
Ordinary shares	10,000	3,000	(3,000)	10,000
Retained earnings (*W2)*	3,450	2,430	(808)	5,072
Non-controlling interests (*W3)*			543	543
Non-current liabilities	2,000	800	250	3,050
Current liabilities	1,960	1,120	345	3,425
Total equity and liabilities	**17,410**	**7,350**	**(2,670)**	**22,090**

(W1) Goodwill	**€000**	**€000**
Cost of investment in S Ltd		3,890
S Ltd at acquisition date:		
Ordinary shares	3,000	
Retained earnings	1,300	
	4,300	
Group's share: 90%		3,870
SoFP		20

(W2) Retained earnings		
P Ltd at reporting date:		3,450
Journal 3 share of JV Ltd post-acquisition earnings		605
S Ltd at reporting date	2,430	
S Ltd at acquisition date	1,300	
Post-acquisition	1,130	
Group's share: 90%		1,017
SoFP		5,072

(W3) Non-controlling interests	**€000**	**€000**
S Ltd at reporting date:		
Ordinary shares	3,000	
Retained earnings	2,430	
	5,430	
NCI × 10%		543

Parent

Consolidated Statement of Financial Position

as at 31 August 2011

Assets		**€000**	**€000**
Non-current assets			
Property, plant and equipment	Group:	15,690	
	Share of JV:	1,960	17,650
Goodwill			30
Current assets	Group:	3,920	
	Share of JV:	490	4,410
Total assets			**22,090**

Equity and liabilities		
Equity		
Ordinary share capital		10,000
Retained earnings		5,072
Total shareholders' equity		15,072
Non-controlling interests		543
Total equity		15,615
Non-current liabilities		
Group	2,800	
Share of JV	250	
		3,050
Current liabilities		
Group	3,080	
Share of JV:	345	
		3,425
Total equity and liabilities		**22,090**

Use of the Equity Method for Joint Ventures

As an alternative to proportionate consolidation, IAS 31 allows a venture to recognise its interest in a jointly controlled entity using the equity method as in the case of an associate. However, the standard does not recommend the use of equity accounting because proportionate consolidation better reflects the substance and economic reality of a venturer's interest in a jointly controlled entity.

Conclusion

Thus far, you have studied the consolidation procedures for a subsidiary, an associate and a joint venture. A unique opportunity to revise all of these at the same time is presented in **Question 6.7**. Do not let this opportunity pass!

SUMMARY

1. There are three types of joint venture specified in IAS 31:
   (a) Jointly controlled operations;
   (b) Jointly controlled assets: and
   (c) Jointly controlled entities.
2. A jointly controlled entity is a joint venture that involves establishing a corporation, partnership or other entity in which each venturer has an interest and a contractual arrangement exists between the venturers establishing joint control over the economic activities of the entity.

3. Proportionate consolidation is the preferred accounting treatment for an interest in a joint venture in consolidated financial statements. The equity method (as for an associate) is also allowed but not encouraged under IAS 31.
4. Under proportionate consolidation in group accounts, the group's share of each asset and liability of a joint venture is consolidated with the assets and liabilities of a parent and subsidiary. The group's share of the post-acquisition reserves of the joint venture is also consolidated.

QUESTIONS

Question 6.1

What is meant by a joint venture in accordance with IAS 31 *Interests in Joint Ventures*?

Solution

A joint venture is a contractual arrangement whereby two or more parties undertake an economic activity that is subject to joint control.

Question 6.2

How many categories of joint ventures are contained in IAS 31?

Solution

IAS 31 recognises three categories of joint ventures:
(a) jointly controlled operations
(b) jointly controlled assets
(c) jointly controlled entities.

Question 6.3

What are the defining characteristics of a joint venture which causes it to be accounted for in consolidated financial statements?

Solution

The defining characteristics are:
(a) the fact that the joint venture is an entity;
(b) there is joint control over the financial and operating activities of the joint venture.

Question 6.4

Describe the method of accounting for a joint venture in consolidated financial statements.

Solution

Proportionate consolidation is used to account for a jointly controlled entity in consolidated financial statements. The venturer's share of each asset and liability of the joint venture is combined with the assets and liabilities of the venturer.

Question 6.5

Explain the alternative accounting treatment for joint ventures in consolidated financial statements.

Solution

The use of the equity method is permitted (but not encouraged) for treating joint ventures in consolidated financial statements.

> ***Note:*** Questions 6.6 and 6.7 are longer, review-type questions. Question 6.6 involves consolidating a parent, a subsidiary and a joint venture. Question 6.7 goes further and also includes an associate and a trade investment. Each solution to these questions contains:
> 1. Journal adjustments
> 2. The T account method workings
> 3. The columnar method workings
> 4. The consolidated SoFP.

Question 6.6

The following are the draft statements of financial position for P Ltd, S Ltd, and JV Ltd as at 31 May 2011:

STATEMENTS OF FINANCIAL POSITION

	P Ltd	S Ltd	JV Ltd
	€000	€000	€000
Assets			
Non-current assets			
Property, plant and equipment	6,720	4,600	2,380
Investment in S Ltd	2,480		–
Investment in JV Ltd	740		
	9,940	4,600	2,380
Current assets			
Inventories	1,240	580	170
Trade receivables	1,020	430	130
Cash at bank and in hand	150	40	10
	2,410	1050	310
Total assets	**12,350**	**5,650**	**2,690**

Equity and liabilities			
Equity			
Ordinary share capital (1 Euro)	3,000	1,000	1,000
Share premium	500	200	–
Retained earnings	4,920	2,290	1,040
Total equity	8420	3,490	2,040
Non-current liabilities	2,000	1,000	300
Current liabilities	1,930	1,160	350
Total equity and liabilities	**12,350**	**5,650**	**2,690**

The following additional information is available:

1. P Ltd acquired 80% of the ordinary shares of S Ltd on 1 November 2008 when S Ltd had the following reserve balances:

	€000
Share premium	200
Retained Profits	1,500

2. P Ltd acquired 50% of the ordinary shares of JV Ltd on 1 December 2009 when the retained earnings of JV were €440,000. The remaining 50% is owned by R Ltd, a company outside the group. P Ltd and R Ltd jointly control JV Ltd.

Requirement Prepare the consolidated statement of financial position as at 31 May 2011.

Solution to Question 6.6

Journal Entries

Accounting for JV Ltd

		€000	**€000**
1.	Dr. Property, plant and equipment	1,190	
	Dr. Inventories	85	
	Dr. Trade receivables	65	
	Dr. Cash	5	
	Cr. Investment in JV Ltd		1,345
	(Share of JV's assets)		
2.	Dr. Investment in JV Ltd	325	
	Cr. Non-current liabilities		150
	Cr. Current liabilities		175
	(Share of JV's liabilities)		
3.	Dr. Investment in JV	300	
	Cr. Retained earnings (P Ltd)		300
	(Being 50% of post-acquisition retained earnings of JV Ltd 50% (1,040 – 440))		

Workings (T account Method)

Property, Plant and Equipment

Debit		Credit	
P	6,720		
S	4,600		
Journal 1 – share of JV	1,190	SoFP	12,510
	12,510		12,510

Investment in S Ltd

Debit		Credit	
P	2,480	Cost of Control	2,480

Investment in JV Ltd

Debit		Credit	
P	740	Journal 1	1,345
Journal 2	325		
Journal 3	300	SoFP -- premium	20
	1,365		1,365

Inventories

Debit		Credit	
P	1,240		
S	580		
Journal 1 – share of JV	85	SoFP	1,905
	1,905		1,905

Trade Receivables

Debit		Credit	
P	1,020		
S	430		
Journal 1 – share of JV	65	SoFP	1,515
	1,515		1,515

Cash

Debit		Credit	
P	150		
S	40		
Journal 1 – share of JV	5	SoFP	195
	195		195

Non-current Liabilities

Debit		Credit	
		P	2,000
		S	1,000
SoFP	3,150	Journal 2: share of JV	150
	3,150		3,150

Current Liabilities

Debit		Credit	
		P	1,930
		S	1,160
SoFP	3,265	Journal 2 – share of JV	175
	3,265		3,265

Ordinary Shares

Debit		Credit	
Cost of control 80%	800	P	3,000
NCI 20%	200	S	1,000
SoFP	3,000		
	4,000		4,000

Share Premium

Debit		Credit	
Cost of control (80% × 200)	160	P	500
NCI (20% × 200)	40	S	200
SoFP	500		
	700		700

Retained Earnings

Debit		Credit	
Cost of control (80% × 1,500)	1,200	P	4,920
NCI (20% × 2,290)	458	S	2,290
SoFP	5,852	Journal 3 (P Ltd)	300
	7,510		7,510

Cost of Control

Debit		Credit	
Investment in S Ltd	2,480	Ordinary shares	800
		Share premium	160
		Retained earnings	1,200
		SoFP Goodwill	320
	2,480		2,480

Non-controlling interests

Debit		Credit	
		Ordinary shares	200
SoFP	698	Share premium	40
		Retained earnings	458
	698		698

Workings (Columnar Method)

	P Ltd	S Ltd	Adjustment	Consol. SoFP
	€000	€000	€000	€000
Property, plant and equipment	6,720	4,600	1,190	12,510
Investment in S Ltd	2,480		(2,480)	
Investment in JV Ltd	740		(1,345) 325 300	20
Goodwill *(W1)*			320	320
Inventories	1,240	580	85	1,905
Trade receivables	1,020	430	65	1,515
Cash	150	40	5	195
Total Assets	**12,350**	**5,650**	**(1,535)**	**16,465**
Ordinary shares	3,000	1,000	(1,000)	3,000
Share premium *(W2)*	500	200	(200)	500
Retained earnings *(W3)*	4,920	2,290	(1,358)	5,852
Non-controlling interests *(W4)*			698	698
Non-current liabilities	2,000	1,000	150	3,150
Current liabilities	1,930	1,160	175	3,265
Total Equity and Liabilities	**12,350**	**5,650**	**(1,535)**	**16,465**

(W1) Goodwill	€000	€000
Cost of investment		2,480
S Ltd at acquisition date:		
Share capital	1,000	
Share premium	200	
Retained earnings	1,500	
	2,700	
Group's share – 80%		2,160
SoFP		320

(W2) Share premium		
P Ltd at reporting date		500
S Ltd at reporting date	200	
at acquisition date	200	
post-acquisition	nil	
Group's share		nil
SoFP		500

(W3) Retained earnings	**€000**	**€000**
P Ltd at reporting date		4,920
Journal 3 share of JV post-acquisition profits		300
S Ltd at reporting date	2,290	
At acquisition date	1,500	
Post-acquisition	790	
Group's share – 80%		632
SoFP		5,852

(W4) Non-controlling interests		
S Ltd at reporting date:		
Ordinary shares	1,000	
Share premium	200	
Retained earnings	2,290	
	3,490	
NCI × 20%		698

P Limited
STATEMENT OF FINANCIAL POSITION
as at 31 May 2011

		€000	**€000**
Assets			
Non-current assets			
Property, plant and equipment	– Group	11,320	
	– Share of JV	1,190	12,510
Goodwill/premium			340
			12,850
Current Assets			
Inventory	Group	1,820	
	Share of JV	85	1,905
Trade receivables	Group	1,450	
	Share of JV	65	1,515
Cash	Group	190	
	Share of JV	5	195
			3,615
Total Assets			**16,465**
Equity and Liabilities			**€000**
Equity			
Ordinary share capital			3,000
Share premium			500
Retained earnings			5,852
Total shareholders' equity			9,352

Non controlling interests			698
Total equity			10,050
Non-current liabilities	Group	3,000	
	Share of JV	150	3,150
Current liabilities	Group	3,090	
	Share of JV	175	3,265
Total equity and liabilities			**16,465**

Question 6.7

The following are the statements of financial position of Peach Plc, Silver Ltd, Amber Ltd and Green Ltd for the year ended 30 June 2011:

	Peach Plc	Silver Ltd	Amber Ltd	Green Ltd
	€000	**€000**	**€000**	**€000**
Assets				
Non-current assets				
Property, plant and equipment	10,350	9,520	16,200	6,400
Investment in Silver Ltd	5,450	–	–	–
Investment in Amber Ltd	4,950	–	–	–
Investment in Green Ltd	3,200	–	–	–
Investment in Blue Ltd	100	–	–	–
	24,050	9,520	16,200	6,400
Current assets	2,720	1,670	1,290	660
Total assets	**26,770**	**11,190**	**17,490**	**7,060**
Equity and liabilities				
Equity				
Ordinary €1 shares	14,500	4,000	8,700	5,000
Share premium	2,200	800	1,500	–
Retained earnings	8,680	5,260	6,440	1,630
Total equity	25,380	10.060	16,640	6,630
Current liabilities	1,390	1,130	850	430
Total equity and liabilities	**26,770**	**11,190**	**17,490**	**7,060**

The following additional information is available:

1. Peach Plc acquired 70% of the ordinary shares of Silver Ltd on 1 July 2008 when its reserves were:

	€000
Share premium account	800
Retained earnings	2,500

2. Peach Plc acquired 30% of the ordinary shares of Amber Ltd on 1 July 2009 when the reserves of Amber Ltd were:

	€000
Share Premium	1,500
Retained earnings	2,600

3. Peach Plc acquired 50% of the ordinary shares of Green Ltd on 1 July 2010. Red Ltd and Peach Ltd jointly own and jointly control the operations of Green Ltd. Retained earnings of Green Ltd at I July 2010 were €970,000.
4. Impairment of goodwill/premium has occurred as follows:

Year ended 30 June 2011	Silver Ltd	€50,000
	Amber Ltd	€100,000

Requirement Prepare the consolidated statement of financial position as at 30 June 2011.

Solution to Question 6.7

Solution Guidelines

- All of Silver's assets and liabilities are consolidated – *full consolidation.*
- None of Amber's assets and liabilities are consolidated – *equity accounting.*
- The groups share of Green's assets and liabilities are consolidated – *proportionate consolidation.*
- The investment in Red is a trade investment and is carried to the consolidated SoFP.

Accounting for Amber Ltd (Associate)

Journal Entries

		€000	€000
1.	Dr. Investment in Amber Ltd	1,152	
	Cr. Share Premium 30% (1,500 – 1,500)		0
	Cr. Retained Earnings 30% (6,440 – 2,600)		1,152
	(Share of post-acquisition reserves of Amber Ltd)		
2.	Dr. Retained earnings (P Ltd)	100	
	Cr. Investment in Amber Ltd		100
	(Premium impaired)		

Accounting for Green Ltd (Joint Venture)

3.	Dr.	Property, plant and equipment	3,200	
	Dr.	Current assets	330	
	Cr.	Investment in Green Ltd		3,530
		(50% share of Green's assets		
4.	Dr.	Investment in Green Ltd	215	
	Cr.	Current liabilities		215
		(50% share of Green's liabilities)		
5.	Dr.	Investment in Green Ltd	330	
	Cr.	Retained Earnings ((P Ltd)		330
		(Share of Green's post-acquisition profits 50% (1,630 – 970))		

Impairment of Goodwill in Silver Ltd

6.	Dr.	Retained earnings (P Ltd)	50	
	Cr.	Cost of Control		50

WORKINGS (T account Method)

Property, Plant and Equipment

Debit		Credit	
P	10,350		
S	9,520		
Journal 3 – Share of G Ltd	3,200	SoFP	23,070
	23,070		23,070

Investment in Silver Ltd

Debit		Credit	
P	5,450	Cost of Control	5,450

Investment in Amber Ltd

Debit		Credit	
P	4,950	Journal 2	100
Journal 1	1,152	SoFP	6,002
	6,102		6,102

Investment in Green Ltd

Debit		Credit	
P	3,200	Journal 3	3,530
Journal 4	215		
Journal 5	330	SoFP	215
	3,745		3,745

Investment in Blue Ltd

Debit		Credit	
P	100	SoFP	100

The investment would be measured in accordance with IFRS 9.

Current Assets

Debit		Credit	
P	2,720		
S	1,670		
Journal 3 – Share of G Ltd	330	SoFP	4,720
	4,720		4,720

Ordinary Shares

Debit		Credit	
Cost of Control (70%)	2,800	P	14,500
NCI (30%)	1,200		
SoFP	14,500	S	4,000
	18,500		18,500

Share Premium

Debit		Credit	
Cost of Control (70% × 800)	560	P	2,200
NCI (30% × 800)	240		
SoFP	2,200	S	800
	3,000		3,000

Retained Earnings

Debit		Credit	
Journal 2 (P Ltd)	100	P	8,680
Journal 6 (P Ltd)	50	S	5,260
Cost of Control (70% × 2,500)	1,750	Journal 1 (P Ltd)	1,152
NCI (30% × 5,260)	1,578	Journal 5 (P Ltd)	330
SoFP	11,944		
	15,422		15,422

Current Liabilities

Debit		Credit	
		P	1,390
		S	1,130
SoFP	2,735	Journal 4 – Share of G	215
	2,735		2,735

Cost of Control

Debit		Credit	
Investment in S Ltd	5,450	Ordinary shares	2,800
		Share premium	560
		Retained earnings	1,750
		Journal 6	50
		Goodwill	290
	5,450		5,450

Non-controlling Interests

Debit		Credit	
		Ordinary Shares	1,200
		Share Premium	240
SoFP	3,018	Retained earnings	1,578
	3,018		3,018

Workings (Columnar Method)

	Peach €000	Silver €000	Adjustments €000	Consol. SoFP €000
Property, plant and equipment	10,350	9,520	3,200	23,070
Investment in Silver Ltd	5,450		(5,450)	-
Investment in Amber Ltd	4,950		1,152 (100)	6,002
Investment in Green Ltd	3,200		(3,530) 215 330	215
Investment in Blue Ltd	100			100
Goodwill (*W1*)			290	290
Current assets	2,720	1,670	330	4,720
Total assets	**26,770**	**11,190**	**(3,563)**	**34,397**
Ordinary shares	14,500	4,000	(4,000)	14,500
Share premium *(W2)*	2,200	800	(800)	2,200
Retained earnings *(W3)*	8,680	5,260	(1,996)	11,944
Non-controlling interests *(W4)*			3,018	3,018
Current liabilities	1,390	1,130	215	2,735
Total equity and liabilities	**26,770**	**11,190**	**(3563)**	**34,397**

(W1) Goodwill	**€000**	**€000**
Cost of investment in Silver Ltd		5,450
Silver Ltd at date of acquisition:		
Ordinary shares	4,000	
Share premium	800	
Retained earnings	2,500	
	7,300	
Group's share – 70%		5,110
Goodwill		340
Impairment of goodwill		(50)
SoFP		290

(W2) Share premium		
Peach Ltd at reporting date		2,200
Silver Ltd at reporting date	800	
at acquisition date	800	
post-acquisition	nil	
Group's share		nil
SoFP		2,200

(W3) Retained earnings		
Peach Ltd at reporting date		8,680
Share of post-acquisition profits of Amber Ltd:		
Amber Ltd at reporting date	6,440	
at acquisition date	2,600	
post-acquisition	3,840	
Group's share × 30%		1,152
Goodwill impaired Silver Ltd		(50)
Premium impaired Amber Ltd		(100)
Share of post-acquisition profits of Green Ltd:		
Green Ltd at reporting date	1,630	
at acquisition date	970	
post-acquisition	660	
Group's share – 50%		330
		10,012
Silver Ltd at reporting date	5,260	
at acquisition date	2,500	
post-acquisition	2,760	
Group's share – 70%		1,932
		11,944

(W4) Non-controlling interest		
Silver Ltd at reporting date:		
Ordinary shares	4,000	
Share premium	800	

Retained earnings		5,260	
		10,060	
NCI × 30%			3,018

Peach Plc
CONSOLIDATED STATEMENT OF FINANCIAL POSITION
as at 30 June 2010

Assets		**€000**	**€000**
Non-current assets			
Property, plant and equipment	Group	19,870	
	Share of Green Ltd	3,200	23,070
Investment in Amber Ltd			6,002
Investment in Blue Ltd			100
Goodwill/premium			505
			29,677
Current assets	Group	4,390	
	Share of Green Ltd	330	4,720
Total assets			**34,397**
Equity and liabilities			
Equity			
Ordinary share capital			14,500
Share premium			2,200
Retained earnings			11,944
Total shareholders equity			28,644
Non-controlling interests			3,018
Total equity			31,662
Current liabilities	Group	2,520	
	Share of Green Ltd	215	2,735
Total equity and liabilities			**34,397**

Chapter 7

The Statement of Comprehensive Income and The Statement of Changes in Equity

Learning Objectives

After studying this chapter you should be able to:

1. Explain the application of full consolidation, equity accounting and proportionate consolidation in the context of the consolidated SoCI and the SoCE;
2. Demonstrate an understanding of the calculation of non-controlling interests in the subsidiary's profit/loss and its total comprehensive income for a reporting period; and
3. Prepare and present a basic consolidated statement of comprehensive income and a consolidated statement of changes in equity incorporating a parent, subsidiary, associate joint venture and trade investment.

Introduction

This chapter shifts the focus from the relative 'comfort zone' of the double entry approach when preparing an SoFP to the largely single entry approach used in the statement of comprehensive income (SoCI) and the statement of changes in equity (SoCE). However, by the end of the chapter, you should have a more complete picture of consolidation.

In **Chapters 3 to 6** we dealt with the preparation and presentation of consolidated statements of financial position (SoFP), including the treatment of:

- investments in subsidiaries;
- investments in associates;
- investments in joint ventures; and
- trade investments.

This chapter will illustrate the preparation and presentation of:
1. the consolidated statement of comprehensive income (SoCI) and
2. the consolidated statement of changes in equity (SoCE)

for each type of investment.

Other Comprehensive Income

It is a fundamental principle of accounting that all gains and losses, other than those arising from transactions with owners acting in their capacity as owners, should be included in the calculation of profit or loss for a reporting period. However, company law and specific international accounting standards allow or require some gains/losses to be taken through other comprehensive income (OCI) to reserves. Any gain/loss taken to reserves is included under **other comprehensive income** in the statement of comprehensive income, for example:

- changes in revaluation reserves (e.g. property revaluation);
- exchange differences on translating foreign operations;
- gains or losses from investments in equity instruments measured at fair value through OCI.

Definition of Other Comprehensive Income

'Other comprehensive income' "comprises items of income and expense (including reclassification adjustments) that are not recognised in profit and loss as required or permitted by other IFRSs" (IAS 1 *Presentation of Financial Statements*, para 7).

Definition of Total Comprehensive Income

'Total comprehensive income' (TCI) comprises all components of 'profit or loss' *and* of 'other comprehensive income'.

The Consolidated Statement of Comprehensive Income

IAS 1 specifies the format and content of the statement of comprehensive income (SoCI) and the statement of changes in equity (SoCE) and requires that particular disclosures are made in these statements or in the notes to the statements.[1]

IAS 1 also states that an entity must present all items of income and expense recognised in a period using either one of two methods:

Method 1: in a single statement of comprehensive income; **or**

Method 2: in two statements:

(a) a statement of income showing components of profit or loss, and

(b) a separate statement of comprehensive income beginning with profit or loss and showing components of other comprehensive income.

> ***Key Note*:** This text adopts Method 1, a single consolidated statement of comprehensive income in its examples, questions and solutions.

[1] See ***Connolly***, Chapter 2 "Presentation of Financial Statements", for a complete discussion of IAS 1.

Non-controlling Interests

The **profit or loss for the reporting period** and the **total comprehensive income** for the same period must be apportioned between the shareholders of the parent and the non-controlling interests as follows:

PRO-FORMA: CONSOLIDATED STATEMENT OF COMPREHENSIVE INCOME

	€
Revenue	X
Cost of sales	(X)
Gross profit	X
Distribution costs	(X)
Administrative expenses	(X)
Finance costs	(X)
Profit before tax	X
Income tax expense	X
Profit for the year	X
Other comprehensive income:	
Gains on property revaluation	X
Total comprehensive income for the year	X
Profit for the year attributable to:	
Owners of the parent	X
Non-controlling interests	X
	X
Total comprehensive income for the year attributable to:	
Owners of the parent	X
Non-controlling interests	X
	X

The Consolidated Statement of Changes in Equity

An entity must present a statement of changes in equity (SoCE) showing:

(a) the carrying amount for each component of equity both at the beginning and the end of each reporting period;

(b) the total comprehensive income for the period showing separately the total amounts attributable to owners of the parent and to non-controlling interests;

(c) transactions with shareholders in their capacity as owners, e.g issues of shares, distributions to owners.

PRO-FORMA: CONSOLIDATED STATEMENT OF CHANGES IN EQUITY

	Share capital	Revaluation reserve	Retained earnings	Total	Non-controlling interests	Total Equity
	€	€	€	€	€	€
Balance at 1 July 2010	X	X	X	X	X	X
Issue of shares	X			X		X
Dividends			(X)	(X)		(X)
Total comprehensive income for the year		X	X	X	X	X
Balance at 30 June 2011	X	X	X	X	X	X

Note: the majority of examination questions involving the preparation of a consolidated SoCI will also require preparation of the consolidated SoCE.

Accounting Treatment of a Subsidiary in the Consolidated SoCI

As previously stated in **Chapter 3,** subsidiaries are accounted for using full consolidation. This means that all the income and expenses of subsidiary S Ltd are consolidated with those of parent company P Ltd.

Key Note: However, a parent can only consolidate the post-acquisition income and expenses of a subsidiary, or any other acquired entity. Therefore, a vital distinction needs to made between:

- a subsidiary acquired *before* the start of a reporting a year (see **Example 7.1**); and
- a subsidiary acquired during a reporting year (see **Example 7.2**).

Accounting Treatment of Non-controlling Interests

The **profit/loss** and the **total comprehensive income** of a subsidiary (S Ltd) for a reporting period must be apportioned between the shareholders of the parent (P Ltd) and the non-controlling interests (NCI). The following points should be noted:

1. The non-controlling interests in the profit/loss of subsidiary S Ltd is based on S Ltd's profit/loss **after tax** (this figure may need to be adjusted for 'complications', e.g. unrealised inventory profits, etc., which will be covered in **Chapter 8**).
2. The non-controlling interests in the total comprehensive income of S Ltd for a reporting period is calculated as follows:

	€
Interest in profit/loss of S Ltd (as in 1 above)	X
Plus/Minus: NCI share of other comprehensive gains and losses	X
NCI in total comprehensive income	X

Example 7.1: Subsidiary Acquired before the Start of the Reporting Period

Statements of Comprehensive Income
Year Ended 31 August 2011

	Pop Ltd €000	**Snap Ltd €000**
Revenue	4,600	1,800
Cost of sales	(3,200)	(1,300)
	1,400	500
Distribution costs	(270)	(70)
Administrative expenses	(320)	(90)
Finance costs	(60)	(30)
Profit before tax	750	310
Income tax expense	(280)	(90)
Profit for the year	470	220
Other comprehensive income		
Property revaluation surplus	100	50
Total comprehensive income for the year	570	270

Pop Ltd acquired 80% of the ordinary shares of Snap Ltd when its retained earnings were €120,000. The date of acquisition was 1 September 2008.

Retained earnings 1 September 2010

Pop Ltd	€860,000
Snap Ltd	€340,000

Requirement Prepare:

(a) The consolidated statement of comprehensive income;

(b) The consolidated statement of changes in equity, for the year ended 31 August 2011, insofar as the information permits.

Solution

WORKINGS (Columnar Method)

	Pop	Snap	Adjustments	Consol. SoCI
	€000	€000	€000	€000
Revenue	4,600	1,800		6,400
Cost of sales	(3,200)	(1,300)		(4,500)
Gross profit	1,400	500		1,900
Distribution costs	(270)	(70)		(340)
Administrative expenses	(320)	(90)		(410)
Finance costs	(60)	(30)		(90)
Profit before tax	750	310		1,060
Income tax expense	(280)	(90)		(370)
Profit for the year	470	220		690
Non-controlling interest:				
In profit of Snap Ltd				
Profit after tax Snap Ltd			220	
NCI × 20%			44	
In total comprehensive income of Snap Ltd			44	
As per above				
Revaluation surplus – Snap Ltd:				
€50,000 × 20%			10	
			54	

Pop Limited

CONSOLIDATED STATEMENT OF COMPREHENSIVE INCOME
for the Year Ended 31 August 2011

	€000
Revenue	6,400
Cost of sales	(4,500)
Gross profit	1,900

Distribution costs	(340)
Administrative expenses	(410)
Finance costs	(90)
Profit before tax	1,060
Income tax expense	(370)
Profit for the year	**690**
Other comprehensive income	
Property revaluation surplus	150
Total comprehensive income for the year	**840**
Profit attributable to:	
Owners of the parent	646
Non-controlling interest	44
	690
Total comprehensive income attributable to:	
Owners of the parent	786
Non-controlling interests	54
	840

Statement of Changes in Equity
for the Year Ended 31 August 2011

	Ordinary Shares €000	**Revaluation Reserve €000**	**Retained Earnings €000**	**NCI €000**	**Total €000**
Balance 1 September 2010			1,036 (W1)		
TCI for the year		140	646	54	840
Balance 31 August 2011			1,682		

(W1) Group retained earnings 1 September 2010

The group retained earnings at the start of a reporting period can be defined as the retained earnings of the parent at that date **plus** the group's share of the post-acquisition retained earnings of the subsidiary to the same date.

		€000
Pop Ltd		860
Snap Ltd	80% (340 − 120)	176
		1,036

(340 = 1/9/10; 120 = Acquisition date)

Subsidiary Acquired during a Reporting Period

It is a basic principle of consolidated financial statements that income and expenses of a subsidiary **are only consolidated from the date of acquisition**. When a subsidiary is acquired during a reporting period, its income and expenses must be **time-apportioned** and only those income and expenses earned and incurred **after the date of acquisition** can be consolidated. ***Beware:*** an income or expense could fall into one period only.

Non-controlling Interest in a Subsidiary Acquired during a Reporting Period

The non-controlling interests in the profits of S Ltd must also be time-apportioned.

Example 7.2: Subsidiary Acquired During a Reporting Period

Statements of Comprehensive Income
for the Year Ended 30 September 2011

	Pit Ltd	**Stop Ltd**
	€	**€**
Revenue	860,000	220,000
Cost of sales	520,000	130,000
Gross profit	340,000	90,000
Distribution costs	(80,000)	(10,000)
Administrative expenses	(90,000)	(30,000)
Finance costs	(30,000)	(5,000)
Profit before tax	140,000	45,000
Income tax expense	(50,000)	(18,000)
Profit for the year	90,000	27,000
Other comprehensive income	nil	nil
Total comprehensive income for the year	90,000	27,000

Pit Ltd acquired 80% of the ordinary shares of Stop Ltd on 31 March 2011.

Retained earnings 1 October 2010	
Pit Ltd	€310,000
Stop Ltd	€186,000

Requirement Prepare:

(a) The consolidated statement of comprehensive income;

(b) The consolidated statement of changes in equity, for the year ended 30 September 2011, insofar as the information permits.

Solution

Stop Ltd became a subsidiary of Pit Ltd on 31 March 2011 (1/2 way through the reporting period), therefore all its income and expenses must be **time-apportioned × 6/12.**

WORKINGS

	Pit	Stop	Adjustments	Consol. SoCI
Revenue	860,000	220,000	(110,000)	970,000
Cost of sales	(520,000)	(130,000)	(65,000)	(585,000)
Gross profit	340,000	90,000	(45,000)	385,000
Distribution costs	(80,000)	(10,000)	(5,000)	(85,000)
Administrative expenses	(90,000)	(30,000)	(15,000)	(105,000)
Finance costs	(30,000)	(5,000)	(2,500)	(32,500)
Profit before tax	140,000	45,000	(22,500)	162,500
Income tax expense	(50,000)	(18,000)	(9,000)	(59,000)
Profit for the year	90,000	27,000	(13,500)	103,500

Non-controlling interests

In profits of Stop Ltd

Post-acquisition profit after tax	€27,000 × 6/12	=	€13,500
NCI × 20%			€2,700

CONSOLIDATED STATEMENT OF COMPREHENSIVE INCOME
y/e 30 September 2011

	€
Revenue	970,000
Cost of sales	(585,000)
Gross profit	385,000
Distribution costs	(85,000)
Administrative expenses	(105,000)
Finance costs	(32,500)
Profit before tax	162,500
Income tax expense	(59,000)
Profit for the year	103,500
Other comprehensive income	nil
Total comprehensive income for the year	103,500
Profit for the year attributable to:	
Owners of the parent	100,800
Non-controlling interest	2,700
	103,500

Total comprehensive income for the year attributable to:	
Owners of the parent	100,800
Non-controlling interest	2,700
	103,500

Consolidated Statement of Changes in Equity

	Ordinary Shares	Ret. Earnings	NCI	Total
Balance at 1 October 2010		310,000 *(W1)*		
TCI for the year		100,800	2,700	103,500
Balance at 30 September 2011		410,800		

(W1) Retained Earnings
Pit Ltd €310,000

Note: S Ltd cannot be included in the opening retained earnings of the group as it was bought during the reporting period, i.e. there were no post-acquisition earnings at the start of the reporting period.

Introducing an Associate

Accounting Treatment

As previously explained in **Chapter 5**, the investment in an associate (A Ltd) is accounted for using the equity method. In the consolidated statement of financial position, the investment in A Ltd is valued as follows:

	€
Cost of investment in A Ltd	X
Plus: group's share of post-acquisition profits and reserves of A Ltd	X
Less: impairment of premium/goodwill	(X)
	X

In the consolidated SoCI **none of the individual income and expenses of associate A Ltd are consolidated**; however, the associate is dealt with through a one line item which is added to the consolidated profit before tax figure, as follows:

	€
Share of profit of associate (profit after tax)	X

Note: The consolidated SoCI would also have to recognise the group share of any OCI of A Ltd.

Example 7.3 illustrates a consolidated SoCI/SoCE involving a parent, a subsidiary and an associate.

Example 7.3: Associate Acquired before the Start of the Reporting Period

Statements of Comprehensive Income
Year Ended 31 July 2011

	Pot Ltd	Stove Ltd	Apron Ltd
	€000	€000	€000
Revenue	4,840	3,610	1,790
Cost of sales	(3,230)	(2,410)	(1,260)
Gross profit	1,610	1,200	530
Distribution costs	(380)	(295)	(110)
Administrative expenses	(350)	(185)	(130)
Finance costs	(140)	(95)	(55)
Profit before tax	740	625	235
Income tax expense	(310)	(250)	(95)
Profit for the year	430	375	140
Other comprehensive income	nil	nil	nil
Total comprehensive income for the year	430	375	140

(a) Pot Ltd acquired 80% of the ordinary shares of Stove Ltd and 40% of the ordinary shares of Apron Ltd when Stove Ltd's retained earnings were €630,000 and those of Apron Ltd were €140,000. The investments were made on 1 November 2008 and 31 August 2009.

(b) The retained earnings of the companies at 1 August 2010 were:

Pot Ltd	€2,650,000
Stove Ltd	€1,410,000
Apron Ltd	€360,000

Requirement Prepare:

(a) the consolidated statement of comprehensive income for the year ended 31 July 2011;

(b) the consolidated statement of changes in equity for the same period, insofar as the information permits.

Solution

Workings

	Pot	Stove	Adjustments	Consol. SoCI
	€000	€000	€000	€000
Revenue	4,840	3,610		8,450
Cost of sales	(3,230)	(2,410)		(5,640)
Gross profit	1,610	1,200		2,810
Distribution costs	(380)	(295)		(675)

Administrative expenses	(350)	(185)		(535)
Finance costs	(140)	(95)		(235)
Share of profit of A *(W1)*			56	56
Profit before tax	740	625	56	1,421
Income tax expense	(310)	(250)		(560)
Profit for the year	430	375	56	861

Consolidated Statement of Comprehensive Income
for the year ended 31 July 2011

	€000
Revenue	8,450
Cost of sales	5,640
Gross profit	2,810
Distribution costs	(675)
Administrative expenses	(535)
Finance costs	(235)
Share of profit of associate *(W1)*	56
Profit before tax	1,421
Income tax expense	(560)
Profit for the year	861
Other comprehensive income for the year	nil
Total comprehensive income for the year	861
Profit attributable to:	
Owners of the parent	786
Non-controlling interests *(W2)*	75
	861
Total comprehensive income attributable to:	
Owners of the parent	786
Non-controlling interests *(W2)*	75
	861

(W1) Share of profit of associate

Profit after tax Apron Ltd	140
Group's Share × 40%	56

(W2) Non-controlling interests

Profit after tax Stove Ltd	375
NCI × 20%	75

CONSOLIDATED STATEMENT OF CHANGES IN EQUITY

	Ordinary Shares €000	Retained Earnings €000	NCI €000	Total €000
Balance 1 August 2010		3,362 (W1)		
TCI for the year		786	75	861
Balance 31 July 2011		4,148		

(W1) Retained Earnings @ 1/8/2010

Pot Ltd	2,650
Share of Post-Acquisition Profits:	
Stove Ltd: Group's Share: 80% (1,410 – 630)	624
Apron Ltd: Group's Share: 40% (360 – 140)	88
	3,362

***Note*:** both Stove Ltd and Apron Ltd are included in the opening retained earnings of the group as both companies were acquired before the reporting period.

Key Note: if an associate is acquired during a reporting period, its profit after tax must be time-apportioned and only the group's share of the post-acquisition element should be included in the consolidated SoCI.

Joint Ventures

Accounting Treatment

As discussed in **Chapter 6**, a joint venture is an entity that is subject to joint control. It is accounted for in consolidated financial statements using proportionate consolidation. What are the implications for the consolidated SoCI? **The group's share of each income and expense item of a joint venture is consolidated as follows:**

PRO-FORMA: CONSOLIDATED STATEMENT OF COMPREHENSIVE INCOME

To include the group's share of joint venture:

		€	€
Revenue	Group	X	
	Share of JV	X	X
Cost of sales	Group	X	
	Share of JV	X	(X)

Example 74: Joint Venture Acquired before the Start of the Reporting Period

The following are the statements of comprehensive income of Pete Ltd, Sue Ltd and JV Ltd for the period ending 31 May 2011:

	Pete Ltd	**Sue Ltd**	**JV Ltd**
	€000	**€000**	**€000**
Revenue	12,600	8,900	4,800
Cost of sales	8,800	6,670	3,600
Gross profit	3,800	2,230	1,200
Distribution costs	(590)	(410)	(150)
Administrative expenses	(1,240)	(530)	(260)
Finance costs	(440)	(220)	(90)
Profit before tax	1,530	1,070	700
Income tax expense	(300)	(210)	(140)
Profit for the year	1,230	860	560
Other comprehensive income	nil	nil	nil
Total comprehensive income for the year	1,230	860	560

Pete Ltd acquired 90% of the ordinary shares of Sue Ltd on 1 November 2008.

Pete Ltd and Rob Ltd each acquired 50% of the ordinary shares of JV Ltd on 1 June 2009. JV Ltd is subject to joint control by its two investing companies.

Requirement Prepare the consolidated statement of comprehensive income for the period ended 31 May 2011.

Solution

Workings

	Pete	**Sue**	**Adjustment**	**Consol. SoCI**
	€000	**€000**	**€000**	**€000**
Revenue	12,600	8,900	2,400	23,900
Cost of sales	(8,800)	(6,670)	(1,800)	(17,270)
Gross profit	3,800	2,230	600	6,630
Distribution costs	(590)	(410)	(75)	(1,075)

Administrative expenses	(1,240)	(530)	(130)	(1,900)
Finance costs	(440)	(220)	(45)	(705)
Profit before tax	1,530	1,070	350	2,950
Income tax expense	(300)	(210)	(70)	(580)
Profit for the year	1,230	860	280	2,370

Consolidated Statement of Comprehensive Income
for the Year Ended 31 May 2011

		€000	€000
Revenue	Group	21,500	
	Share of JV	2,400	23,900
Cost of sales	Group	15,470	
	Share of JV	1,800	17,270
Gross profit			6,630
Distribution costs	Group	1,000	
	Share of JV	75	(1,075)
Administrative expenses	Group	1,770	
	Share of JV	130	(1,900)
Finance costs	Group	660	
	Share of JV	45	(705)
Profit before tax			2,950
Income tax expense	Group	510	
	Share of JV	70	(580)
Profit for the year			2,370
Other comprehensive income			Nil
Total comprehensive income for the year			2,370
Profit for the year attributable to:			
Owners of the parent			2,284
Non-controlling interests (*W1*)			86
			2,370
Total comprehensive income for the year attributable to:			

Owners of the parent	2,284
Non-controlling interests	86
	2,370

(W1) Non-controlling interests
Sue Ltd – profit after tax 860 × 10% = 86

> ***Key Note:*** when a joint venture is acquired during a reporting period, the group's share of each income and expense must be time-apportioned.

Trade (or Simple) Investments

A trade investment occurs when the investor acquires less than 20% of the voting rights of the investee (see **Chapter 2**). In a consolidated statement of comprehensive income a group records as income dividends received or receivable from a trade investment.

Conclusion

At this stage of your progress through the text you have studied a significant proportion of the preparation of consolidated financial statements, and if you have attempted all of the questions so far in the text you should now be proficient in what many students call, simply, 'consolidation'.

SUMMARY

1. In accordance with IAS 1 the statement of comprehensive income must be either:
   (a) a single statement; or
   (b) two statements comprising an income statement and a statement of comprehensive income.
2. In the consolidated SoCI all the income and expenses of subsidiary S Ltd are consolidated with those of the parent.
3. The following must be disclosed in respect of non-controlling interests in a subsidiary:
   (a) profit for the year attributable to NCI;
   (b) total comprehensive income for the year attributable to NCI.
4. Non-controlling interests in a subsidiary's profit for the year are calculated on its profit after tax.

5. Under the equity method none of the individual income and expenses of an associate are consolidated with those of a parent and subsidiary. The group's share of the profit after tax of an associate is included as a line item in the consolidated SoCI as follows:

   Share of profit of associate €X

6. The group's share of each income and expense of a joint venture is consolidated with those of the parent and subsidiary in accordance with the principles of proportionate consolidation.
7. The consolidated statement of changes in equity must disclose:
   (a) the opening and closing balances for each item classed as equity;
   (b) total comprehensive income for the reporting period split between reserves, retained earnings and non-controlling interests; and
   (c) transactions with shareholders in their capacity as owners.
8. The group retained earnings at the beginning of a reporting period can be defined as:
   The retained earnings of P Ltd at the start of the reporting date
   Plus
   The group's share of the post-acquisition retained earnings of the other group entities at the same date.

   A subsidiary, associate or joint venture acquired during a reporting period cannot be included in the group retained earnings at the beginning of that period.

QUESTIONS

Question 7.1

How is a subsidiary accounted for in a consolidated statement of comprehensive income and how is such treatment effected?

Solution

A subsidiary is accounted for in a consolidated SoCI using full consolidation. This means that all the income and expenses of subsidiary S Ltd earned and incurred after the date of acquisition are consolidated with those of the parent.

Question 7.2

Explain how non-controlling interests are disclosed both in the consolidated SoCI and SoCE.

Solution to Question 7.2

SoCI There must be disclosed:

(a) the profit/loss of subsidiary S Ltd, for the reporting period attributable to the non-controlling interests; and

(b) the total comprehensive income of S Ltd for the period attributable to the non-controlling interests.

SoCE Normally, the consolidated SoCE discloses with regard to the non-controlling interests:

(a) the opening and closing balances; and

(b) their share of the total comprehensive income of subsidiary S Ltd for the year.

Question 7.3

Explain the effect of the equity method on the consolidated SoCI.

Solution

An associate is accounted for using the equity method, which means that the group's share of the profit after tax of associate A Ltd is included as a line item in the consolidated SoCI.

Question 7.4

How is a joint venture accounted for in a consolidated statement of comprehensive income and how is such treatment effected?

Solution

A joint venture is accounted for using proportionate consolidation and, consequently, the group's share of each item of income and expense of joint venture (JV Ltd) is consolidated.

Question 7.5

List the usual components of a consolidated SoCE.

Solution

The usual components are

- the opening and closing balances for each component of equity;
- the total comprehensive income for the year; and
- transactions with shareholders in their capacity as owners.

> ***Note:*** Questions 7.6 and 7.7 are longer review-type questions. Question 7.6 and its solution provides a comprehensive coverage of the consolidated SoCI and SoCE as it incorporates a parent, a subsidiary, an associate, a joint venture and a trade investment.
>
> Question 7.7 will test your knowledge of how to prepare a SoCE only, while incorporating a parent, a subsidiary and an associate.

Question 7.6

STATEMENTS OF COMPREHENSIVE INCOME
for the Year Ended 31 July 2011

	Wind Ltd €000	**Rain Ltd €000**	**Ice Ltd €000**	**Hail Ltd €000**
Revenue	15,850	12,680	9,510	6,340
Cost of sales	11,880	9,490	7,130	4,760
Gross profit	3,970	3,190	2,380	1,580
Dividend received	80			
Distribution costs	(320)	(250)	(190)	(120)
Administrative expenses	(510)	(400)	(290)	(180)
Finance costs	(130)	(110)	(70)	(50)
Profit before tax	3,090	2,430	1,830	1,230
Income tax expense	(620)	(480)	(350)	(240)
Profit for the year	2,470	1,950	1,480	990
Other comprehensive income:				
Property revaluation surplus	400			
Movement in financial asset of FV through OCI		(100)		
Total comprehensive income for the year	2,870	1,850	1,480	990

1. Wind Ltd has made the following investments:
   (a) 60% of the ordinary shares of Rain Ltd on 1 April 2007 when the retained earnings of Rain Ltd were €450,000;
   (b) 30% of the ordinary shares of Ice Ltd on 1 February 2011;
   (c) 50% of the ordinary shares of Hail Ltd on 1 August 2010 when its retained earnings were €1,010,000. Weather Ltd acquired the other 50% on the same date. Wind Ltd and Weather Ltd exercise joint control over the policies of Hail Ltd;
   (d) 10% of the ordinary shares of Storm Ltd on 1 August 2010;
   (e) the dividend received by Wind Ltd was from Storm Ltd.
2. Retained earnings at 1 August 2010

	€000
Wind Ltd	8,130
Rain Ltd	1,970

Ice Ltd	930
Hail Ltd	1,250

Requirement Prepare for the year ended 31 July 2011:
(a) the consolidated statement of comprehensive income; and
(b) the consolidated statement of changes in equity.

Solution to Question 7.6

WORKINGS

	Wind	Rain	Adjustments	Consol. SoCI
	€000	**€000**	**€000**	**€000**
Revenue	15,850	12,680	3,170	31,700
Cost of sales	(11,880)	(9,490)	(2,380)	(23,750)
Gross profit	3,970	3,190	790	7,950
Dividend received	80			80
Distribution costs	(320)	(250)	(60)	(630)
Administrative expenses	(510)	(400)	(90)	(1,000)
Finance costs	(130)	(110)	(25)	(265)
Share of profit of associate *(W1)*			222	222
Profit before tax	3,090	2,430	837	6,357
Income tax expense	(620)	(480)	(120)	(1,220)
Profit for the year	2,470	1,950	717	5,137

(W1) Share of profit of associate:
Profit after tax of Ice Ltd: €1,480 × 6 months × 30% = 222

Wind Ltd
CONSOLIDATED STATEMENT OF COMPREHENSIVE INCOME
for the Year Ended 31 July 2011

		€000	€000
Revenue	Group	28,530	
	Share of joint venture	3,170	31,700
Cost of sales	Group	21,370	
	Share of joint venture	2,380	(23,750)
Gross profit			7,950
Dividend received			80
Distribution costs	Group	570	
	Share of joint venture	60	(630)
Administrative expenses	Group	910	
	Share of joint venture	90	(1,000)
Finance costs	Group	240	
	Share of joint venture	25	(265)
Share of profit of associate			222

Profit before tax			6,357
Income tax expense	Group	1,100	
	Share of joint venture	120	(1,220)
Profit for the year			5,137
Other comprehensive income:			
Property revaluation surplus			400
Loss on available for sale investments			(100)
Total comprehensive income for the year			5,437
Profit for the year attributable to:			
Owners of the parent			4,357
Non-controlling interests *(W2)*			780
			5,137
Total comprehensive income attributable to:			
Owners of the parent			4,697
Non-controlling interests *(W3)*			740
			5,437

(W2) Non-controlling Interests – Profit

Profit after tax of Rain Ltd €1,950 × 40%	=	780

(W3) Non-controlling Interests – TCI

Profit after tax of Rain Ltd €1,950 × 40%	=	780
Less: Share of loss on available for sale investments €100 × 40%		(40)
		740

Consolidated Statement of Changes in Equity
for the Year Ended 31 July 2011

	Ord. Shares €000	Rev. Res. €000	Ret. Earnings €000	NCI €000	Total €000
Balance 1 August 2010			9,042 *(W4)*		
TCI for the year		340*	4,357	740	5,437
Balance 31 July 2011			13,399		

(W4) Retained Earnings @ 1/8/2010

Wind	8,130
Rain 60% (1,970 – 450)	912
Ice	nil
Hail	nil
	9,042

* 400 – (100 × 60%)

Question 7.7

1. The following extracts have been taken from the consolidated statement of comprehensive income for the year ended 30 June 2011:

	€000
Profit for the year attributable to:	
Owners of the parent	3,160
Non-controlling interests	220
	3,380
Total comprehensive income for the year attributable to:	
Owners of the parent	3,430
Non-controlling interests	250
	3,680

2. Munster Ltd acquired 90% of the ordinary shares of Leinster Ltd on 1 December 2008 when the retained earnings of Leinster Ltd were €850,000.
3. Munster Ltd acquired 45% of the ordinary shares of Connaught Ltd on 1 May 2010 when the retained earnings of Connaught Ltd were €300,000.
4. Retained earnings 1 July 2010

	€000
Munster Ltd	3,154
Leinster Ltd	2,100
Connaught Ltd	700

5. The property of Leinster Ltd was revalued at the reporting date showing a surplus of €300,000.

Requirement Prepare the consolidated statement of changes in equity for the year ended 30 June 2011.

Solution to Question 7.7

Group retained earnings 1 July 2010	€000
Munster Ltd	3,154
Leinster Ltd 90% (2,100 – 850)	1,125
Connaught Ltd 45% (700 – 300)	180
	4,459

CONSOLIDATED STATEMENT OF CHANGES IN EQUITY
for the Year Ended 30 June 2011

	Ord. Shares €000	**Reval. Reserve €000**	**Ret. Earnings €000**	**NCI €000**	**Total €000**
Balance 1 July 2010			4,459		
TCI for the year		270	3,160	250	3,680
Balance 30 June 2011			7,619		

Chapter 8

Statement of Comprehensive Income and Statement of Changes in Equity: Complications

Learning Objectives

Having studied this chapter you should be able to:

- demonstrate an understanding of the rationale for each complication or adjustment;
- explain the accounting treatment for each complication in the preparation of the SoCI and the SoCE; and
- undertake a question with complications that will demonstrate a comprehensive understanding of the preparation of a consolidated SoCI and SoCE.

Introduction

It is time to deal with 'Complications' again. In this instance, however, we will examine how each one affects the consolidated SoCI and/or the consolidated SoCE.

At end of this chapter, you should be in a position to understand, within the context of consolidated financial statements, the link between the SoFP, on one hand, and the SoCI/SoCE, on the other, and, in particular, the effect of complications.

As discussed in **Chapter 4**, in the world of business, group entities trade with one another and subsidiaries pay dividends to parents. As a consequence adjustments may need to be made to **consolidated** financial statements to reflect intragroup trading and other items such as intragroup dividends or amounts owing by one group entity to another at the reporting date. These adjustments are more commonly known as 'complications'.

The complications relevant to this chapter are:

1. Unrealised inventory profit
2. Unrealised profit on sale of tangible non-current assets
3. Revaluation of a subsidiary's net assets at acquisition date
4. Intragroup dividends
5. Dividends paid out of pre-acquisition profits of a subsidiary
6. Intragroup transactions
7. Impairment of goodwill. Gain from a bargain purchase.

Statement of Changes in Equity (SoCE)

The statement of changes in equity is the link between the statement of comprehensive income and the statement of financial position, particularly in the case of retained earnings and non-controlling interests.

> ***Key Note:*** The retained earnings at a reporting date per the SoCE must equal the corresponding figure in the SoFP. Accordingly, **any complication that affects retained earnings in the consolidated SoFP workings must have the same cumulative effect on the consolidated SoCI and the SoCE.**

In **Chapter** 7, we saw that the **group retained earnings brought forward** were defined as:

The retained earnings of the parent P Ltd at the start of a reporting period

Plus

The **group's share** of the post-acquisition retained earnings of a subsidiary S Ltd and any other group companies as at that date.

Therefore, any complication that changes the opening retained earnings of the group must be accounted for accordingly:

(a) If the adjustment affects P Ltd – account for all of the adjustment.
(b) If the adjustment affects another group company – account for the group's share.

In dealing with each complication as listed above, we will show:

(a) the effect on the consolidated SoFP for **revision** purposes and, more importantly, to demonstrate the **link** between the SoFP and the SoCI/SoCE; and
(b) the combined effect on the consolidated SoCI and SoCE.

(***Note***: The examples used in **Chapter 4** are repeated where relevant.)

Complication 1 – Unrealised Inventory Profit

This complication arises where one group company sells goods at a profit to another group company and some or all of those goods are in the inventory of the buying entity at the reporting date. This results in an element of unrealised profit being included in the closing inventory of the buying company. This would be in contravention of IAS 2 *Inventories* if no adjustment were made in preparing the group accounts because the standard states that inventories should be valued at the **lower** of cost and net realisable value.

Example 8.1: Treatment of Unrealised Inventory Profit

A parent (P Ltd) buys goods for €100 and sells them to a subsidiary (S Ltd) for €150. At the reporting date, S Ltd still has these goods in inventory and has valued them at cost (€150) in accordance with IAS 2. However, if the inventory of S Ltd were consolidated (without adjustment) with the inventory of P Ltd the result would be that the group bought these goods for €100 and valued its inventory at €150 which contravenes IAS 2. There is unrealised profit from a group perspective of €50.

Statement of Financial Position

Problem: The retained earnings of P Ltd and the group inventories are overstated by €50.

Accounting Adjustment

Eliminate all the unrealised profit

		€	€
Dr.	Retained Earnings (selling Company P Ltd)	50	
Cr.	Inventory		50

Statement of Comprehensive Income and Statement of Changes in Equity

Problem: The profits of P Ltd are overstated. The adjustment will affect the SoCI only.
The revenue and cost of sales are both overstated by the intragroup sales.

Accounting Adjustment

Add the unrealised profit €50 to the cost of sales of the selling company P Ltd.
Reduce revenue and cost of sales by €150.

Complication 2 – Unrealised Profit on Sale of Tangible Non-current Assets

This second complication arises where one group company sells property, plant and equipment to another at a profit and the asset is in the SoFP of the buying entity at the reporting date.

IAS 16 *Property, Plant and Equipment* states that an asset should be carried at:

1. **Cost**, less accumulated depreciation and impairment; **or**
2. **Revaluation**, being its fair value at the date of revaluation less subsequent depreciation and impairment, provided that fair value can be measured reliably.

The inclusion of the asset at the selling price results in an overstatement of the non-current assets of the group and of the profits of the selling company (with the profit on the disposal of the asset). The depreciation charge may also be overstated by the buying company as the charge would be based on the incorrectly inflated group asset value.

Example 8.2: Unrealised Profit on Sale of Tangible Non-current Assets

A parent, P Ltd, bought an item of property, plant and equipment (PPE) on 1 August 2008 at a cost of €300,000 and is depreciating it at 10% straight line. On 1 August 2010 P Ltd sold the asset to S Ltd for €280,000 who is currently depreciating it over the remaining eight years. Consolidated financial statements are prepared as at 31 July 2011.

1 August 2010

	€
Carrying value of asset (€300,000 − 2 years' depreciation)	240,000
Sale proceeds	280,000
Profit on disposal	40,000

Statement of Financial Position

Problem: The retained earnings and the property, plant and equipment (PPE) as at 31 July 2011 are overstated by the profit on disposal of €40,000.

Accounting Adjustment

Eliminate unrealised profit in the selling company's accounts

Dr.	Retained Earnings (P Ltd)	€40,000	
Cr.	PPE		€40,000

Statement of Comprehensive Income and Statement of Changes in Equity

Problem: The profits of P Ltd for the year ended 31 July 2011 are overstated by €40,000.

Accounting Adjustment

Deduct €40,000 in the SoCI from the profit of P Ltd.

This transaction is further complicated by the fact that the asset in question is subject to depreciation. Currently, **the depreciation is overstated from a group perspective** calculated as follows:

Year Ended 31 July 2011

			€
Depreciation per S Ltd financial statements	280,000 ÷ 8	=	35,000
Depreciation if asset not sold at a profit	300,000 @ 10%	=	30,000
Over-provision			5,000

Statement of Financial Position

Problem: At 31 July 2011 both the carrying value of PPE and the retained earnings of S Ltd. are understated.

Accounting Adjustment

Write back the over-provision of depreciation in the buying company.

Dr.	PPE	€5,000	
Cr.	Retained Earnings (S Ltd)		€5,000

Statement of Comprehensive Income and Statement of Changes in Equity

Problem: The depreciation charge for the year ended 31 July 2011 in the SoCI of S Ltd is overstated by €5,000.

Accounting Adjustment

Decrease the relevant expense (e.g. cost of sales) in S Ltd by €5,000, which will increase its profit.

Complication 3 – Revaluation of a Subsidiary's Net Assets at Acquisition Date

When a parent (P Ltd) acquires a subsidiary (S Ltd) the purchase consideration is based on the **fair value** of the subsidiary's net assets and not the carrying values, which are frequently significantly different, particularly in the case of tangible assets such as property.

IFRS 3 *Business Combinations* requires that the net assets of S Ltd must be revalued to **fair value** for consolidation purposes at the date of acquisition. IFRS 3 defines fair value as "the amount for which an asset could be exchanged, or a liability settled, between knowledgeable, willing parties in an arm's length transaction".

Example 8.3: Revaluation of Net Assets

Summarised Statement of Financial Position of S Ltd on 1 June 2009

	€000
Property, plant and equipment	4,400
Current assets	1,300
Total Assets	**5,700**
Ordinary share capital	2,000
Retained earnings	1,800
Non-current liabilities	1,000
Current liabilities	900
Total Equity and Liabilities	**5,700**

P Ltd acquired 60% of the ordinary shares of S Ltd on the 1 June 2009. At the date of acquisition the fair value of the property, plant and equipment (PPE) exceeded the carrying value by €300,000, while those assets had an average remaining useful life of five years. S Ltd did not record the revaluation.

Statement of Financial Position

Problem: In the consolidated workings as at 31 May 2011, the PPE must be revalued to reflect the surplus as at the date of acquisition and two years' additional depreciation on the surplus must be provided.

Accounting Adjustment

(a) Account for surplus

		€000	**€000**
Dr.	PPE	300	
Cr.	Cost of Control (60%)		180
Cr.	Non-controlling Interests (40%)		120

(b) Account for additional depreciation

Dr.	Retained Earnings (S Ltd)	120	
Cr.	Accumulated Depreciation – PPE		120

With the cumulative additional depreciation, i.e. €300,000 × $\frac{2}{5}$

Statement of Comprehensive Income and Statement of Changes in Equity

Problem: The depreciation charge for both 31 May 2010 and 31 May 2011 in the SoCI of S Ltd is understated.

Accounting Adjustment

In the consolidated SoCI for the year ended 31 May 2011 add €60,000 to depreciation charge. (This adjustment will affect the NCI.)

In the consolidated SoCE for the year ended 31 May 2011 reduce the opening group retained earnings by 60% × €60,000 = €36,000 (this being the group's share, as explained above, and will recur in other complications).

Complication 4 – Intragroup Dividends

When a subsidiary (S Ltd) declares a dividend, part of it is payable to its parent (P Ltd) and the remainder to non-controlling interests, the intragroup amounts must be eliminated in the consolidated workings, otherwise both the assets and liabilities of the group would be overstated.

Example 8.4: Intragroup Dividends included in Subsidiary and Parent Accounts

A parent (P Ltd) owns 80% of the preference shares of subsidiary (S Ltd) and S Ltd has proposed a preference dividend of €50,000 for year ended 31 August 2011. Both S Ltd and P Ltd have accounted for the proposed dividend in their respective financial statements.

Extract from Statements of Financial Position
as at 31 August 2011

	P Ltd	S Ltd
Assets		
Dividends receivable	€40,000	
Liabilities		
Proposed dividends		€50,000

Extract from Statements of Comprehensive Income
for the Year Ended 31 August 2011

	P Ltd	S Ltd
Dividends receivable	€40,000	

Statement of Financial Position

Problem: The assets and liabilities of the group would be overstated if the intragroup dividend was not eliminated.

Adjustment

Dr. Proposed dividends	€40,000	
Cr. Dividends receivable		€40,000

STATEMENT OF COMPREHENSIVE INCOME AND STATEMENT OF CHANGES IN EQUITY

Problem: The dividend receivable in the SoCI of P Ltd is an intragroup dividend and the group profits would be overstated if the intragroup dividend was not eliminated.

ADJUSTMENT

Do not include the dividend €40,000 in the consolidated SoCI.

Complication 5 – Dividends Paid Out of Pre-Acquisition Profits of a Subsidiary

As explained in **Chapter 4**, occasionally, a subsidiary (S Ltd) pays a dividend to a parent (P Ltd) out of profits accumulated at the date of acquisition by S Ltd. IAS 27 states that **such a dividend should be included in the profits of the parent and eliminated as an intragroup item**.

At present, company law does not permit P Ltd to treat such a dividend as revenue; it should be credited against the investment in S Ltd.

This complication only affects the SoCI workings when P Ltd has taken the dividend to profit and **the issue is accounted for under company law,** and in that instance the dividend would have to be eliminated from the profits and credited against the cost of the investment in S Ltd.

Complication 6 – Intragroup Transactions

It is perfectly legitimate for a group company to sell goods to another group company at a profit and for companies in a group to charge the other group companies for management charges, interest on loans, etc. When preparing consolidated group accounts these 'internal' or 'intragroup' transactions must be eliminated from the consolidated figures to avoid any overstatement of income or expenditures.

EXAMPLE 8.5: INTRAGROUP TRANSACTIONS

During the year ended 31 July 2011, P Ltd sold goods valued at €300,000 to S Ltd while S Ltd paid a management fee of €100,000 to P Ltd. None of the goods were in S Ltd inventory at the end of the year and P Ltd accounted for the management fee received in 'Other Income'.

STATEMENT OF FINANCIAL POSITION

Problem: As there are no sums outstanding at the end of the year, no problem arises.

Statement of Comprehensive Income and Statement of Changes in Equity

Problem: Without adjustment, the revenue and cost of sales figures in the consolidated SoCI would both be overstated by €300,000 being the amount of the intragroup sales in P Ltd and the intragroup purchases in S Ltd. 'Other Income' (in P Ltd) would also be overstated by €100,000 as would the "Management Fee" in the administrative expenses (in S Ltd).

Accounting Adjustment (SoCI only)

Dr.	Revenue	€300,000	
Cr.	Cost of Sales		€300,000

Reduce revenue and cost of sales by intragroup sales of €300,000.

Dr.	Other Income	€100,000	
Cr.	Administrative Expenses		€100,000

Reduce other income and administrative expenses by management charge paid of €100,000.

Complication 7 – Impairment of Goodwill. Gain from a Bargain Purchase

As explained in **Chapter 3**, goodwill arises when the fair value of the consideration given to acquire a subsidiary exceeds the fair value of the net assets (capital and reserves) acquired. Under IAS 36 *Impairment of Assets* goodwill must be tested annually for impairment. IAS 36 defines an 'impairment loss' as *the amount by which the carrying amount of an asset or a cash generating unit exceeds its recoverable amount.*[1] If impairment occurs, the reduction in the carrying value of goodwill should be written off in the consolidated SoCI.

Example 8.6: Goodwill Impairment

Port Ltd acquired 75% of the ordinary shares of Storm Ltd on 1 September 2009 at a cost of €1.4 million when the ordinary share capital of Storm Ltd was €1 million and the retained earnings €600,000. The goodwill has been impaired as follows:

Year Ending 31 August 2010	€30,000
Year Ending 31 August 2011	€50,000

[1] Impairment losses have a much wider impact than those covered by this text. See ***Connolly***, Chapter 10, 'Impairment'.

STATEMENT OF FINANCIAL POSITION
Year Ended 31 August 2011

Problem: Goodwill must be reduced by €80,000 as at 31 August 2011.

ACCOUNTING ADJUSTMENT

Dr.	Retained earnings (Port Ltd)	€80,000	
Cr.	Cost of control		€80,000

STATEMENT OF COMPREHENSIVE INCOME AND STATEMENT OF CHANGES IN EQUITY
Year Ended 31 August 2011

Problem: The impairment for 2011 must be written off in the consolidated SoCI. The impairment for 2010 must be accounted for in the consolidated SoCE.

ACCOUNTING ADJUSTMENT

1. Charge €50,000 against 2011 profits:
   Impairment of goodwill €50,000
2. Reduce opening group retained earnings as at
   September 2010 in consolidated SoCE by €30,000

Gain from a Bargain Purchase

Where the amount paid for the investment is less than the fair value of the net assets acquired, this is classified by IFRS 3 *Business Combinations* as a "**bargain purchase**" and the resulting "**gain**" should be taken in full to the consolidated SoCI at the acquisition date.

EXAMPLE 8.7: GAIN FROM A BARGAIN PURCHASE

Using the same information as in Example 8.6 above, except that Port Ltd paid €1.1 million for the investment in Storm Ltd on 1 September 2009:

Cost of investment	€1,100,000
Acquired 75% (1,000,000 + 600,000)	€1,200,000
Gain from a bargain purchase	€100,000

STATEMENT OF FINANCIAL POSITION
Year Ended 31 August 2011

Problem: At 31 August 2011, the gain of €100,000 must be dealt with.

ADJUSTMENT

Dr.	Cost of control	€100,000	
Cr.	Retained earnings (Port Ltd)		€100,000

Statement of Comprehensive Income and Statement of Changes in Equity
Year Ended 31 August 2011

Problem: The gain should be added to group retained profit at 1 September 2010.

Adjustment

Increase the group retained profit in consolidated SoCE at the start of the year by €100,000.

Summary

1. Any complication which causes an adjustment to retained earnings in the consolidated SoFP must cause the same cumulative adjustment to the consolidated SoCI and the SoCE. An adjustment which changes the current year's profits will affect the consolidated SoCI only, whereas an adjustment which changes the group retained earnings at the reporting period should be accounted for in the consolidated SoCE.
2. Unrealised inventory profit during a reporting period is added to the cost of sales of the selling entity.
3. Additional depreciation on a revaluation surplus on the net assets of a subsidiary at acquisition date is accounted for as follows:
   (a) any amount relating to the current year is added to the relevant expense of S Ltd.
   (b) the group's share of any amount relating to prior years is deducted in arriving at the group retained earnings brought forward.
4. When one group entity sells an item of property, plant and equipment at a profit to another the unrealised profit must be deducted from the seller's profits on consolidation. Any consequential over provision of depreciation should be treated as follows:
   (a) any amount relating to the current year is deducted from the relevant expense of the buying entity;
   (b) the group's share of any amount relating to prior years is added in arriving at the group retained earnings brought forward if S Ltd is the buyer, or all the amount relating to prior years if P Ltd is the buyer.
5. Any dividend received/receivable from S Ltd in the SoCI of the parent must be excluded from consolidation.
6. Impairment of goodwill is treated as follows:
   (a) the current year's charge is included as a separate line item in the consolidated SoCI.
   (b) the amount relating to prior periods is deducted in arriving at group retained earnings brought forward in the consolidated SoCE.
7. Any adjustment which affects the profit of S Ltd must be taken into account when calculating non-controlling interests in the profits of S Ltd for the year.

Conclusion

Chapters 4 and **8** combined will give you a comprehensive understanding of all the complications and the impact on consolidated financial statements, i.e. SoFP, SoCI and SoCE, and you should now be in a position to tackle examination-style questions (see **Appendix 1**).

Recommended Reading

Chapter 28, "Consolidated Statement of Comprehensive Income", of *International Financial Accounting and Reporting* (3rd Edition) by Ciaran Connolly.

Questions

Question 8.1

Explain the adjustments to the consolidated SoCI and/or the consolidated SoCE for each of the following transactions relating to different groups, **each of which has a reporting date at 30 September 2011**:

> Blue Ltd, a subsidiary, sold goods at invoice value of €250,000 to its parent Green Ltd. In July 2011, Blue Ltd made a gross profit of 20% on the sale and 40% of the goods were in the inventory of Green Ltd at the reporting date.

Solution

Problem: There is unrealised profit included in the inventory of Green Ltd: 250,000 × 1/5 × 40% = €20,000. Group revenue and cost of sales are also overstated.

Adjustment

Increase cost of sales of Blue Ltd by €20,000 (note impact on NCI).
Reduce group revenue and cost of sales by €250,000.

Question 8.2

Pan Ltd acquired 70% of the ordinary shares of Slice Ltd on 1 October 2009. At that date, the fair value of the property, plant and equipment (PPE) of Slice Ltd exceeded the carrying value by €200,000 while the average remaining useful lives of the PPE was four years. The group depreciates PPE on a straight-line basis. Slice Ltd did not record the revaluation.

Solution

Problem: Group depreciation is understated by €50,000 each year ended 30 September 2010 and 2011.

ADJUSTMENT

Increase expenses of Slice Ltd by €50,000 (€200,000 × ¼) for y/e 30 September 2011 in SoCI (note impact on NCI).

Decrease group retained profits at 1 October 2010 by (€50,000 × 70% (group's share)) in SoCE.

Question 8.3

Purple Ltd acquired 100% of the ordinary shares of Silver Ltd on 1 December 2009. The consideration included goodwill of €150,000. The goodwill has been impaired as follows:

y/e 30 September 2010	€25,000
y/e 30 September 2011	€35,000

Solution

Problem: Impairment of goodwill €60,000 must be written off

ADJUSTMENT

Charge €35,000 in consolidated SoCI for year ended 30 September 2011, as follows:

Impairment of goodwill	€35,000

Reduce group retained profits brought forward at 1 October 2010 by €25,000 in consolidated SoCE.

Question 8.4

Pop Ltd acquired 90% of the ordinary shares of Snap Ltd, at a gain from a bargain purchase of €130,000. The date of acquisition was 1 November 2009.

Solution

Problem: Increase the retained profit brought forward at 1 October 2010 by €130,000 in the consolidated SoCE.

Question 8.5

Pip Ltd, a parent, sold an item of property, plant and equipment (PPE) to its 80% owned subsidiary Seed Ltd on 1 October 2009 at a profit of €55,000. The depreciation on this asset in the SoCI of Seed Ltd. was €12,000 per year for each of the years ended 30 September 2010 and 2011. The annual charge would have been €9,000 based on historic cost.

Solution

Problem (a) The unrealised profit of €55,000 on the sale of the PPE must be eliminated in the September 2011 accounts.

ADJUSTMENT

Reduce the group retained profits brought forward by €55,000 in the consolidated SoCE.

Problem (b): The depreciation is overstated from a group perspective by €3,000 for each of two years, i.e. year-ended 30 September 2010 and year-ended 30 September 2011.

ADJUSTMENT

Increase the profit of Seed Ltd by €3,000 in the consolidated SoCI.
Increase the group retained earnings brought forward by (80% × €3,000 (group's share)) = €2,400 in the consolidated SoCE.

> ***Note:*** Questions 8.6 and 8.7 are longer, review-type questions. **Question 8.6** requires the preparation of both a consolidated SoCI and SoCE of a parent, subsidiary and associate, including many of the complications discussed in this chapter. **Question 8.7** will assist you to revise virtually all of the principles outlined in this chapter as it involves a parent, a subsidiary, associate, a joint venture and a trade investment with a combination of complications.
>
> The solutions to both questions contain the columnar method workings and an explanation of how to account for each complication.

Question 8.6

The following are the statements of comprehensive income of Pear Plc, Sloe Ltd and Apple Ltd for the year ended 30 June 2011:

STATEMENTS OF COMPREHENSIVE INCOME

	Pear Plc €000	**Sloe Ltd €000**	**Apple Ltd €000**
Revenue	14,000	9,750	6,870
Cost of sales	(8,400)	(5,850)	(2,620)
Gross profit	5,600	3,900	4,250
Dividends receivable – Sloe Ltd	20		
– Red Ltd	10		
Distribution costs	(480)	(450)	(160)
Administrative expenses	(1,490)	(650)	(460)
Finance costs	(350)	(180)	(70)
Profit before tax	3,310	2,620	3,560
Income tax expense	(1,350)	(1,050)	(420)
Profit for the year	1,960	1,570	3,140
Other comprehensive income	500	nil	nil
Total comprehensive income for the year	2,460	1,570	3,140

The following additional information is available.

1. Pear Plc acquired 70% of the ordinary shares of Sloe Ltd on 1 July 2008 when its reserves were:

	€000
Share premium account	800
Retained earnings	2,500

2. At 1 July 2008, the fair value of the property, plant and equipment of Sloe Ltd exceeded the carrying value by €160,000. This surplus has not been reflected in the financial statements of Silver Ltd. At that date the average remaining useful life of the non-current assets was four years.
3. Pear Plc acquired 30% of the ordinary shares of Apple Ltd on 1 July 2009 when the reserves of Apple Ltd were:

	€000
Share Premium	1,500
Retained earnings	2,600

4. During March 2011 Sloe Ltd sold goods to Pear Plc at invoice value €200,000 on which Sloe Ltd made a gross profit of 20%. One half of these goods remained in the inventory of Pear Plc at 30 June 2011.
5. Impairment of goodwill/premium (attributable to Pear Plc) has occurred as follows:

Year ended 30 June 2010	Sloe Ltd	€30,000
	Apple Ltd	€20,000
Year ended 30 June 2011	Sloe Ltd	€50,000
	Apple Ltd	€40,000

6. Pear Plc had 10 million ordinary shares of €1 each in issue on 1 July 2010. On the 31 March 2011, the company made a bonus issue of 1 for 4 out of share premium which stood at €4,000,000 on the 1 July 2010.
7. Pear Plc revalued its property during the reporting period under review giving rise to a revaluation surplus of €500,000.
8. Retained earnings at 1 July 2010:

	€000
Pear Plc	€6,750
Sloe Ltd	€3,690
Apple Ltd	€3,300

9. Pear Ltd owns 10% of the ordinary shares of Red Ltd.

Requirement:

(a) Prepare the consolidated statement of comprehensive income for the Pear Plc group for the year ended 30 June 2011.

(b) Prepare the consolidated statement of changes in equity for the year ended 30 June 2011 in so far as the information permits.

Solution to Question 8.6

ADJUSTMENTS (as required by the additional information)

2. Provide for additional depreciation of €40,000 per annum for three years.
   Charge €40,000 to current year's administrative expenses (note impact on NCI).
   Reduce opening retained earnings in SoCE by 2 × €40,000 × 70% = €56,000.

3. Disclose in consolidated SoCI share of profit of associate Apple Ltd.

Profit after tax: 3,140 × 30%	=	942	
Less premium impairment for 2011		(40)	902

4. Reduce group revenue and cost of sales by intragroup sales €200,000.
   Add unrealised inventory profit €200,000 × 1/5 × ½ = €20,000 to cost of sales Sloe Ltd (note impact on NCI).
5. Charge to consolidated SoCI impairment in Sloe Ltd for current year €50,000.
   Reduce group retained earnings brought forward in SoCE by:
   2010 impairment (30,000 + 20,000) = €50,000.

6. In the SoCE reduce share premium and increase ordinary share capital of Pear Plc by €2.5 million.
7. Include €500,000 under other comprehensive income in consolidated SoCI.
9. The dividend received by Pear Plc from Red Ltd must be included in the consolidated SoCI as it is a dividend from outside the group.

WORKINGS

	Pear	Sloe	Adjustment	Consol. SoCI
	€000	€000	€000	€000
Revenue	14,000	9,750	(200)	23,550
Cost of sales	8,400	5,850	(200) 20	(14,070)
Gross profit	5,600	3,900	(20)	9,480
Dividends receivable from Red	10			10
Distribution costs	(480)	(450)		(930)
Administrative expenses	(1,490)	(650)	(40)	(2,180)
Finance costs	(350)	(180)		(530)
Impairment of goodwill			(50)	(50)
Share of profit of associate			902	902
Profit before tax	3,290	2,620	792	6,702
Income tax expense	(1,350)	(1,050)		(2,400)
Profit for the year	1,940	1,570	792	4,302

CONSOLIDATED STATEMENT OF COMPREHENSIVE INCOME
for Year Ended 30 June 2011

	€000
Revenue	23,550
Cost of Sales	(14,070)
Gross profit	9,480

Dividends receivable	10
Distribution costs	(930)
Administrative expenses	(2,180)
Finance costs	(530)
Impairment of goodwill	(50)
	5,800
Share of profit of associate	902
Profit before tax	6,702
Income tax expense	(2,400)
Profit for the year	4,302
Other Comprehensive Income	
Property revaluation surplus	500
Total Comprehensive Income for the year	**4,802**
Profit for year attributable to	
Owners of the parent	3,849
Non-controlling interests	453
	4,302
Total comprehensive income for the year attributable to:	
Owners of the parent	4,349
Non-controlling interests	453
	4,802
Non-controlling interests	
Profit after tax (Sloe Ltd)	1,570
Less extra depreciation (1 year)	(40)
Unrealised inventory profit	(20)
	1,510
NCI × 30%	453

Consolidated Statement of Changes in Equity

	Ordinary Shares	Share Premium	Reval. Reserves	Retained Earnings	NCI	Total
	€000	**€000**	**€000**	**€000**	**€000**	**€000**
At 1 July 2010	10,000	4,000	–	7,687 *(W1)*	X	X
TCI for year			500	3,849	453	4,802
Bonus issue	2,500	(2,500)				0

(W1) Retained earnings at 1 July 2010	**€000**
Pear Plc	6,750
Goodwill written off 2010 – Sloe Ltd	(30)
Goodwill written off 2010 – Apple Ltd	(20)
Sloe Ltd	
(3,690 – 2,500) × 70%	833
extra depreciation – 2 years (80) × 70% (group's share)	(56)
Apple Ltd	
(3,300 – 2,600) × 30%	210
	7,687

Question 8.7

STATEMENTS OF COMPREHENSIVE INCOME
for the Year Ended 30 September 2011

	Cork Ltd	Kerry Ltd	Louth Ltd	Meath Ltd
	€000	€000	€000	€000
Revenue	15,460	12,370	7,700	6,180
Cost of sales	(10,820)	(8,680)	(5,400)	(4,320)
Gross profit	4,640	3,690	2,300	1,860
Other income	300	–	–	–
Distribution costs	(930)	(740)	(400)	(370)
Administrative expenses	(1,110)	(880)	(500)	(440)
Finance costs	(390)	(310)	(100)	(170)
Profit before tax	2,510	1,760	1,300	880
Income tax expense	(750)	(530)	(400)	(260)
Profit for the year	1,760	1,230	900	620
Other comprehensive income:				
Property revaluation surplus	1,000	800	–	500
Total comprehensive income for the year	2,760	2,030	900	1,120

The following additional information is available:

1. Cork Ltd acquired 90% of the ordinary shares of Kerry Ltd on 1 October 2008 when the retained earnings of Kerry Ltd were € 900,000.
2. During August 2011 Kerry Ltd sold goods to Cork Ltd at invoice value €120,000 on which Kerry Ltd made a mark-up of 1/3. All the goods were in the inventory of Cork Ltd at the reporting date. Total sales from Kerry Ltd to Cork Ltd during the year amounted to €600,000.
3. Cork Ltd received a management fee of €300,000 from Kerry Ltd for the year under review.
4. Cork Ltd and Limerick Ltd jointly control the policies of Louth Ltd each having purchased 50% of the voting rights on 1 July 2011.

5. Cork Ltd acquired 25% of the voting rights of Meath Ltd on 1 October 2010.
6. Goodwill/premium on acquisition has been impaired as follows:
   y/e 30 September 2010 – on acquisition of Kerry Ltd €40,000
   y/e 30 September 2011 – on acquisition of Meath Ltd €20,000
7. Retained earnings at 1 October 2010:

	€000
Cork Ltd	8,460
Kerry Ltd	3,500
Louth Ltd	1,500
Meath Ltd	1,940.

Requirement Prepare for the year ended 30 September 2011:
(a) the consolidated statement of comprehensive income; and
(b) the consolidated statement of changes in equity.

Solution to Question 8.7

Adjustments (as required by the additional information)
2. Unrealised inventory profit €120,000 × ¼ = €30,000
   Add €30,000 to cost of sales of Kerry Ltd (note impact on NCI).
   Intragroup sales €600,000
   Reduce revenue and cost of sales in consolidated SoCI by €600,000.
3. Management fee
   Reduce other income Cork Ltd by €300,000
   Reduce administrative expenses Kerry Ltd by €300,000.
4. Joint venture Louth Ltd acquired nine months into reporting period. Time apportion income and expenses. Consolidate each income and expense $\times \frac{3}{12} \times$ 50%.
5. Share of profit of associate Meath Ltd

Profit after tax	€620,000 × 25%	=	€155,000	
Impairment of premium (see 6)			€20,000	€135,000

6. Reduce group retained earnings at 1 October 2010 by €40,000
   Reduce share of profit of associate (see 5) by €20,000.

Workings

	Cork Ltd €000	**Kerry Ltd €000**	**Adjustments €000**	**Consol. SoCI €000**
Revenue	15,460	12,370	(600) 962.5	2,819,2.5
Cost of sales	10,820	8,680	(600) 30 675	(19,605.0)
Gross profit	4,640	3,690	257.5	8,587.5
Other Income	300		(300.0)	0.0
Distribution costs	(930)	(740)	(50.0)	(1,720.0)
Administrative expenses	(1,110)	(880)	300.0 (62.5)	(1,752.5)
Finance costs	(390)	(310)	(12.5)	(712.5)
Share of profit of associate			135.0	135.0
Profit before tax	2,510	1,760	267.50	4,537.5

Income tax expense	(750)	(530)	(50)	(1,330.0)
Profit for the year	1,760	1,230	217.50	3,207.5

Consolidated Statement of Changes in Equity

	Ordinary Shares €000	Revaluation Reserve €000	Retained Earnings €000	NCI €000	Total €000
Balance 1 October 2010 *(WX)*			10,760.0		
TCI for the year *(W1/W2)*		1,845.0	3,087.5	200.0	5,132.5
Balance 30 September 2011					

(WX) Retained earnings 1 October 2010

Cork Ltd	8,460
Impairment of goodwill Kerry Ltd	(40)
Kerry Ltd: 90% (3,500 – 900)	2,340
	10,760

(***Note:*** Neither Louth Ltd nor Meath Ltd are included in the group retained earnings at 1 October 2010, as both were acquired during the year under review.)

Cork Ltd

Consolidated Statement of Comprehensive Income
for the Year Ended 30 September 2011

		€000	€000
Revenue	Group	27,230.0	
	Share of JV	962.5	28,192.5
Cost of sales	Group	18,930.0	
	Share of JV	675.0	19,605.0
Gross profit			8,587.5
Distribution costs	Group	1,670.0	
	Share of JV	50.0	(1,720.0)
Administrative expenses	Group	1,690.0	
	Share of JV	62.5	(1,752.5)
Finance costs	Group	700.0	
	Share of JV	12.5	(712.5)
Share of profit of associate			135
Profit before tax			4,537.50
Income tax expense	Group	1,280.0	
	Share of JV	50.0	(1,330.0)
Profit for the year			3,207.50
Other comprehensive income			
Property revaluation surplus			1,925.0

Total comprehensive income for the year	5,132.50
Profit for the year attributable to:	
Owners of the parent	3,087.5
Non-controlling interests *(W1)*	120.0
	3,207.50
Total comprehensive income attributable to:	
Owners of the parent	4,932.5
Non-controlling interests	200.0
	5,132.5

(W1) NCI	**€000**
Non-controlling interests in Kerry Ltd profit for the year	
Profit after tax Kerry Ltd	1,230
Less unrealised inventory profit	(30)
Adjusted	1,200
NCI × 10%	120

(W2) NCI	
Non-controlling interests in Kerry Ltd total comprehensive income.	
Interest in profit for the year *(W1)*	120
Share of property revaluation surplus Kerry Ltd (800 × 10%)	80
	200

Chapter 9

IFRS 3 *Business Combinations*

Learning Objectives

After reading this chapter you should be able to:

- give the appropriate accounting treatment for business combinations and explain how this accounting treatment is applied;
- explain how the component parts of the purchase consideration should be valued;
- give guidance on which assets and liabilities of the subsidiary should be recognised in the consolidated statement of financial position and how they should be valued;
- demonstrate an understanding of how goodwill is calculated and discuss a gain from a bargain purchase; and
- explain how goodwill can be attributable to non-controlling interests.

Introduction

IFRS 3 *Business Combinations* could be aptly entitled the 'Umbrella Standard for the Preparation of Consolidated Financial Statements of a Parent and Subsidiaries'. Chapters 3 to 6 inclusive contain several examples of how to calculate goodwill (attributable to P Ltd)/gain from a bargain purchase, and how to treat these items in consolidated financial statements. The cost of control account (T account method) and alternative workings have been used in this text to calculate goodwill/gain from a bargain purchase. IFRS 3 extends this topic further as it contains the principles for valuing each component part used in the calculations. The standard informs us:

(a) how to value the investment in a subsidiary;
(b) how to value the net assets of the subsidiary at the date of acquisition;
(c) how to identify which net assets should be recognised in the calculation; and
(d) how to measure the non-controlling interests in the net assets of a subsidiary at the date of acquisition.

IFRS 3 also introduces a new concept of goodwill, i.e. goodwill attributable to non-controlling interests (NCI).

The objective of IFRS 3 is to improve the relevance, reliability and comparability of the information that a reporting entity provides in its financial statements about business combinations and their effects.

IFRS 3 details how the parent/acquirer (P Ltd):

1. recognises and measures in its financial statements *the identifiable assets* acquired, the liabilities assumed and any *non-controlling interests* in the *acquiree;*
2. recognises and measures any *goodwill* acquired or a *gain from a bargain purchase*;
3. determines the information to be disclosed to enable the users of its financial statements to evaluate the nature and financial effects of a business combination.

Note: The content of this chapter does not represent an exhaustive coverage of IFRS 3.

Accounting Treatment for Business Combinations (the Acquisition Method)

IFRS 3 states that all business combinations shall be accounted for using the acquisition method. (***Note:*** The **acquisition method** is the method that has been used in this text.)

There are five steps involved in applying the acquisition method (IFRS 3, para 5):

Step **1** Identify the acquirer
Step **2** Determine the acquisition date
Step **3** Ascertain the identifiable assets and liabilities of the entity being acquired, and determine how these assets and liabilities are to be measured
Step **4** Determine the non-controlling interests in the subsidiary and the attributable valuation
Step **5** Calculate the amount of goodwill or gain from a bargain purchase.

Step 1: Identify the Acquirer

The acquirer is the entity that obtains control over the other combining entity. Control is the power to govern the financial and operating policies of an entity so as to gain benefits from its activities. In **Chapter 2**, it was explained that control is achieved when a parent (P Ltd) acquires more than half of the voting power of a subsidiary (S Ltd). However, control can also exist, under IAS 27 *Consolidated and Separate Financial Statements,* where a parent owns less than 50% of the voting power of an entity but, for example, has **power over** more than 50% of the voting rights by virtue of an agreement with other investors.

Step 2: Determine the Acquisition Date

The acquisition date is the date on which the acquirer gets **control** over the subsidiary. This is generally the date on which the acquirer legally transfers the consideration, acquires the assets and assumes the liabilities of the acquiree.

Step 3: Assets Acquired and Liabilities Assumed: Recognition and Measurement

The acquirer must recognise the identifiable assets acquired and the liabilities assumed at the acquisition date. To qualify for recognition, the identifiable assets acquired and liabilities assumed must meet the definitions of assets and liabilities in the International Accounting Standards Board's (IASB) *Conceptual Framework for Financial Reporting 2010* i.e.:

Asset A resource controlled by an entity as a result of past events and from which future economic benefits are expected to flow to the entity.

Liability A present obligation of the entity arising from past events, the settlement of which is expected to result in an outflow from the entity of economic benefits.[1]

Recognising Contingent Liabilities The acquirer should recognise, as of the date of acquisition, any contingent liability assumed in a business combination if it is a present obligation that arises from past events and its fair value can be measured reliably.

Valuing the Assets Acquired and Liabilities Assumed The identifiable assets acquired and all liabilities assumed should be measured at their **fair values,** i.e. the amount for which an asset could be exchanged, or a liability settled, between knowledgeable willing parties in an arm's length transaction.

Step 4: Non-controlling Interests

Non-controlling interests at the date of acquisition were traditionally measured as follows:

Share Capital plus Reserves of subsidiary (S Ltd)* × Non-controlling interests %

*Share Capital and Reserves of S Ltd = Net Assets of S Ltd, which are valued at fair value.

This could be titled the proportion of net assets method.

IFRS 3 now also permits the **non-controlling interests** in the net assets of the subsidiary at the date of acquisition to be valued at fair value, which would impact on the value of goodwill and NCI, and which is dealt with later in this chapter.

This could be titled the fair value method.

Purchase Consideration The amount of the purchase consideration is a major component in the calculation of goodwill. The valuation of the purchase consideration may not always be self-evident or straightforward as a purchase consideration can have many components, e.g. an issue of shares, a cash payment, a transfer of an asset, deferred consideration and contingent consideration. There is, however, one overriding principle: all elements of the purchase consideration should be valued at fair value as at the date of acquisition, e.g.:

- shares issued – valued at **market value**;
- cash paid – valued at the **actual** amount;
- deferred consideration – valued at the **present value** of the future payment.

---

[1] For a complete discussion of the Conceptual Framework for Financial Reporting, see ***Connolly***, Chapter 1, "Framework for Financial Reporting".

Example 9.1: Calculation of Purchase Consideration

Pat Plc acquired 90% of the ordinary shares of Susan Ltd on 1 September 2010 for the following consideration:
(a) the issue of 2 million €1 ordinary shares at market value €1.80;
(b) an immediate cash payment of €200,000; and
(c) a cash payment of €500,000, three years after the date of the acquisition.

Pat Plc can borrow funds at 10%.

Journal entry to record the purchase consideration in the financial statements of Pat Plc:

	€000	**€000**
Dr. Investment in Susan Ltd	4,175	
Cr. Ordinary Shares		2,000
Cr. Share premium (€0.80 × 2 million)		1,600
Cr. Cash		200
Cr. Deferred consideration		375

The deferred consideration is recorded at present value, at a discount factor of 0.751.*
(*As per generally available present value tables.)

The total deferred consideration discount (500 – 375) €125,000 is unwound over three years and accounted for in the consolidated financial statements in the year ended 31 August 2011 as follows:

	€000	**€000**
Dr. Finance costs	37.5	
Cr. Deferred consideration (€ 375,000 × 10%)		37.5

Contingent Consideration Occasionally, the cost of acquisition contains an element of contingent consideration, where the amount payable is contingent on the outcome of future events, e.g. an additional amount if the subsidiary achieves a certain level of performance.

If the purchase consideration contains an element of contingent consideration this must be valued at fair value at the date of acquisition. If the amount of contingent consideration changes as the result of a post-acquisition event, e.g. meeting a profit target, accounting for the changed consideration depends on whether the additional consideration is equity or cash/other asset. Equity instruments are not re-measured: if the additional amount is cash/other asset it is recognised in profit or loss.

If the fair value changes because of new information relating to events at the acquisition date, the cost of acquisition must be re-measured.

Example 9.2(A): Payment in Cash

Assume that in acquiring Susan Ltd above, Pat Plc had agreed to pay a further €360,000 in cash at the end of five years provided that the cumulative profits of Susan Ltd exceed €4 million. When the probabilities of reaching the target are evaluated the **fair value of the contingent consideration** at the date of acquisition is calculated at €100,000. At the end of Year 1 (31 August 2011), the probability of reaching the target has improved and the fair value is now estimated at €120,000. The additional €20,000 is expensed to profit and loss. This evaluation is carried out at the end of each reporting period and any change to the fair value is taken to profit and loss.

Journal Entry in Consolidated Accounts

Dr. SoCI	€20,000	
Cr. Contingent Consideration		€20,000

Example 9.2(B): Payment in Fixed Number of Shares

Assume that Pat Plc had agreed to give a further 200,000 shares (fair value of €360,000 at acquisition date) at the end of five years provided that the cumulative profits of Susan Ltd exceed €4 million. When the probabilities of reaching the target are evaluated the **fair value of the contingent consideration** at the date of acquisition is calculated at €100,000. The contingent consideration is classed as equity and is not re-measured each year.

Acquisition Costs Incremental costs of acquisition, such as general administration costs, any professional fees, cost of the acquisition department, etc., cannot be included as part of the acquisition costs. All such costs must be expensed to the statement of comprehensive income as incurred.

Step 5: Calculating Goodwill (attributable to a Parent) or a Gain from a Bargain Purchase

IFRS 3 defines situations where:

1. the consideration paid exceeds the share of net assets (capital + reserves) acquired, both at fair value as goodwill

   and

2. the consideration is less than the share of the net assets acquired as a gain from a bargain purchase.

Example 9.3: Calculation of Goodwill

Shrub Ltd
Statement of Financial Position
as at 31 August 2011

	€000
Property, plant and equipment	4,600
Current assets	2,200
Total assets	6,800
Equity and liabilities	
Equity	
Ordinary shares €1	2,500
Retained earnings	2,600
Total equity	5,100
Current liabilities	1,700
Total equity and liabilities	6,800

Scenario 1:
Petal Plc acquires 80% of the ordinary shares of Shrub Ltd on 31 August 2011 at a cost of €4.8 million. The fair values of the assets and liabilities of Shrub Ltd are the same as their carrying values except for property, plant and equipment, the fair value of which is €5 million.

Scenario 2:
Petal Plc acquires 80% of the ordinary shares of Shrub Ltd at a cost of €3,780,000. The carrying values of all the assets and liabilities of Shrub Ltd are the same as their book values.

Solution – Scenario 1

Journal Entry

		€000	**€000**
1. Dr.	PPE	400	
Cr.	Cost of control (80%)		320
Cr.	NCI (20%)		80

Cost of Control

Debit		**Credit**	
		Journal 1	320
Investment in Shrub Ltd	4,800	Ordinary shares (80%)	2,000
		Retained earnings (80% × 2,600)	2,080
		Goodwill	400
	4,800		4,800

Non-controlling Interests

Debit		**Credit**	
		Journal 1	80
		Ordinary shares (20%)	500
SoFP	1,100	Retained earnings	520
	1,100	(20% × 2,600)	1,100

The goodwill (€400,000) is treated as a non-current intangible asset in the consolidated SoFP and is only written down when impaired.

Solution – Scenario 2

Cost of Control

Debit		**Credit**	
Investment in Shrub Ltd	3,780	Ordinary shares	2,000
Gain from a bargain purchase	300	Retained earnings	2,080
	4,080		4,080

Non-Controlling Interests

Debit		**Credit**	
		Ordinary shares	500
SoFP	1,020	Retained earnings	520
	1,020		1,020

Gain from a Bargain Purchase Before recognising a gain from a bargain purchase, the acquirer must:

(a) **re-assess** whether it has correctly identified all the assets acquired and all the liabilities assumed;
(b) **review** the measurement of the purchase consideration; and
(c) **re-assess** the fair values attributed to the assets acquired and the liabilities assumed.

A bargain purchase might happen, for example, in a business combination that is a forced sale in which the seller is acting under compulsion.

Treatment of a Gain from a Bargain Purchase If the gain remains after steps (a), (b) and (c) above have been carried out, the acquirer should take the gain to profit or loss at the date of acquisition:

Journal Entry (for SoFP)
Dr. Cost of Control
Cr. Retained Earnings of P Ltd

Non-controlling Interests and Goodwill Traditionally, goodwill on consolidation was only attributable to the parent company's investment, i.e. if the fair value of the purchase consideration exceeded the group's share of the net assets of the subsidiary at fair value, no goodwill was attributable to the non-controlling interests.

IFRS 3 now permits the non-controlling interests in the net assets of subsidiary at the date of acquisition to be measured in two ways:

1. **The 'Traditional Method'** – non-controlling interests at the date of acquisition are measured as follows:

   Net assets of subsidiary S Ltd (at fair value) × Non-controlling Interests %.

   Or

2. **The 'New Method'** – the non-controlling interest itself is measured at fair value at the acquisition date.

See **Example 9.4** for the application of both methods.

Example 9.4: Valuation of Non-controlling Interests

Recalling **Example 9.3** above, Shrub Ltd (Scenario 1), the non-controlling interest at the date of acquisition was valued using the **traditional method**:

Non-controlling Interests

Debit		**Credit**	
		Journal 1(Revaluation PPE)	80
		Ordinary shares (20%)	500
SoFP	1,100	Retained earnings	520
	1,100	(20% × 2,600)	1,100

This could alternatively be stated as follows:	**€000**	**€000**
Net assets		
At acquisition date	5,100	
Revaluation surplus	400	
	5,500	
NCI × 20%		1,100

Non-Controlling Interests measured under 'New Method'

Assume that the directors of Petal Plc engaged an independent consultant who determined that the fair value of the 20% non-controlling interest in Shrub Ltd was €1.2 million at the date of acquisition.

Solution

Journal

		€000	**€000**
1. Dr.	PPE	400	
Cr.	Cost of control (80%)		320
Cr.	NCI (20%)		80
	Increase in value of Shrub Ltd's property, plant and equipment to fair value.		

2. Dr. Goodwill	100	
Cr. NCI		100
Goodwill attributable to NCI		

Goodwill attributable to NCI:

	€000
Net assets of Shrub Ltd at acquisition date	5,100
Revaluation surplus	400
	5,500
NCI × 20%	1,100
Independently attributed fair value	1,200
Goodwill NCI	100

Cost of Control (Petal Plc)

Debit		Credit	
Investment in Shrub Ltd	4,800	Journal 1	320
		Ordinary shares (80%)	2,000
		Retained earnings (80% × 2,600)	2,080
		Goodwill	400
	4,800		4,800

Non-Controlling Interests

Debit		Credit	
		Journal 1	80
		Ordinary shares (20%)	500
		Retained earnings (20% × 2,600)	520
SoFP	1,200	Journal 2	100
	1,200		1,200

Goodwill

Debit		Credit	
Transfer – cost of control	400		
Journal 2	100	SoFP	500
	500		500

Any future impairment of goodwill would be apportioned 80 : 20 and the entry will be:

Dr.	Retained Earnings (Petal Plc)	80% (of impairment)
Dr.	NCI	20% (of impairment)
Cr.	Goodwill	100% (of impairment)

Conclusion

In Chapters 3 to 6, we calculated goodwill (attributable to a parent) using a cost of control account. Having studies this chapter, you should now be able to appreciate how each figure in the cost of control was valued. The new method of valuing non-controlling interests at date of acquisition can give rise to additional goodwill with a corresponding increase in non-controlling interests.

Summary

1. The acquisition method is the only method permitted by IFRS 3 to account for business combinations, i.e. where a parent gains control over the operating and financial policies of a subsidiary.
2. All elements of the purchase consideration must be recorded at fair value in the financial statements of the parent.
3. The assets and liabilities of a subsidiary must be revalued to fair value for consolidation purposes as at the date of acquisition.
4. The acquirer should recognise, as of the date of acquisition, a contingent liability assumed in a business combination if it is a present obligation that arises from past events and its fair value can be measured reliably.
5. Goodwill (attributable to a parent) arises if the fair value of the consideration to acquire a subsidiary is greater than the group's share of the capital and reserves (net assets at fair value) at the date of acquisition.
6. A gain from a bargain purchase arises when the fair value of the consideration to acquire a subsidiary is less than the group's share of the capital and reserves (net assets) at the date of acquisition.
7. Traditionally goodwill was only attributable to the parent's investment but IFRS 3 now permits goodwill to be attributed to the non-controlling interests. This can arise where a fair value is attributed to the non-controlling interests at the acquisition date and this amount is greater than their share of the net assets of subsidiary S Ltd at fair value.

Recommended Reading

As stated throughout this text, you are encouraged to read alternative texts, as the opinions and methods of others can only help to develop a greater understanding of all topics. To this end, and in the context of this chapter, it is recommended that you also read Chapter 26, "Business Combinations and Consolidated Financial Statements", of *International Financial Accounting and Reporting* (3rd Edition) by Ciaran Connolly.

QUESTIONS

Question 9.1

What is the recognised method for accounting for business combinations in accordance with IFRS 3?

Solution

The acquisition method should be used to account for business combinations.

Question 9.2

Explain the term 'deferred consideration' and how it is measured as part of a purchase consideration.

Solution

Deferred consideration refers to a known amount payable at a future date. Deferred consideration should be recorded at the present value of the future payment. The discount is unwound in the consolidated financial statements over the period of deferral.

Question 9.3

What is contingent consideration? How is it measured?

Solution

Contingent consideration is a component of the cost of investment in subsidiary S Ltd where the amount payable is dependent on a future event. Contingent consideration is measured at fair value as at the date of acquisition.

Question 9.4

Pete Ltd acquired an 80% interest in Sharon Ltd at the following cost:

(a) the issue of 500,000 ordinary €1 shares when the market value of each share was €2.
(b) a cash payment of €300,000 two years later. Pete Ltd can borrow funds at 8%.
(c) a cash payment of €350,000 after three years if Sharon Ltd produces total profits of €280,000 over that period. When the probabilities of reaching the target are evaluated the **fair value** at the date of acquisition is calculated at €120,000.

Requirement Show the entry to record the purchase consideration in the financial statements of Pete Ltd at the date of acquisition.

Solution

Present value of deferred consideration:	€	€
€300,000 × 100/108 × 100/108 = say €257,000		
Dr. Investment in Sharon	1,377,000	
Cr. Ordinary shares		500,000
Cr. Share premium (500 × €1)		500,000
Cr. Non-current liabilities (257 + 120)		377,000

Question 9.5

Explain how goodwill can be attributed to the non-controlling interests.

Solution

IFRS 3 now permits goodwill to be attributed to non-controlling interests. This can occur where a **fair value** is attributed to the non-controlling interests at acquisition date which is **greater** than the NCI share of the **net assets** of subsidiary S Ltd (at fair value) at the same date.

> ***Note:*** The following questions, Questions 9.6 and 9.7, are longer, review-type questions. These questions afford an opportunity to implement the new method of attributing goodwill to non-controlling interests and to record a purchase consideration according to IFRS 3.
>
> Each solution contains:
> 1. Journal entries
> 2. The T account method workings
> 3. The columnar method workings

Question 9.6

The following are the statements of financial position of Pilot Plc and its subsidiary Steward Ltd as at 30 September 2011:

	Pilot Plc €000	**Steward Ltd €000**
Assets		
Non-current assets		
Property, plant and equipment	16,560	13,240
Investment in Steward Ltd	8,300	
Current assets	4,970	3,950
Total assets	**29,830**	**17,190**

Equity and liabilities		
Equity		
Ordinary share capital (€0.50)	10,000	6,000
Retained earnings	15,840	8,030
Total equity	25,840	14,030
Current liabilities	3,990	3,160
Total equity and liabilities	**29,830**	**17,190**

Notes to the Statements of Financial Position:

1. Pilot Plc acquired 9,000,000 ordinary shares (75%) in Steward Ltd on 1 October 2010 when the retained earnings of Steward Ltd were €4,800,000.
2. The non-controlling interests in the net assets of Steward Ltd were independently valued at €2,800,000 and this should be reflected in the consolidated financial statements.
3. Goodwill was impaired in the amount of €40,000 for the year ended 30 September 2011.

Requirement:

(a) Prepare the consolidated statement of financial position as at 30 September 2011.

(b) Explain any differences to the consolidated SoFP as in (a) if non-controlling interests at acquisition date were measured using the traditional share of the net assets of Steward Ltd valued at fair value.

Solution to Question 9.6

(a) Non-controlling Interests measured using 'New Method'

Non-controlling interests	**€000**	**€000**
Valuation		2,800
Share of net assets (capital and reserves)		
Steward Ltd at acquisition date:		
Ordinary shares	6,000	
Retained earnings	4,800	
	10,800	
NCI share 25%		2,700
Attributable goodwill		100

Journal Entries:

		€000	**€000**
1.	Dr. Goodwill	100	
	Cr. Non-controlling interests		100
	Goodwill attributed to NCI		
2.	Dr. Retained earnings (Pilot Plc)	30	
	Dr. NCI	10	
	Cr. Goodwill		40
	Impairment of goodwill in ratio 75% : 25%		

Workings (T account Method)

Property, Plant and Equipment

Debit		Credit	
Pilot	16,560		
Steward	13,240	SoFP	29,800
	29,800		29,800

Investment in Steward Ltd

Debit		Credit	
Pilot	8,300	Cost of control	8,300
	8,300		8,300

Current Assets

Debit		Credit	
Pilot	4,970		
Steward	3,950	SoFP	8,920
	8,920		8,920

Ordinary Shares

Debit		Credit	
Cost of control (75%)	4,500	Pilot	10,000
NCI (25%)	1,500		
SoFP	10,000	Steward	6,000
	16,000		16,000

Retained Earnings

Debit		Credit	
Cost of control			
(75% × 4,800)	3,600.0	Pilot	15,840.0
NCI			
(25% × 8,030)	2,007.5		
Journal 2	30.0		
SoFP	18,232.5	Steward	8,030.0
	23,870.0		23,870.0

Current Liabilities

Debit		Credit	
		Pilot	3,990
SoFP	7,150	Steward	3,160
	7,150		7,150

Cost of Control

Debit		Credit	
Investment in Steward Ltd	8,300	Ordinary shares	4,500
		Retained earnings	3,600
		Transfer – goodwill	200
	8,300		8,300

Non-controlling Interests

Debit		Credit	
Journal 2	10.0	Journal 1	100.0
		Ordinary shares	1,500.0
SoFP	3,597.5	Retained earnings	2,007.5
	3,607.5		3,607.5

Goodwill

Debit		Credit	
Journal 1	100	Journal 2	40
Cost of control	200	SoFP	260
	300		300

WORKINGS (Columnar Method)

	Pilot Plc €000	**Steward Ltd €000**	**Adjustments €000**	**Consol. SoFP €000**
PPE	16,560	13,240		29,800
Investment in Steward Ltd	8,300		(8,300)	0
Goodwill *(W1)*			260	260
Current assets	4,970	3,950		8,920
Total assets	**29,830**	**17,190**	**(8,040)**	**38,980**
Ordinary shares	10,000	6,000	(6,000)	10,000
Retained earnings *(W2)*	15,840	8,030	(5,637.50)	18,232.50
Non-controlling interests *(W3)*			3,597.50	3,597.50
Current liabilities	3,990	3,160		7,150
Total equity and liabilities	**29,830**	**17,190**	**(8,040)**	**38,980**

(W1) Goodwill	**€000**	**€000**
Cost of investment in Steward Ltd		8,300
at acquisition date:		
Ordinary shares	6,000	
Retained earnings	4,800	
	10,800	

Group's share 75%			8,100
Goodwill attributable to Pilot Plc			200
Attributable to NCI Journal 1			100
Goodwill Impairment			(40)
SoFP			260

(W2) Retained earnings

Pilot Plc at reporting date			15,840.0
Goodwill impairment (75%)			(30.0)
			15,810.0
Steward Ltd at reporting date	8,030		
At acquisition date	4,800		
Post-acquisition	3,230		
Group's Share 75% =			2,422.5
SoFP			18,232.5

(W3) Non-controlling interests

Steward Ltd at reporting date:	**€000**	**€000**
Ordinary shares	6,000	
Retained earnings	8,030	
	14,030	
NCI × 25%		3,507.5
Goodwill attributed		100.0
Goodwill impairment (25% × 40)		(10.0)
SoFP		3,597.5

Pilot Plc

Statement of Financial Position

as at 30 September 2011

Assets	**€000**
Non-current assets	
Property, plant and equipment	29,800.0
Goodwill	260.0
Current assets	8,920.0
Total assets	**38,980.0**
Equity and liabilities	
Equity	
Ordinary shares	10,000.0
Retained earnings	18,232.5
Total shareholders' equity	28,232.5
Non-controlling interests	3,597.5
Total equity	31,830.0
Current liabilities	7,150.0
Total equity and liabilities	**38,980.0**

(b) Non-controlling Interests measured using the 'Traditional Method'

Non-controlling Interests	**€000**	**€000**
Share of net assets (capital and reserves)		
Steward Ltd		
Ordinary shares	6,000	
Retained earnings (at year-end)	8,030	
	14,030	
NCI share 25%		3,507.50

There would not have been any goodwill (€100) attributable to the NCI and no impairment (€10). The NCI in the consolidated statement of financial position would amount to €3,507.50.

Goodwill

Goodwill would not include any NCI share and will be as follows:

	€000	**€000**
Cost of Control (Pilot Ltd)	200	
Less: Goodwill Impairment (total)	(40)	
SoFP		160

Question 9.7

Polish Ltd acquired 60% of the ordinary shares of Shine Ltd on 1 September 2011 when the issued share capital of Shine Ltd was €3 million and its retained earnings €1 million. The consideration is as follows:

(a) the issue of 1 million ordinary €1 shares in Polish Ltd at market value €2.20;
(b) a cash payment of €400,000 on 1 September 2013.

Polish Ltd can borrow funds at 10%.

The non-controlling interests in the net assets of Shine Ltd as at 1 September 2011 is professionally valued at €1,650,000.

Requirement:

(a) Show the journal entry to record the purchase consideration in the financial statements of Polish Ltd at 1 September 2011.
(b) Calculate the following as at 1 September 2011:
   (i) Goodwill
   (ii) Non-controlling interests

Solution to Question 9.7

(a) Journal Entry to Record Purchase Consideration:

		€000	€000
Dr.	Investment in Shine Ltd	2,530	
Cr.	Ordinary shares		1,000
Cr.	Share premium (1m x €1.20)		1,200
Cr.	Non-current liabilities (Deferred consideration)		330

Deferred Consideration:
€400,000 × 100/110 × 100/110 say €330,000

(b) Goodwill Attributable to NCI:

	€000	€000
Fair Value of NCI at 1 September 2011		1,650
Share of net assets (capital and reserves) Shine Ltd at acquisition date:		
Ordinary shares	3,000	
Retained earnings	1,000	
	4,000	
NCI share 40%		1,600
Attributable goodwill		50

Workings (T account Method)

Cost of Control

Debit		**Credit**	
Investment in Shine Ltd	2,530	Ordinary shares	1,800
		Retained earnings (1,000 × 60%)	600
		Transfer-goodwill	130
	2,530		2,530

Non-controlling Interests

Debit		**Credit**	
		Goodwill	50
		Ordinary shares (40%)	1,200
SoFP	1,650	Retained earnings (40%)	400
	1,650		1,650

Goodwill

Debit		**Credit**	
Cost of control	130		
NCI	50	SoFP	180
	180		180

Workings (Columnar Method)

Goodwill	**€000**	**€000**
Investment in Shine Ltd		2,530
Shine at acquisition date		
Ordinary shares	3,000	
Retained earnings	1,000	
	4,000	
Group's share 60%		2,400
Goodwill		130
Goodwill attributable to NCI		50
SoFP		180

Non-controlling interests

Shine Ltd at acquisition date		
Ordinary shares	3,000	
Retained earnings	1,000	
	4,000	
NCI × 40%		1,600
Goodwill		50
		1,650

Chapter 10

Foreign Operations

Learning Objectives

After reading this chapter you should be able to:

- Identify the only recognised method for translating the financial statements of a foreign operation;
- Demonstrate an understanding of the rules contained in IAS 21 for translating income, expenses, assets and liabilities of a foreign operation;
- Account for exchange differences which arise under the presentation currency method; and
- Prepare and present a complete set of consolidated financial statements which include the results and financial position of a foreign operation.

Introduction

Thus far, this text has focused on preparing consolidated financial statements where a parent has invested in entities whose financial statements are denominated in the same currency as the parent. This chapter now introduces a 'foreign operation', the accounts of which must be translated into the same currency as the parent before consolidation.

The emphasis of the chapter is on:

1. how to translate the financial statements of a foreign operation; and
2. how to calculate and treat resultant exchange differences.

> ***Key Note:*** An important point to remember is that the principles and practices of 'consolidation' do not change just because there is a foreign operation. These principles remain the same and what you have learned thus far is totally relevant to this chapter.

IAS 21 *The Effects of Changes in Foreign Exchange Rates* deals with two broad areas:

1. where an **individual company** engages in transactions that are denominated in a foreign currency (this area is outside the scope of this text[1]); and

[1] See ***Connolly***, Chapter 31, "Foreign Currency Transactions and Translations of Foreign Operations".

2. where an entity has an interest in a foreign operation, whose financial statements are denominated in a foreign currency (this is the focus of this chapter).

A foreign operation would normally prepare its financial statements in its local currency (its *functional currency* – see definition below). These financial statements must be translated into the functional currency of the reporting parent entity (P Ltd). This chapter will focus on the principles for the translation of the financial statements of a foreign operation into the functional currency of the reporting parent and the accounting treatment for the resultant exchange differences.

Note: The functional currency of a parent is invariably the same as its presentation currency (see definition of presentation currency below).

Relevant Definitions

Presentation Currency This is the currency in which the financial statements are **presented**. Though an entity is allowed to present its financial statements in any currency it chooses, of course, practicalities will tend to determine that the entity will use its functional currency.

Functional Currency This is the currency of the primary economic environment in which the reporting entity operates (see below for the factors that determine a functional currency).

Foreign Currency A currency other than the functional currency of the entity.

Foreign Operation An entity that is a subsidiary, associate, joint venture or branch of a reporting entity, the activities of which are conducted in a country or currency different from the reporting entity.

Spot Exchange Rate The exchange rate for immediate delivery.

Closing Rate The spot exchange rate at the end of the reporting period (i.e. the reporting date).

Monetary Items These are units of currency held and assets/liabilities to be received/ paid in a fixed or determinable number of units of currency.

Exchange Differences The difference resulting from translating a given number of units of one currency into another currency at different exchange rates.

Functional Currency

IAS 21 *The Effects of Changes in Foreign Exchange Rates*, at paragraph 9, states that:

A reporting entity should consider certain factors when determining its functional currency, i.e.:

- the currency that **mainly influences sales prices** for goods and services, i.e. the currency in which prices are denominated and settled;
- the currency of the country whose **competitive forces and regulations** mainly determine the sales prices of its goods and services;

- the currency that **mainly influences labour, material and other costs** of providing goods/services;
- the currency in which funds from **financing activities are generated**;
- the currency in which **receipts from operating activities** are usually retained.

An entity's functional currency reflects the underlying transactions, events and conditions that are relevant to it. In most cases, the functional currency of a reporting entity is the currency of the country in which it is situated and in which it carries out most of its transactions.

Translation of a Foreign Operation

Under IAS 21, a parent company must translate the financial statements of a foreign operation into its own functional currency before preparing the consolidated accounts (as explained above, the functional currency is normally the same as the presentation currency). The financial statements of the foreign operation should be translated into the functional currency of the reporting entity using the presentation currency method. Specifically, this method is used **where a foreign operation has a different functional currency than that of the reporting entity (parent company)**.

Translation Rules: Presentation Currency Method

The financial statements of a foreign operation should be translated into the functional currency of the reporting entity using the following rules as per IAS 21, paragraph 39:

- **Assets** and **liabilities** should be translated at the **closing rate**.
- **Income** and **expenses** should be translated at the exchange rates at the **dates of the transactions** or at an **average rate** for the period when this is a **reasonable approximation**. (**Note:** the average rate is normally used in examination questions as using the actual rates would be very impractical.)
- All resulting **exchange differences** (see **Example 10.1**) should be **recognised in other comprehensive income**. These differences are not recognised through profit and loss because they have little or no direct effect on the present and future cash flows from operations.

> ***Key Note*:** The above translation rules apply equally to foreign subsidiaries, associates and joint ventures.

Translation Differences Arising under the Presentation Currency Method

Two exchange differences naturally arise:

1. the difference caused by the retranslation of the opening net assets of the foreign operation (see **Example 10.1**);
2. the difference caused by using the average rate for income and expenses while using the closing rate for assets and liabilities (see **Example 10.1**).

In the absence of such items as revaluations of property, plant and equipment, issues of shares for cash, etc., the following accounting equation is true:

Opening Net Assets + Retained Earnings for a Reporting Period = Closing Net Assets

EXAMPLE 10.1: CALCULATION OF EXCHANGE DIFFERENCES

Assume a foreign operation at a reporting date 31 August 2011. Exchange rates:

1 September 2010	€1 = 5.00 Zicos
Average y/e 31 August 2011	€1 = 4.50 Zicos
31 August 2011	€1 = 4.00 Zicos

Foreign Operation

	Opening Net Assets	+	Retained Earnings	=	Closing Net Assets
(A) Zicos	200		100		300
(B) Exchange rates	5		4.50 Av		4
(C) Euros (A/B)	40	+	22	≠	75

The equation stands up when the figures are expressed in Zicos but does not when translated into Euros, therefore, the two exchange differences must be taken into account.

Exchange Difference 1	**Zicos**	**€**
Opening net assets	200	
At opening rate 5		40
At closing rate 4		50
Difference		10

Exchange difference 2	**Zicos**	**€**
Retained earnings for year	100	
At average rate 4.50		22
At closing rate 4.00		25
Difference		3
Total exchange difference		13

The accounting equation now reads:
Opening net assets + retained earnings + net exchange difference = closing net assets or 40 + 22 + 13 = 75.

A **third** difference arises as follows. IAS 21 at paragraph 47 states:

> "Any goodwill arising on the acquisition of a foreign operation and any fair value adjustments to the carrying amounts of assets and liabilities arising on the acquisition of that foreign operation shall be treated as assets and liabilities of the foreign operation.

Thus, they shall be expressed in the functional currency of the foreign operation and retranslated at **the closing rate.**"

Therefore:

Goodwill in the consolidated statement of financial position should be retranslated at each reporting date using the closing rate, as shown in **Example 10.2.**

Example 10.2: Consolidation of a Parent (Functional Currency Euros) with a Foreign Subsidiary (Functional Currency Bingos)

From the following information prepare:

1. the consolidated statement of comprehensive income;
2. the consolidated statement of changes in equity;
3. The consolidated statement of financial position.

Statement of Comprehensive Income
for the Year Ended 31 July 2011

	Ireland Ltd €000	**Joburg Inc. Bingos 000**
Revenue	6,400	1,300
Cost of sales	(4,500)	(780)
Gross profit	1,900	520
Distribution costs	(350)	(90)
Administrative expenses	(250)	(120)
Finance costs	(100)	(40)
Profit before taxation	1,200	270
Income tax expense	(130)	30
Profit for the year	1,070	240
Other comprehensive income	–	–
Total comprehensive income for the year	1,070	240

Statement of Financial Position
as at 31 July 2011

	Ireland Ltd €000	**Joburg Inc. Bingos 000**
Assets		
Non-current assets		
Property, plant and equipment	5,050	900
Investment in subsidiary	500	–
	5,550	900

Current assets		
Inventory	480	150
Other current assets	1,600	700
	2,080	850
Total assets	**7,630**	**1,750**
Equity		
Capital and reserves		
Share capital	2,000	300
Retained earnings	4,650	1,010
	6,650	1,310
Non-current liabilities		
Long-term loan	–	120
Current liabilities	980	320
Total equity and liabilities	**7,630**	**1,750**

Exchange Rates

			Bingos
1 August 2009	€1	=	1.60
31 July 2010			1.50
Average for reporting year			1.80
31 July 2011			2.00

Ireland Ltd purchased 80% of Joburg Inc. on 1 August 2009 when the retained earnings of Joburg Inc. were 540,000 Bingos.

Non-controlling interests are valued at acquisition date using the share of net assets method.

Solution

Translation of Joburg Inc. SoCI at Average Rate

	Bingos 000	Rate	Euro €000
Revenue	1,300	1.80	722
Cost of sales	780	1.80	433
Gross profit	520		289
Distribution costs	(90)	1.80	(50)

Administrative expenses	(120)	1.80	(67)
Finance costs	(40)	1.80	(22)
Profit before tax	270		150
Income tax expense	(30)	1.80	(17)
Profit for year	240		133

Remember: IAS 21 states that under the presentation currency method income and expenses should be translated using the rates at the dates of the transactions but the average rate for the reporting period could be used when this gives a close approximation. If an examination question includes actual rates for:

- opening inventories;
- closing inventories; and
- depreciation;

then those rates should be used, while using the average rate for all other income and expenses.

WORKINGS (for the consolidated statement of comprehensive income)

	Ireland Ltd	Joburg Inc.	Adjustments	Consol. SoCI
	€000	**€000**	**€000**	**€000**
Revenue	6,400	722		7,122
Cost of sales	(4,500)	(433)		(4,933)
Gross profit	1,900	289		2,189
Distribution costs	(350)	(50)		(400)
Administrative expenses	(250)	(67)		(317)
Finance costs	(100)	(22)		(122)
Profit before taxation	1,200	150		1,350
Income tax expense	(130)	(17)		(147)
Profit for the year	1,070	133		1,203

CONSOLIDATED STATEMENT OF COMPREHENSIVE INCOME
for the Year Ended 31 July 2011

	€000
Revenue	7,122
Cost of sales	(4,933)
Gross profit	2,189
Distribution costs	(400)
Administrative expenses	(317)
Finance costs	(122)
Profit before tax	1,350

Income tax expense		(147)
Profit for the year		1,203
Other comprehensive income		
Exchange difference on translating foreign operation (*W5*)		(212)
Total comprehensive income for the year		991
Profit attributable to:		
Owners of the parent		1,176
Non-controlling interests *(W1)*		27
		1,203
Total comprehensive income attributable to:		
Owners of the parent		1,002
Non-controlling interests *(W2)*		(11)
		991

(W1) Non-controlling Interest

Profit after tax of Joburg Inc.	(133 × 20%) =	27

(W2) Non-controlling Interest

NCI in profit for the year		27
Foreign exchange difference *(W5)*	(191 × 20%)	(38)
		(11)

Translation of Joburg Inc. Statement of Financial Position using Closing Rate

	Bingos 000		**Rate**	**€000**
Property, plant & equipment	900		2.00	450
Inventories	150		2.00	75
Other current assets	700		2.00	350
Long-term loan	(120)		2.00	(60)
Current liabilities	(320)		2.00	(160)
	1,310			655
Capital	300			
Pre-acq. retained earnings	540			
	840		1.60	525
Post-acq. retained earnings	470	Bal. fig.		130
	1,310			655

Note: The capital and pre-acquisition reserves of Joburg are translated using the exchange rate at the date of acquisition. The post-acquisition reserves represent the balancing figure.

Workings (T account Method)

Property Plant and Equipment

Debit		Credit	
Irl	5,050		
Joburg	450	SoFP	5,500
	5,500		5,500

Investment in Joburg Inc.

Debit		Credit	
Irl	500	Cost of control	500
	500		500

Inventories

Debit		Credit	
Irl	480		
Joburg	75	SoFP	555
	555		555

Other Current Assets

Debit		Credit	
Irl	1,600		
Joburg	350	SoFP	1,950
	1,950		1,950

Long-term Loan

Debit		Credit	
SoFP	60	Joburg	60

Current liabilities

Debit		Credit	
		Irl	980
SoFP	1,140	Joburg	160
	1,140		1,140

Capital and Reserves

Debit		Credit	
Cost of control (80% × 525)	420	Irl Ltd Sh.cap	2,000
Non-controlling interests		Irl. Ltd Retained earnings	4,650
(20% × 655) (Note 1)	131	Joburg Cap & pre-acq.	525
Share capital SoFP	2,000	Joburg post-acq. earnings	130
Goodwill diff *(Wa)*	16		
SoFP (Note 2)	4,738		
	7,305		7,305

Note 1: NCI have an interest in all capital and reserves of Joburg.
Note 2: The balance 4,738 involves an exchange loss (121) which is transferred to other equity component (see SoCE).

Cost of Control

Debit		**Credit**	
Inv. in Joburg	500	Share cap. and pre-acquisition reserves	420
		Goodwill *(Wa)* SoFP	64
		Trans. FX diff to ret. earn.	16
	500		500

Non-controlling Interest

Debit		**Credit**	
SoFP	131	Cap. & reserves	131

WORKINGS (Columnar Method)

	Ireland	**Joburg**	**Adjusts.**	**Consol. SoFP**
Assets	**€000**	**€000**	**€000**	**€000**
PPE	5,050	450		5,500
Investment in Joburg	500		(500)	-
Goodwill (*Wa*)			64	64
Inventories	480	75		555
Other current assets	1,600	350		1,950
Total Assets	**7,630**	**875**	**(436)**	**8,069**
Equity and Liabilities				
Ordinary shares & reserves (*Wb*)	6,650	655	(567)	6,738
Non-controlling interests (*Wc*)			131	131
Long-term loan		60		60
Current liabilities	980	160		1,140
Total Equity and Liabilities	**7,630**	**875**	**(436)**	**8,069**

(Wa) Goodwill

Cost of investment in Joburg			500
Joburg at acquisition date			
Ordinary shares	300		
Retained earnings	540		
	840/ 1.60	525	
Group's share 80%			420
Original goodwill			80
Retranslated at 31 July 2011			
80 × 1.60/2.00			64
Difference			**16**

(Wb) Share capital & reserves

Share capital Ireland Ltd		2,000
Retained earnings Ireland Ltd at reporting date		4,650
Post-acquisition of Joburg	130 × 80%	104
Group's share of exchange differences		(16)*
		6,738

(*This represents the exchange difference on the goodwill only.)

(Wc) Non-controlling interests

Joburg at reporting date		
Capital and reserves	655 × 20%	131

Statement of Changes in Equity

	Share Capital	Other Equity Comp.	Retained Earnings	NCI
	€000	**€000**	**€000**	**€000**
Balance at 1 August 2010	2,000	53 (*W7*)	3,682 (*W3*)	142 (*W4*)
TCI for the year		(174)	1,176	(11)
Balance at 31 July 2011	2,000	(121)*	4,858	131

(*The notes should explain that this is a foreign exchange difference.)

(W3) ***Retained earnings b/f at 1 August 2010:***

		€000
Ireland: Retained earnings at 31/7/11		4,650
Retained earnings y/e 31/7/11		(1,070)
➪ Retained earnings at 1/8/10		3,580
Joburg: Capital and reserves:		
At 1/8/10 (*See W4*)	713	
At acquisition date	525	
Post-acquisition	188	
Group × 80%		150
Goodwill translation 80 × 1.6/1.5= 85		5
		3,735

Summary:

Retained earnings at 1/8/10	3,735	
Exchange difference	53	*(W7)* – shown as other equity component
Opening Balance Reserves	3,682	

(W4) ***NCI at 1 August 2010***

Joburg	**Bingos 000**	**€000**
Net assets at 31 July 2011	1,310	
Retained earnings y/e 31 July 2011	(240)	
Net assets 31 July 2010	1,070	

At then rate 1.50				
Net Assets Joburg 1 August 2010				713
NCI × 20%				142

(W5) Exchange difference arising y/e 31/7/2011

		Bingos 000	**€000**	
1. Capital and reserves (net assets) of Joburg at 31/7/10 (*W4*)		1,070		
At opening rate 1/8/10	1.50		713	
At closing rate	2.00		535	
Difference			**(178)**	**NC1 20% (35.6)**
2. Profit after tax y/e 31/7/11		240		
At average rate	1.80		133	
At closing rate	2.00		120	
Difference			**(13)**	**NCI 20% (2.6)**
Exchange loss taken to Other Comprehensive income			**(191)**	**(38)**
3. Retranslation of goodwill.				
Goodwill 1/8/10 *(W3)*		85		
× 1.50/2.00 =		64		
Taken to other comprehensive income			(21)	
Net differences taken to other comprehensive income			**(212)**	

Summary – Exchange Difference y/e 31 July 2011

Group	**(174)**
NCI	**(38)**
Total	**(212)**

(*W6*) ***Cumulative exchange difference to 31/7/11***

		Bingos 000	**€000**	**€000**
Net assets of Joburg at acquisition date		840		
At opening rate	1.60		525	
At closing rate	2.00		420	
Difference (i)			(105)	
– NCI 20%				(21)
Net assets Joburg 31/7/11		1,310		
Net assets Joburg at acquisition date		840		
Cumulative retained earnings		470		
At average rate	1.80		261	
At closing rate	2.00		235	
Difference (ii)			(26)	
– NCI 20%				(5)

Goodwill *(W5.3)* 80 – 64 (iii)	(16)
Cumulative (i)+(ii)+(iii)	(147)

Group = (121)
NCI = (26)

(W7) Group's Share of Exchange Difference 1 August 2010

Group's share of cumulative exchange difference as at 31/7/11 (*W6*)	(121)
Group's share of exchange difference y/e 31/7/11 *(W5)*	(174)
Group's share at 1/8/10	53

Ireland Ltd
CONSOLIDATED STATEMENT OF FINANCIAL POSITION
as at 31 July 2011

Assets	**€000**
Non-current assets	
Property, plant and equipment	5,500
Goodwill	64
	5,564
Current assets	
Inventories	555
Other	1,950
	2,505
Total assets	**8,069**
Equity and Liabilities	
Equity	
Ordinary share capital	2,000
Exchange difference other equity component	(121)
Retained earnings	4,859
	6,738
Non-controlling interest	131
	6,869
Non-current liabilities	
Long-term loan	60
Current liabilities	1,140
Total equity and liabilities	**8,069**

Conclusion

There is only one method recognised in IAS 21 for translating the financial statements of a foreign operation into the functional currency (normally also the presentation currency) of the reporting entity namely: the presentation currency method. The need for this method arises when the functional currency of the foreign operation is different from that of the reporting entity. Though a reporting entity can present its financial statements in any currency, in almost all cases its functional currency is the same as its presentation currency.

Recommended Reading

As stated throughout this text, you are encouraged to read alternative texts, as the opinions and methods of others can only help to develop a greater understanding of all topics. To this end and in the context of this chapter, it is recommended that you also read Chapter 31, "Foreign Currency Transactions and Translation of Foreign Operations", in *International Financial Accounting and Reporting* (3rd Edition) by Ciaran Connolly.

Summary

1. The presentation currency method is the only method recognised under IAS 21 for translating a foreign operation into the functional currency of the investor. The functional currency is invariably the same as the presentation currency.
2. Assets and liabilities are translated at the closing rate.
3. Share capital and pre-acquisition reserves are translated at the rate at the date of acquisition to facilitate the calculation of goodwill/gain from a bargain purchase.
4. Income and expenses should be translated at the rates at the dates of the transactions but for practical reasons an average rate for the period is often used. However, if exchange rates fluctuate significantly, the use of the average rate for a period is inappropriate.
5. Exchange differences are taken to reserves being shown as other comprehensive income in the statement of comprehensive income.
6. Cumulative exchange differences to the reporting date are shown under 'Other Equity Components' in the consolidated SoFP and explained in the notes.

Questions

Question 10.1

What is the only recognised method for translating the financial statements of a foreign operation into the functional currency of the reporting entity?

Solution

The presentation currency method is the only method recognised under IAS 21 for translating the financial statements of a foreign operation.

Question 10.2

What rate(s) are applied to translate the following:
(a) the assets and liabilities of a foreign operation;
(b) the share capital and pre-acquisition reserves of a foreign operation;
(c) the income and expenses of a foreign operation and is there any alternative allowed?

Solution

(a) the assets and liabilities are translated using the closing rate;
(b) the capital and pre-acquisition reserves of a foreign operation are translated using the rate at the date of acquisition;
(c) ideally, the income and expenses are translated using the rates at the dates of the transactions but an average rate for the reporting period can be used when this rate approximates to the actual rates.

Question 10.3

Explain the exchange differences that arise:
(a) on translating the financial statements of a foreign operation;
(b) on the preparation of the resultant consolidated financial statements.

Solution

There are two differences that naturally arise on the translation of the financial statements of a foreign operation:

1. The difference caused by the retranslation of the opening net assets of a subsidiary calculated as follows:

	€		€
Opening net assets at opening rate	X		
at closing rate	X		
Difference	X	× group's share	Y
2. Profit after tax at average rate	X		
at closing rate	X		
Difference	X	× group's share	Y
Total			2Y

A third difference arises on the preparation of the consolidated financial statements which is caused by the requirement of IAS 21 to retranslate the goodwill/premium on acquisition at each reporting date using the closing rate.

Question 10.4

What is the accounting treatment for exchange differences which arise under the presentation currency method?

Solution

All exchange differences under the presentation currency method are recognised as other comprehensive income in the consolidated SoCI.

> ***Note:*** Question 10.5 is a longer, review-type question and includes a foreign operation which is an associate. The solution contains:
> 1. journal adjustments
> 2. the T account method workings
> 3. the columnar method workings
> 4. the consolidated SoFP; and
> 5 the consolidated SoCI and SoCE.

Question 10.5

Chartered Accountants Ireland, P3, Summer 2005, Question 1

You are with Gold Group plc (Gold) an Irish company involved in mining precious metals. You have responsibility for the consolidation of Gold's financial statements, and you have just received draft financial statements for the year ended 31 December 2010 in respect of Gold, Silver Limited (Silver) and Copper Incorporated (Copper).

Draft Statements of Comprehensive Income
for the year ended 31 December 2010

	Gold €000	Silver €000	Copper $000
Revenue	600,000	105,000	33,000
Cost of sales	(360,000)	(63,000)	(20,000)
Gross profit	240,000	42,000	13,000
Net operating expenses	(120,000)	(21,000)	6,000
Profit before tax	120,000	21,000	7,000
Income tax expense	(54,000)	(7,000)	(3,000)
Profit for the year	66,000	14,000	4,000
Other comprehensive income	nil	nil	nil
Total comprehensive income for the year	66,000	14,000	4,000

Draft Statement of Financial Position
as at 31 December 2010

	Gold €000	Silver €000	Copper $000
Assets			
Non-current assets			
Property, plant and machinery	130,000	30,000	10,000

Investment in Silver	30,000		
Investment in Copper	12,000		
	172,000	30,000	10,000
Current assets			
Inventories	12,000	1,500	-
Receivables	22,500	5,000	3,000
Bank and cash	4,500	1,000	500
	39,000	7,500	3,500
Total Assets	**211,000**	**37,500**	**13,500**
Equity and Liabilities			
Ordinary shares	12,000	5,000	1,000
Retained earnings	76,000	25,000	7,000
Total shareholders' equity	88,000	30,000	8,000
Current liabilities			
Payables	50,000	1,500	1,000
Taxation	73,000	6,000	4,500
	123,000	7,500	5,500
Total Equity and Liabilities	**211,000**	**37,500**	**13,500**

The following additional information is available:

1. On 1 January 2010 Gold acquired 80% of the ordinary shares of Silver. On this date the carrying value of the net assets of Silver approximated to their fair value.
2. On 1 January 2008 Gold purchased 30% of the ordinary shares of Copper when there was a credit balance of $2 million on the retained earnings of Copper. There was no difference between the carrying value of the net assets of Copper and the fair value at this date.
3. The directors of Gold believe that the goodwill arising on the acquisition of Silver and Copper was impaired for the first time during the year under review by €1,720,000 and €312,500 respectively. NCI is measured at the date of acquisition using the share of the net assets method.
4. The rates of exchange were as follows:

1 January 2008	$2 : €1	31 December 2010	$1.50 : €1
1 January 2010	$1.80 : €1	Average rate 2010	$ 1.60 : €1

5. Retained earnings 1 January 2010

Gold	€36,000
Silver	€11,000
Copper	$3,000

6. The directors of Gold proposed a dividend of €26 million at the year end and this amount is included under payables.

Requirement Prepare for the reporting year of Gold:

(a) the consolidated statement of comprehensive income;
(b) the consolidated statement of financial position; and
(c) the consolidated statement of changes in equity.

Solution to Question 10.5

TRANSLATION OF COPPER SOFP
at 31 December 2010 (using closing rate)

	$000	Rate	€000
Assets			
Non-current assets			
Property, plant and machinery	10,000	1.50	6,667
Current assets			
Inventories	–		
Receivables	3,000	1.50	2,000
Bank and cash	500	1.50	333
Current liabilities			
Payables	(1,000)	1.50	(667)
Taxation	(4,500)	1.50	(3,000)
Net assets	8,000		5,333
Ordinary shares	1,000		
Pre-acq. profits	2,000		
	3,000	2.00	1,500
Post-acq. profits	5,000	Bal. Fig.	3,833
	8,000		5,333

Workings (Consolidated SoFP)

(W1) Premium on acquisition of Copper	€000
Cost of investment	12,000
Share Capital and Reserves of Copper at date of acquisition 30% × €1,500	450
Premium	11,550
Retranslated at 31 December 2010 × 2.00/1.50	15,400
Gain to SoCI	3,850

Analysed as follows:

Gain to 31.12.09 11,550 × 2.00/1.80	=	12,833.3	1,283
Gain to 31.12.10 12,833.3 × 1.80/1.50	=	15,400	2,567
			3,850

(*W2*) Copper is an associate of Gold. In the consolidated SoCI there will be disclosed the group's share of the profit after tax of Copper. There is, therefore, no need to translate the full SoCI of Copper, only its **profit after tax**:

		€000
Profit after tax $4,000 at average rate for 2010 of 1.60	=	2,500.00
Group's share 30%	=	750.00
Less impairment of premium (Journal 3)		312.50
Credit to consolidated SoCI		437.50

Journal Entries

		€000	€000
1.	Dr. Investment in Copper	1,150	
	Cr. Retained earnings Gold		1,150
	With 30% of the post-acquisition retained earnings of Copper 30% × 3,833 = 1,150 (see translated SoFP)		
2.	Dr. Retained earnings Gold	1,720	
	Cr. Cost of control		1,720
	Impairment of goodwill on acquisition of Silver		
3.	Dr. Retained earnings Gold	312.50	
	Cr. Investment in Copper		312.50
	Impairment of premium/goodwill on acquisition of Copper		
4.	Dr. Payables	26,000	
	Cr. Retained earnings Gold		26,000
	With reversal of proposed dividend by Gold		

There is no indication that this dividend was approved before the reporting date. In accordance with IAS 10 such dividends should not be provided for but disclosed in the notes.

		€000	€000
5.	Dr. Investment in Copper	3,850	
	Cr. Retained earnings Gold		3,850
	Gain on retranslation of premium on acquisition of Copper *(W1)*		

This gain will eventually be disclosed under Other Equity Component.

Workings (T account method)

Property, Plant and Equipment

Debit		**Credit**	
Gold	130,000		
Silver	30,000	SoFP	160,000
	160,000		160,000

Investment in Silver

Debit		**Credit**	
Gold	30,000	Cost of control	30,000

Investment in Copper

Debit		**Credit**	
Gold	12,000	Journal 3 (impairment)	312.5
Journal 1(post-acq. earnings)	1,150		
Journal 5 (retranslation)	3,850	SoFP	16,687.5
	17,000		17,000.0

Inventory

Debit		Credit	
Gold	12,000		
Silver	1,500	SoFP	13,500
	13,500		13,500

Receivables

Debit		Credit	
Gold	22,500		
Silver	5,000	SoFP	27,500
	27,500		27,500

Bank and Cash

Debit		Credit	
Gold	4,500		
Silver	1,000	SoFP	5,500
	5,500		5,500

Ordinary Shares

Debit		Credit	
Cost of control 80%	4,000	Gold	12,000
NCI 20%	1,000		
SoFP	12,000	Silver	5,000
	17,000		17,000

Retained Earnings

Debit		Credit	
Cost of control			
80% × (25,000 – 14,000)	8,800.0	Gold	76,000
NCI 20% × 25,000	5,000.0	Silver	25,000
		Journal 1 (Gold)	1,150
Journal 2 (Gold)	1,720.0		
Journal 3 (Gold)	312.5	Journal 4 (Gold)	26,000
SoFP	116,167.5	Journal 5 (Gold)	3,850
	132,000.0		132,000

Balance	116,167.5	
Less exchange gains (*W8)*	4,143.0	Shown as other equity component
SoFP	112,024.50	

Payables

Debit		Credit	
Journal 4	26,000	Gold	50,000
SoFP	25,500	Silver	1,500
	51,500		51,500

Taxation

Debit		Credit	
		Gold	73,000
SoFP	79,000	Silver	6,000
	79,000		79,000

Cost of Control

Debit		Credit	
Investment in Silver	30,000	Ordinary shares	4,000
		Retained earnings	8,800
		Journal 2	1,720
		SoFP (Goodwill)	15,480
	30,000		30,000

Non-controlling Interests

Debit		Credit	
		Ordinary shares	1,000
SoFP	6,000	Retained earnings	5,000
	6,000		6,000

Workings (Columnar Method)

	Gold	Silver	Adjustments	Consol. SoFP
	€000	**€000**	**€000**	**€000**
PPE	130,000	30,000		160,000
Investment in Silver	30,000		(30,000)	-
Investment in Copper (*W3*)	12,000		1,150 3,850 (312.50)	16,687.5
Goodwill (*W4*)			15,480	15,480
Inventory	12,000	1,500		13,500
Receivables	22,500	5,000		27,500
Bank and cash	4,500	1,000		5,500
Total Assets	**211,000**	**37,500**	**(9,832.5)**	**238,667.5**
Ordinary shares	12,000	5,000	(5,000)	12,000
Retained earnings (*W5*)	76,000	25,000	15,167.5 (4,143)	112,024.5
Other equity component			4,143	4,143
Non-controlling interests (*W6*)			6,000	6,000
Payables	50,000	1,500	(26,000)	25,500
Taxation	73,000	6,000		79,000
Total Equity and Liabilities	**211,000**	**37,500**	**(9,832.5)**	**238,667.5**

(W3) Investment in Copper

	€000
Cost of investment	12,000
Share of post-acquisition profits	1,150
Gain on retranslation of premium on acquisition	3,850

Impairment of premium	(312.50)	
SoFP	16,687.50	

(W4) Goodwill

	€000	€000
Cost of investment in Silver		30,000
Silver at acquisition date		
Ordinary shares	5,000	
Retained earnings	11,000	
	16,000	
Group's share 80%		(12,800)
Impairment		(1,720)
SoFP		15,480

(W5) Retained earnings

Gold at reporting date		76,000.0
Jnl. 1 share of post-acq. profit of Copper		1,150.0
Jnl. 2 impairment of goodwill Silver		(1,720.0)
Jnl. 3 impairment of premium		(312.5)
Jnl. 4 reversal of proposed dividend		26,000.0
Jnl. 5 Gain on retranslating premium		3,850.0
Silver at reporting date	25,000	
at acquisition date	11,000	
	14,000	
Group Share × 80%		11,200.0
Balance includes exchange differences 4,143 *(W8)* shown separately on SoFP as Other Equity Component		116,167.5

(W6) Non-controlling interests

Silver at reporting date		
Ordinary shares	5,000	
Retained earnings	25,000	
	30,000	
NCI × 20%		6,000

Consolidated Statement of Financial Position
as at 31 December 2010

	€000
Assets	
Non-current assets	
Property, plant and equipment	160,000.0
Goodwill	15,480.0
Investment in associate	16,687.5
	192,167.5

	€000
Current assets	
Inventory	13,500.0
Receivables	27,500.0
Bank and cash	5,500.0
	46,500.0
Total assets	238,667.5
Equity and liabilities	
Equity	
Ordinary share capital	12,000.0
Other equity component (*W6*)	4,143.0
Retained earnings	112,024.5
Total shareholders' equity	128,167.5
Non-controlling interests	6,000.0
Total equity	134,167.5
Current liabilities	
Payables	25,500.0
Taxation	79,000.0
	104,500.0
Total equity and liabilities	**238,667.5**

COLUMNAR WORKINGS (Consolidated SoCI)

	Gold	**Silver**	**Adjustments**	**Consol. SoCI**
	€000	**€000**	**€000**	**€000**
Revenue	600,000	105,000		705,000
Cost of sales	(360,000)	(63,000)		(423,000)
Gross profit	240,000	42,000		282,000
Operating expenses	(120,000)	(21,000)		(141,000)
Impairment of goodwill			(1,720)	(1,720)
Share of profit of associate *(W2)*			437.5	437.5
Profit before tax	120,000	21,000	(1,282.5)	139,717.5
Income tax expense	(54,000)	(7,000)		(61,000)
Profit for the year	66,000	14,000	(1,282.5)	78,717.5

CONSOLIDATED STATEMENT OF COMPREHENSIVE INCOME
for the Year Ended 31 December 2010

	€000
Revenue	705,000.0
Cost of sales	(423,000.0)
Gross profit	282,000.0
Operating expenses	(141,000.0)
Impairment of goodwill	(1,720.0)
Share of profit of associate *(W2)*	437.5
Profit before tax	139,717.5
Income tax expense	(61,000.0)
Profit for the year	78,717.5

Other comprehensive income	
Exchange difference on translating foreign operations	2,750.6
Total comprehensive income for the year	81,468.1
Profit for the year attributable to:	
Owners of the parent	75,917.5
Non-controlling interests *(W10)*	2,800.0
	78,717.5
Total comprehensive income for the year attributable to:	
Owners of the parent	78,668.1
Non-controlling interests *(W10)*	2,800.0
	81,468.1

Consolidated Statement of Changes In Equity
for the Year Ended 31 December 2010

	Ord. Shares €000	**Other Equity Components €000**	**Ret. Earnings €000**	**NCI €000**
Balance at 1 January 2010	12,000	1,392	36,107.6 (*W5*)	–
Acquired				3,200
TCI for the year		2,751	75,917.5	2,800
Balance at 31 December 2010		4,143	112,025.1	6,000

(W7) ***Retained earnings 1.1.2010***		**€000**	**€000**
Gold after proposed dividend addback			36,000.0
Exchange differences – premium on acquisition of Copper *(W1)*			1,283.0
Copper: Net assets 1.1.2008	$3,000		
At rate 1/1/08 2 : 1		1,500	
Net assets 1.1.2010	$4,000		
At rate 1/1/10 1.80 : 1		2,222	
Post-acq. to 1/11/10		722	
Group's share × 30%			216.6
			37,499.6
Shown as other component of equity			1,392.0
			36,107.6

(W8) Exchange differences ***cumulative to 31/12/10***

1. Retranslation of net assets

		€000
Net assets at 1.1.2008	$3,000	
At rate 1.1.2008 2 : 1	€1,500	
At rate 31.12.2010 1.50 : 1	€2,000	
Exchange difference	500 × 30% =	150

			€000	
2. On cumulative profits 1.1.08 to 31.12.10.				
(7,000–2,000) 5,000				
At average rate 1.75 : 1	€2,857			
At closing rate 1.50 : 1	€3,333			
	476 × 30%		143	
3. On retranslation of Goodwill *(W1)*			3,850	
			4,143	

(W9) Exchange differences arising y/e 31 December 2010

			€000
Net assets of Copper 1.1.2010.			
($8,000 – 4,000)	$4,000		
At opening rate 1.80 : 1	€2,222		
At closing rate 1.50 : 1	€2,667		
Difference		445 × 30%	133.5
Profit after tax Copper	$4,000		
At average rate 1.60 : 1	€2,500		
At closing rate 1.50 : 1	€2,667		
Difference		167 × 30%	50.1
Retranslation of Goodwill *(W1)*			2,567.0
			2,750.6

(W10) Profit after tax Silver	14,000
× 20%	2,800

Chapter 11

Consolidated Statements of Cash Flows

Learning Objectives

After reading this chapter you should be able to:

- demonstrate an understanding of the issues which are particular to the preparation of a consolidated SoCF;
- explain the effects of non-controlling interests on the consolidated SoCF;
- account for the effects of an associate, a joint venture and a trade investment;
- explain the impact of acquisitions and disposals of subsidiaries and associates on the consolidated SoCF;
- account for a foreign operation; and
- prepare and present a consolidated statement of cash flows.

Introduction

The issues dealt with in this chapter involve a combination of skills namely:

1. utilising your knowledge of preparing consolidated financial statements; and
2. preparing statements of cash flows.

Before reading this chapter you must

- have prior knowledge and practice of the preparation of statements of cash flows for individual entities in accordance with the provisions of IAS 7 *Statement of Cash Flows*;[1]
- be proficient in the preparation of consolidated financial statements.

IAS 7 requires that all entities prepare a statement of cash flows (SoCF) as an integral part of the entity's financial statements for each financial period. Information about the cash flows of an entity is useful in providing users of financial statements with a basis to assess the ability of the entity to generate cash and cash equivalents, and the needs of the entity to utilise those cash flows. The economic decisions that are taken by users of financial statements require an evaluation of the ability of an entity to generate cash and cash equivalents. IAS 1 *Presentation of Financial Statements* includes

[1] See ***Connolly***, Chapter 19, "Statement of Cash Flows: Single Company", for an in-depth treatment of the preparation and presentation of statements of cash flows for individual entities.

a statement of cash flows as one of the components of a complete set of financial statements.

Relevant Definitions

Cash This comprises cash on hand and demand deposits.

Cash equivalents Short-term, highly liquid investments, which are readily convertible to known amounts of cash and which are subject to an insignificant risk of changes in value.

Cash flows Inflows and outflows of cash and cash equivalents.

The Statement of Cash Flows

IAS 7 requires that all cash flows are classified by activity, which provides information to users of the financial statements allowing them to assess the impact of those activities on the cash, cash equivalents and the financial position of the entity.

The three types of activity under which IAS 7 classifies cash flows are as follows:

1. **Operating activities**, which are the principal revenue activities of an entity (e.g. cash receipts from sales; cash payments made to suppliers, employees, etc.).

   An entity can report cash flows from operating activities using either:

   (a) **the direct method:**

		€000
Cash received from customers		X
Cash paid to suppliers		(X)
Cash paid to or on behalf of employees		(X)
Other cash payments		(X)
Cash generated from operations	(say)	1,546

   or

   (b) **the indirect method:**

		€000
Profit before tax		X
Adjustments		
Depreciation		X
Interest charge		X
Profit on disposal of PPE		(X)
Increase in inventories		(X)
Increase in receivables		(X)
Increase in payables		X
Cash generated from operations	(say)	1,546

From your studies of the presentation of statements of cash flows for individual entities (which is outside the scope of this text), you should now be familiar with both the direct and indirect methods.

> ***Key Note:*** IAS 7 permits either of the above methods to be used. When answering examination questions you are entitled to use either method, unless one of them is specified. **This text adopts the indirect method as it is the more traditional of the two and, in the author's opinion, the one more familiar to students.**

2. **Investing activities,** which are the acquisition and disposal of long-term assets and other investments which are not cash equivalents. These are expenditures made to acquire resources intended to generate future income and cash flows (for example: payments to acquire property, plant and equipment).
3. **Financing activities**, which are those that result in changes in the size and composition of the contributed equity and borrowings of an entity (e.g. proceeds from the issue of shares; repayment of long-term loans, etc.).

Issues Peculiar to the Consolidated Statement of Cash Flow

In general, the principles applied in the preparation of a consolidated statement of cash flows are the same as those of an individual entity. However, there are issues that only arise with consolidated statements of cash flows and which need special attention. These are:

- dealing with the non-controlling interests in subsidiaries,
- dealing with associates;
- an acquisition of a subsidiary during an accounting period;
- a disposal of a subsidiary during an accounting period;
- an acquisition or disposal of shares in an associate during an accounting period;
- dealing with a joint venture which is an entity and which has been accounted for using proportionate consolidation;
- dealing with a foreign operation.

Before dealing with the above issues, it is important to highlight three principles:

1. A consolidated SoCF should only include inflows and outflows of cash that are **external to the group**. Internal cash flows, such as payment of dividends by a subsidiary to its parent, should be eliminated. This problem should only arise if a consolidated SoCF is being prepared from the individual financial statements of the group entities.
2. If an undertaking (e.g. an associate) is accounted for under the **equity method** of accounting in the consolidated financial statements, only the cash flows between the group and the undertaking should be included in the group SoCF.
3. If a subsidiary is acquired or disposed of during an accounting period, the consolidated SoCF should only include the cash flows of that subsidiary for the same period as its results are included in the consolidated statement of comprehensive income.

Dealing with Non-controlling Interests

A subsidiary is fully consolidated; therefore, all its assets and liabilities, income and expenses are included in the consolidated financial statements, whether or not there is a non-controlling interest. This means that cash flows for subsidiaries, relating to such items as operating activities, taxation, acquisition or disposal of non-current assets, are combined with those of the parent undertaking, However, certain items need special attention i.e.:

1. issue of shares for cash to non-controlling interests (NCI);
2. redemption of shares owned by non-controlling interests; and
3. dividends paid to non-controlling interests.

Cash flows relating to items 1 and 2 would appear in the group statement of cash flows under 'Financing activities'. In the absence of the acquisition or disposal of a subsidiary during the period (part of which is owned by the non-controlling interests), dividends paid to non-controlling interests is the balancing figure between the opening and closing values for non-controlling interests in the statements of financial position plus the NCI share of total comprehensive income (TCI) for the financial period (see **Example 11.1**). The following Pro-Forma 'T' account shows the calculation:

PRO-FORMA: T ACCOUNT FOR NCI

Non-controlling Interests			
Debit	**€**	**Credit**	**€**
Cash (dividends) paid		Opening Balance	
(balancing figure)	X	(opening SoFP)	X
Closing balance		Share of TCI	
(closing SoFP)	X	(per consolidated SoCI)	X
	X		X

EXAMPLE 11.1: CALCULATION OF DIVIDENDS PAID TO NCI

EXTRACTS FROM CONSOLIDATED STATEMENT OF FINANCIAL POSITION

	2011	**2010**
	€000	**€000**
Equity and liabilities		
Equity		
Ordinary share capital		
Retained earnings		
Total shareholders' equity		
Non-controlling interests	860	670

EXTRACTS FROM CONSOLIDATED STATEMENT OF COMPREHENSIVE INCOME

	2011 €000
Profit for the year attributable to:	
Owners of the parent	1,160
Non-controlling interests	280
	1,440
Total comprehensive income for the year attributable to:	
Owners of the parent	1,240
Non-controlling interests	300
	1,540

Non-controlling Interests

Debit		**Credit**	
Dividends paid (bal.fig)	110	Opening Balance	670
Closing Balance	860	TCI – Consolidated SoCI	300
	970		970

The dividends paid to non-controlling interests, €110,000, can be included under either:
(a) cash flows from **operating** activities; ***or***
(b) cash flows from **financing** activities,
in the statement of cash flows (IAS 7).

(***Note:*** This text adopts the option (b) method because dividends paid are a cost of obtaining financial resources and the author considers this to be a more appropriate presentation.)

If a subsidiary was acquired or disposed during a reporting period, the above T account would be credited with the non-controlling interest in the net assets of the subsidiary at the date of acquisition, or debited with the share of the net assets of the subsidiary at the date of disposal.

Dealing with Associates

Associates are accounted for in the consolidated financial statements using the **equity method of accounting** (see **Chapter 5** (SoFP) and **Chapter** 7 (SoCI/SoCE)). This means that the consolidated statement of comprehensive income includes the group's share of the profit of the associate after tax. This entry does not involve cash flows, but the *group* cash flow is affected by the dividends received from associates. Dividends received from associates can be calculated as follows (see also **Example 11.2**):

Pro-Forma: T Account Investment in Associate

Investment in Associate

Debit	**€**	**Credit**	**€**
Opening balance (opening SoFP)	X	Dividends received from A (balancing figure)	X
Share of profit of A (Consol. SoCI)	X	Closing balance (closing SoFP)	X
	X		X

Example 11.2: Calculation of Dividend Received from Associate

Extracts from Consolidated Statement of Financial Position

	2011 €000	**2010 €000**
Non-current assets		
Property, plant and equipment		
Investment in Associate	390	240

Extract from Consolidated Statement of Comprehensive Income

	2011 €000
Share of profit of Associate	180

Investment in Associate

Debit		**Credit**	
Balance b/d	240	Dividend received	30
Share of profit	180	Balance c/d	390
	420		420

The dividends received from the associate, €30,000, can be included under either:
(a) cash flows from **investing** activities; ***or***
(b) cash flows from **operating** activities,
in the statement of cash flows (IAS 7).

(***Note:*** this text adopts the option (a) method only because the author considers it preferable to show this cash flow as a return on investment.)

If the parent acquired an interest in an associate during a reporting period, the above T account would be debited with the cash outflow.

Acquisition of a Subsidiary during a Reporting Period

The **net cash flow** from the acquisition of a subsidiary must be shown separately and should be dealt with in the group statement of cash flows under 'Investing activities'. Any cash paid as part of the consideration would be included as a cash outflow, while any balances of cash and overdrafts acquired as part of the combination should be offset against the cash consideration paid.

Example 11.3: Acquisition of a Subsidiary

During the period under review, Pat Ltd acquired 90% of the ordinary shares of Sarah Ltd.

Details of the acquisition:

Net assets acquired	**€000**
Property, plant and equipment	800
Inventories	280
Trade receivables	190
Cash	50
Trade payables	(180)
	1,140
Non-controlling interest @ 10%	(114)
Goodwill: 1200 – (90% × 1,140)	174
	1,200
Discharged by	
Issue of shares	400
Cash paid	800
	1,200

Extract from Consolidated Statement of Cash Flows

Investing activities	**€000**
Purchase of subsidiary	
(Cash paid €800 *less* cash acquired €50)	(750)

It should be noted that property, plant and equipment, €800,000, inventories €280,000, receivables, €190,000, and payables, €180,000, acquired with Sarah Ltd should be excluded from changes in these items in the cash flow statement (see **Question 11.2**). A note to the cash flow statement should show a summary of the effects of the acquisition, for example:

Acquisition of subsidiary undertaking

During the year under review Pat Ltd acquired 90% of the voting shares of Sarah Ltd. Details of the acquisition were:

	€000
Net assets acquired:	
Property, plant and equipment	800
Inventories	280
Receivables	190
Cash	50
Payables	(180)
	1,140
Non-controlling interest 10%	(114)
Goodwill	174
	1,200
Satisfied by	
Cash paid	800
Issue of shares	400
	1,200

Disposal of a Subsidiary

When a subsidiary is disposed of during an accounting period any cash received from the sale of the investment should be shown separately under 'Investing activities', with any balance of cash and overdrafts transferred as part of the sale being offset against the cash consideration received (see **Example 11.4** and **Question 11.3**).

Example 11.4: Disposal of a Subsidiary

During the accounting period, Driver Plc sold 80% of its holding in Screw Ltd for €140,000 cash. The balance sheet of Screw Ltd at the date of disposal was:

	€000
Property, plant and equipment	115
Inventories	55
Receivables	36
Cash	14
Payables	(60)
	160
Ordinary shares €1	50
Reserves	110
	160

EXTRACT FROM CONSOLIDATED STATEMENT OF CASH FLOWS

	€000
Investing Activities	
Sale of subsidiary (Cash received 140 less cash transferred 14)	126
A note should be given showing the effects of the disposal.	

Note: **Disposal of subsidiary undertaking**
During the reporting year Driver Plc sold its entire holding in Screw Ltd. Details of the disposal were:

	€000
Net assets disposed of:	
Property, plant and equipment	115
Inventories	55
Receivables	36
Cash	14
Payables	(60)
	160
Non-controlling interest 20%	(32)
Profit on disposal	12
	140
Satisfied by cash	140

Dealing with Joint Ventures

As stated in Chapter 6, proportionate consolidation is currently the preferred method under IAS 31 *Interests in Joint Ventures* for treating a joint venture (JV) in consolidated financial statements. Accordingly, the group's share of each income, expense, asset and liability of a JV is included in the consolidated financial statements. **The group's share of a JV's cash flows must be included in the consolidated SoCF on a line-by-line basis**, i.e. the group's share of the JV's cash flows from operating, investing and financing activities. This can be achieved quite readily from the figures in the consolidated financial statements.

Dealing with Foreign Operations

IAS 7, paragraph 26 states that "the cash flows of a foreign subsidiary shall be translated at the exchange rates between the functional currency and the foreign currency at the dates of the cash flows". However, a weighted average rate for the reporting period can be used (see **Example 11.5**).

Example 11.5: Accounting for a Foreign Subsidiary

The following are the draft financial statements of Boston Inc. (Boston), a 100%-owned subsidiary of Cork Ltd (Cork), which has other subsidiaries, all of whose functional currency is the Euro. The functional currency of Boston is US Dollars.

Statement of Financial Position
as at 30 September 2011

	2011 $000	2010 $000
Property, plant and equipment	1,120	960
Inventories	150	130
Receivables	250	220
Cash	50	40
	1,570	**1,350**
Ordinary shares ($1)	1,000	1,000
Retained earnings	400	200
Payables	170	150
	1,570	**1,350**

Statement of Comprehensive Income
for the year ended 30 September 2011

	€000
Operating profit	300
Interest	(50)
Profit before tax	250
Income tax expense	(50)
Profit for the year	200
Other comprehensive income	0
Total comprehensive income for the year	200

Relevant information:

1. During the year under review Boston incurred depreciation charges of $140,000 and paid for additions to property, plant and equipment of $300,000.
2. Exchange rates:

1 October 2010	€1 = $1.50
30 September 2011	€1 = $2.50
Average y/e 30 September 2011	€1 = $2.00

If Cork was preparing consolidated financial statements for the year ended 30 September 2011, the financial statements of Boston would be translated from its functional currency (dollars) into the functional currency (and most likely the presentation currency) of Cork using the following translation rules:

- income and expenses at actual rates preferably but most likely at the average rate (as explained in **Chapter 10**);
- assets and liabilities at the closing rate.

However, IAS 7 requires all cash flows of a foreign subsidiary to be translated at the exchange rates between the functional currency and the foreign currency at the dates of the cash flows, or at the average rate if that approximates to actual rates. As a result, it is more practical if the statement of cash flows of the foreign operation is first prepared in its own functional currency and then translated using the average rate before incorporation into the SoCF of the group.

STATEMENT OF CASH FLOWS OF BOSTON
using average rate €1 = $2 for translation

Cash flows from operating activities	**€000**	**€000**
Profit before tax (250/2)	125	
Adjustments		
Depreciation (140/2)	70	
Interest charge (50/2)	25	
Increase in inventories (20/2)	(10)	
Increase in receivables (30/2)	(15)	
Increase in payables (20/2)	10	
Cash generated from operations	205	
Interest paid	(25)	
Tax paid (50/2)	(25)	155
Net cash flow from operating activities		
Cash flows from investing activities		
Payments to acquire PPE (300/2)	(150)	
Net cash flow used in investing activities		(150)
Cash flows from financing activities		0
Effects of exchange rates on cash and cash equivalents		(12)
Net decrease in cash and cash equivalents		(7)
Cash and cash equivalents at beginning of year (40/1.50)		27
Cash and cash equivalents at end of year *(50/2.50)		20

* The cash and cash equivalents both at the beginning and the end of the reporting period are included here and in the consolidated SoCF at the respective closing rates, even though the actual cash flows of the foreign subsidiary are included at the average rate, being a close approximation to the actual rates as discussed above.

Calculation: effect of exchange rates on cash and cash equivalents

		€000	€000
Opening balance $40 at opening rate 1.50	=	26.70	
At closing rate 2.50		16.00	
Difference			(10.70)
Increase during year $10 at opening rate 1.50	=	6.70	
At average rate 2.00		5.00	
Difference			(1.70)
Total difference			(12.40)

Note: **the above statement of cash flows of Boston can now be consolidated with the rest of the Cork group and must include the effects of exchange rates on cash and cash equivalents of (€12,000).**

The Treatment of Trade Investments

A company in which a group has a trade investment is not part of that group and, consequently, its cash flows would have little impact on the consolidated SoCF. The effects on the consolidated SoCF would be:

- dividends received from a trade investment would be included under 'Investing activities' as a cash inflow;
- any cash paid to acquire a trade investment would be shown as a cash outflow under 'Investing activities';
- if a group sold a trade investment during a reporting period, any cash received as part of the proceeds would be included under 'Investing activities' as a cash inflow.

Conclusion

You should now appreciate that it is vital that you must be familiar with the preparation of consolidated financial statements before undertaking the study of the preparation of consolidated statements of cash flows and how important it is to study IAS 7 (the individual entity) beforehand. The treatment of non-controlling interests, associates, joint ventures and trade investments is a logical progression of your previous studies. However, dealing with a foreign operation in the group statement of cash flows is a more complex area. Regular revision of this chapter is advised as the topic is frequently examined.

Recommended Reading

As stated throughout this text, you are encouraged to read alternative texts, as the opinions and methods of others can only help to develop a greater understanding of all topics. To this end, and in the context of this chapter, it is recommended that you also read Chapter 33, "Statements of Cash Flow-Consolidated", of ***Connolly***. Furthermore, as stated, it is recommended that you study Chapter 19 of ***Connolly***, in order to first understand the preparation of statements of cash flow for individual entities. Individual companies are not the subject of this text.

SUMMARY

Though the preparation of a consolidated statement of cash flows is similar to that of an individual entity, there are specific issues that are particular to the consolidated SoCF namely:

1. Dealing with a non-controlling interest. A **subsidiary** is fully consolidated with a parent, therefore, cash flows relating to such items as operating activities, interest paid, acquisitions of property, plant and machinery and taxation are **automatically included with those of the parent whether or not there is a non-controlling interest**. However, specific items such as the NCI share of a subsidiary acquired or disposed of during a reporting period as well as any dividends paid to them must be accounted for.
2. An **associate** is accounted for under the equity method, which means that none of **its assets, liabilities, income and expenses are consolidated.** An associate **has little** effect on the consolidated SoCF, except that dividends paid by **A** Ltd to a group must be included or where an interest in an associate is acquired or sold during the reporting period.
3. The **acquisition of a subsidiary** during a reporting period should be accounted for under 'Investing activities' as the net of any cash paid as part **of the** consideration and any cash/cash equivalents acquired with the new subsidiary i.e.:
   Purchase of subsidiary €X
4. The **disposal of a subsidiary** is similarly disclosed except as the net cash inflow of any cash proceeds received and any cash/cash equivalents transferred i.e.:
   Disposal of subsidiary €X
5. **If an associate is acquired during a reporting year any cash payment which is** part of the purchase price would be included under 'Investing activities' as follows:
   Purchase of associate €X
6. **Any cash proceeds on the disposal of an associate would also be disclosed** under 'Investing activities' as follows:
   Disposal of associate €X
7. The group's share of joint venture cash flows must be included in the consolidated SoCF on a line by line basis.
8. The cash flows of a **foreign subsidiary** must be translated at the exchange rates between the functional currency and the foreign currency **at the date of the cash flow**, but a weighted average rate for the reporting period can be used.

QUESTIONS

Question 11.1

The following extracts have been taken from the consolidated financial statements of the Pupil Ltd group for the year ended 30 September 2011 with comparative figures for the previous year:

	2011	2010
SoFP	**€000**	**€000**
Investment in Associate	480	390
Non-controlling interests	570	450
SoCI		
Share of profit of Associate	140	110
Total comprehensive income attributable to non-controlling interests	120	90

During the year ended 30 September 2011, Pupil Ltd acquired an 80% interest in Student Ltd whose net assets at the date of acquisition amounted to €500,000, including a cash balance of €20,000. The purchase consideration comprised:

- An issue of ordinary shares at market value €300,000
- A deferred cash payment in 2013 €180,000

Pupil Ltd can borrow funds at 8%.

NCI at date of acquisition is measured at their share of net assets of Student Ltd.

Requirements:

(a) Show the extract from the consolidated statement of cash flows for the year ended 30 September 2011 regarding the associate.

(b) Show the extract from the consolidated statement of cash flows for the year ended 30 September 2011, to account for any dividends paid to the non-controlling interests.

(c) Show the entry in the same SoCF to reflect the acquisition of the subsidiary.

(d) Pot Ltd, who has two subsidiaries, acquired an associate Kettle Ltd in October 2010 by making a cash payment of €700,000. How is the acquisition recorded in the consolidated SoCF for the year ended 30 September 2011?

Solution to Question 11.1

(a)

Investment in Associate

Debit		**Credit**	
Balance b/d	390	Dividend received (Bal. Fig.)	50
Share of profit	140	Balance c/d	480
	530		530

Investing activities

	€000
Dividend received from associate	50

(b)

Non-controlling interests

Debit		**Credit**	
Dividends (bal fig.)	100	Balance b/d	450
		TCI	120
Balance c/d	570	Acquisition 20% × 500K	100
	670		670

Financing activities	**€000**
Dividends paid to non-controlling interests	100

(c)
Investing activities

	€000
Purchase of subsidiary	20*

* There was no cash paid during the reporting year as the payment is deferred, but a cash balance of €20,000 was acquired.

(d)
Investing activities

	€000
Purchase of associate	700

> ***Note:*** Questions 11.2 and 11.3 are longer, review-type questions. **Question 11.2** involves non-controlling interests, an associate and the acquisition of a subsidiary during a reporting period. **Question 11.3** contains the disposal of a subsidiary as well as non-controlling interests and an associate.
>
> Each solution contains
> 1. T account workings where necessary;
> 2. The consolidated SoCF.
>
> The Solution to Question 11.3 contains the required notes to the consolidated SoCF.

Question 11.2

Institute of Certified Public Accountants in Ireland (CPA), Professional 1 Stage 1 Corporate Reporting Examination, (August 2010) Question 2.

Splash Plc has a number of subsidiaries, one of which, Muck Ltd, was acquired during the year ended 31 December 2009. The draft consolidated financial statements for the year ended 31 December 2009 are as follows:

Consolidated Statement of Comprehensive Income of Splash Plc
for the year ended 31 December 2009

	€000
Profit from operations	1,210
Interest	(100)
	1,110
Share of profits of associates	240
Profit before taxation	1,350
Taxation	(482)
Profit for the year	868
Other comprehensive income	–
Total comprehensive income for the year	868
Profit for the year attributable to:	
Owners of the parent	764
Non-controlling interest	104
	868
Total comprehensive income for the year attributable to:	
Owners of the parent	764
Non-controlling interest	104
	868

Statements of Financial Position are as follows:

	Splash Plc Consolidated 2009	2008	Muck Ltd at acquisition 31/12/2008
	€000	**€000**	**€000**
Assets			
Non-current assets			
Property, plant and equipment	4,730	2,610	610
Intangibles	350	310	-
Investment in associates	520	500	-
	5,600	3,420	610
Current assets			
Inventories	740	610	150
Trade and other receivables	390	350	85
Cash and cash equivalents	40	85	20
Total assets	6,770	4,465	865
Equity and liabilities			
€1 ordinary shares	1,400	1,000	500
Share premium	300	200	100

Retained earnings	1,615	865	80
	3,315	2,065	680
Non-controlling interest	580	610	–
	3,895	2,675	680
Non-current liabilities			
Long-term loans	1,900	1,100	–
Current liabilities			
Trade payables	520	480	75
Taxation	455	210	110
Total Equity and Liabilities	6,770	4,465	865

Additional information:

1. Splash Plc issued 400,000 €1 ordinary shares at a premium of 25 cent and paid a cash consideration of €197,500 to acquire 75% of Muck Ltd. At the date of acquisition, Muck Ltd's assets and liabilities were recorded at their fair value with the exception of some plant which had a fair value of €90,000 in excess of its carrying value. Goodwill on acquisition was €120,000.
2. The property, plant and equipment during the year to 31 December 2009 shows plant with a carrying value of €800,000 which was sold for €680,000. Total depreciation for the year was €782,000.

Requirement Prepare a consolidated statement of cash flows in accordance with IAS 7 *Statement of Cash Flows* for the year ended 31 December 2009.

Solution to Question 11.2

Consolidated Statement of Cash Flows
for the year ended 31 December 2009

	€000	€000
Net cash flow from operating activities:		
Profit before tax	1,350	
Depreciation	782	
Amortisation	80	
Loss on sale of tangible non-current assets	120	
Interest payable	100	
Share of profit of associate	(240)	
Decrease in inventories	20	
Decrease in trade receivables	45	
Decrease in trade payables	(35)	
Cash generated from operations	2,222	

Interest paid	(100)	
Tax paid	(347)	
Net cash flow from operating activities		1,775.0
Cash flows from investing activities:		
Payments to acquire tangible non-current assets	(3,002)	
Receipts from sale of tangible non-current assets	680	
Purchase of subsidiary company (197.5 – 20)	(177.5)	
Dividends received from associate	220	
Net cash flow from investing activities		(2,279.5)
Cash flows from financing activities:		
Long-term loan received	800	
Dividends paid to owners of the parent	(14)	
Dividends paid to non-controlling interest	(326.5)	
Net cash flow from financing		459.5
Decrease in cash and cash equivalents		(45)
Cash and cash equivalents at 1 January 2009		85
Cash and cash equivalents at 31 December 2009		40

Workings

Property, Plant and Equipment

Debit		**Credit**	
Balance b/d 1/1/09	2,610	Disposal	800
		Depreciation	782
Additions (Bal. Fig.)	3,702	Balance c/d	4,730
	6,312		6,312

Additions	3,702
Acquired Muck at fair value (610 + 90)	(700)
Consolidated SoCF	3,002

Intangible Assets

Debit		**Credit**	
Balance b/d 1/1/09	310	Amortisation (Bal. Fig.)	80
Goodwill on Muck	120	Balance c/d	350
	430		430

Investment in Associates

Debit		Credit	
Balance b/d 1/1/09	500	Dividends received (Bal. Fig.)	220
Share of profit for year	240	Balance c/d	520
	740		740

Non-controlling interests

Debit		Credit	
Dividends paid (Bal. Fig.)	326.5	Balance b/d 1/1/09	610.0
		SoCI share of TCI	104.0
Balance c/d	580.0	Share of net assets of Muck*	192.5
	906.5		906.5

*Net assets of Muck at acquisition date	680
Surplus on property, plant and equipment	90
	770 × 25% = 192.50

Taxation

Debit		Credit	
Cash (Bal. Fig.)	347	Balance b/d 1/1/09	210
Balance c/d*	345	SoCI charge for year	482
	692		692

* Closing balance per Consolidated SoFP	455
Less acquired with Muck	(110)
	345

Net Movement in Inventories, Receivables and Payables:

	Inventories €000	Receivables €000	Payables €000
31 December 2009	740	390	520
31 December 2008	610	350	480
Increase	130	40	40
Less: Acquired with Muck	(150)	(85)	(75)
Consolidated SoCF	20	45	(35)

Dividends paid to owners of the parent:	**€000**
Retained earnings per consolidated SoFP 31.12.08	865
Total comprehensive income y/e 31.12.09	764
	1,629
Retained earnings per consolidated SoFP 31.12.09	1,615
Difference – proposed dividend	14

This dividend was paid as it is not on the consolidated SoFP at 31 December 2009.

Question 11.3

Tango Ltd

CONSOLIDATED STATEMENT OF FINANCIAL POSITION
as at 31 August 2011

	2011 €000	2010 €000
Assets		
Non-current assets		
Property, plant & equipment	3,615	1,970
Goodwill	50	50
Investment in associate	990	860
	4,655	2,880
Current assets		
Inventory	1,570	1,015
Trade receivables	1110	830
Cash	30	18
	2,710	1,863
Total assets	**7,365**	**4,743**
Equity and Liabilities		
Ordinary share capital	2,500	1,800
Share premium	400	100
Revaluation reserve	500	--
Retained earnings	1,680	1,090
Total Shareholders' equity	5,080	2,990
Non-controlling interest	124	180
Total equity	5,204	3,170
Non-current liabilities		
Deferred taxation	500	360
Current- liabilities		
Trade payables	747	583
Bank overdraft	84	20
Corporation tax	580	460
Proposed dividends (approved pre-year end)	250	150
	1,661	1,213
Total equity and liabilities	**7,365**	**4,743**

CONSOLIDATED STATEMENT OF COMPREHENSIVE INCOME
for the year ended 31 August 2011

	€000
Revenue	9,675
Cost of sales	(5,805)

Gross profit	3,870
Operating expenses	(2,550)
	1,320
Profit on disposal of subsidiary	76
Share of profit of associate	160
Profit before tax	1,556
Income tax expense	590
Profit for the year	966
Other comprehensive income	
Property revaluation surplus	500
Total comprehensive income for the year	1,466
Profit for year attributable to:	
Owners of the parent	836
Non-controlling interest	130
	966
Total comprehensive income attributable to:	
Owners of the parent	1,336
Non-controlling interests	130
	1,466

NOTES TO THE FINANCIAL STATEMENTS

1. **Profit before tax**

	€000
The following have been included:	
Depreciation of property, plant and equipment	220
Interest payable	205

2. **Property, plant and equipment**
   During the year under review plant with a carrying value of €180,000 was sold at a loss of €30,000.

3. All proposed dividends were approved before the respective reporting dates. Tango has proposed a dividend of €246,000 for the year under review.

4. **Disposal of Subsidiary: Waltz Limited**
   On 30 April 2011 Tango Ltd disposed of its entire 70% holding in Waltz Ltd Details of the disposal were:

	€000
Net assets disposed	
Property, plant and equipment	220
Inventories	60
Receivables	80
Cash	30

Payables	(70)
	320
Non-controlling interests (30% × 320)	(96)
Profit on disposal	76
	300
Settled by	
Cash received	300

Requirement Prepare a consolidated statement of cash flows in accordance with IAS 7 *Statement of Cash Flows* for the year ended 31 August 2011.

Solution to Question 11.3

Tango Ltd
CONSOLIDATED STATEMENT OF CASH FLOWS
for the year ended 31 August 2011

	€000	€000
Net cash flow from operating activities		
Profit before tax	1,556	
Depreciation	220	
Loss on sale of tangible non-current assets	30	
Interest payable	205	
Profit on disposal of subsidiary	(76)	
Share of profit of Associate	(160)	
Increase in inventories *(W2)*	(615)	
Increase in trade receivables *(W2)*	(360)	
Increase in trade payables *(W2)*	234	
Cash generated from operations	1,034	
Interest paid	(205)	
Tax paid *(W4)*	(330)	
Net cash flow from operating activities		499
Cash flows from investing activities		
Payments to require tangible non-current assets *(W6)*	(1,765)	
Receipts from sale of tangible non-current assets	150	
Disposal of subsidiary company (300 – 30)	270	
Dividends received from associate (*W1*)	30	
Net cash flow from investing activities		(1,315)
Cash flows from financing activities		
Issue of share capital at a premium	1,000	
Dividends paid by Tango Plc *(W5)*	(146)	
Dividends paid to non-controlling interest *(W3)*	(90)	

Net cash flow from financing	764
Decrease in cash and cash equivalents	(52)
Cash and cash equivalents at 1 September 2010	(2)
Cash and cash equivalents at 31 August 2011	(54)

WORKINGS

(W1)

Investment In Associate

Debit		**Credit**	
Bal b/d (Opening SoFP)	860	Dividend (bal. fig)	30
Share of profit (SoCI)	160	Bal c/d (Closing SoFP)	990
	1,020		1,020

(W2)

	Inventory €000	**Receivables €000**	**Payables €000**
at 1 September 2010	1,015	830	583
at 31 August 2011	1,570	1,110	747
Increase	555	280	164
Add: disposed of with subsidiary Waltz Ltd	60	80	70
Consol. SoCF	(615)	(360)	234

(W3)

Non-controlling Interest

Debit		**Credit**	
Cash dividend (balancing figure)	90	Bal b/d (Opening SoFP)	180
Bal c/d (CL SoFP)	124	SoCI	130
Disposal – Waltz	96		
	310		310

(W4)

Taxation (Current and Deferred)

Debit		**Credit**	
Taxation paid (Bal. Fig.)	330	Bal b/d (460 + 360)	820
Bal c/d (580 + 500)	1,080	SoCI	590
	1,410		1,410

(W5)

Dividends paid by Tango

Debit		**Credit**	
Cash payment (balance)	146	Balance b/d	150
Balance c/d	250	SoCE	246
	396		396

(W6)

Property, Plant and Equipment

Balance b/d	1,970	Disposals	180
Revaluation	500	Depreciation	220
Additions (bal. fig.)	1,545	Balance c/d	3,615
	4,015		4,015

Property, plant and equipment	**€000**
Additions during year	1,545
Add disposed of with Waltz Ltd	220
Consolidated SoCF	1,765

NOTES TO CONSOLIDATED STATEMENT OF CASH FLOWS

Note 1

During the period the group sold its entire holding (70%) in Waltz Ltd. Details of the disposal were:

Net assets at date of disposal	**€000**
Property, plant and equipment	220
Inventories	60
Receivables	80
Payables	(70)
	290
Non-controlling interests	(96)
Profit on disposal	76
Total proceeds received in cash	270
Cash balance of subsidiary disposed	30
Cash received on disposal	300

Note 2

Cash and cash equivalents	2011	2010
	€000	**€000**
Cash on hand and bank overdrafts	(54)	(2)

Chapter 12

Disposal of Subsidiaries

Learning Objectives

After reading this chapter you should be able to:

- demonstrate an understanding of the importance of **'control'** in determining the accounting for disposal of shares in a subsidiary; and
- prepare a set of financial statements *where*, during a reporting year:
  1. a parent disposes of its entire holding in a subsidiary;
  2. a parent sells part of its holding in a subsidiary but does not lose control over that subsidiary;
  3. a parent sells sufficient shares in a subsidiary to lose control but the former subsidiary becomes an associate; and
  4. a parent sells most of its shares in a subsidiary and the remaining investment is a simple/trade investment.

Introduction

This chapter is the final step in your mastering of the principles and techniques of preparing and presenting consolidated financial statements. Though accounting for disposal of shares in a subsidiary is a complex area, the provisions of IAS 27 *Consolidated and Separate Financial Statements* are very specific with regard to the treatment of such disposals. The term **control** (see also **Chapter 2**), i.e. "the power to govern the financial and operating policies of an entity so as to obtain benefits from its activities" plays a central role in the correct application of accounting principles to each disposal.

Accounting for Disposals

(a) Changes to a parent's ownership interest in a subsidiary **that do not result in a loss of control** are accounted for as **equity transactions** (transactions with owners in their capacity as owners). No profit or loss on disposal is reported in the consolidated statement of comprehensive income.

(b) If a parent **loses control** over one of its subsidiaries the following must occur:
   1. the subsidiary's assets and liabilities, as well as the non-controlling interests in those net assets, must be derecognised from the consolidated SoFP at their carrying amounts at the date control is lost;

2. the parent must recognise the fair value of the consideration received, which results in the loss of control in the subsidiary;
3. the parent must recognise any gain or loss on the disposal, attributable to the parent, in the consolidated SoCI; and
4. the parent must recognise any remaining investment in the former subsidiary at fair value on the date control is lost.

Levels of Disposals

A parent can sell shares in a subsidiary, which can give rise to different structures after the disposal. The following examples are used for illustration purposes:

Example 12.1: Examples of Different Levels of Disposal

Peel Ltd (Peel) acquired 80% of the 1 million ordinary shares in issue by Skin Ltd (Skin) on 1 September 2008. The reporting date for the group is 31 August.

Scenario 1: Disposal of total investment in Skin Ltd
On 1 February 2011 Peel sold its entire holding in Skin for cash. **Control is lost.** Skin is a subsidiary of Peel until 31 January 2011 and its results must be consolidated with the results of Peel until that date. At the reporting date, i.e. 31 August 2011 Skin is no longer a subsidiary and the SoFP as at that date will comprise the assets (excluding the investment but including the sale proceeds and profit on disposal) and liabilities of Peel only.

Scenario 2: Partial disposal of investment in Skin Ltd without loss of control
On 1 June 2011 Peel sells 200,000 of its shares in Skin. In this instance, **control is not lost** as Peel still retains 60% of the share capital of Skin and Skin is, therefore, a subsidiary for the full reporting year ending on 31 August 2011. The non-controlling interests in the profits of Skin change from 20% for the first 9 months to 40% for the last three months. Skin Ltd is still a subsidiary at the reporting date so all its assets and liabilities must be consolidated with those of Peel at that date.

Scenario 3: Partial disposal of investment in Skin Ltd with loss of control
On 1 March 2011, Peel sells 400,000 of its shares in Skin. **Control is lost** as Peel now only owns 40% of the share capital of Skin. Skin is a subsidiary for half of the reporting year and an associate for the remainder. In the consolidated SoCI for the year ended 31 August 2011, full consolidation is applied to Skin for six months to 28 February 2011 and equity accounting as an **associate** from then until the reporting date. The SoFP as at 31 August 2011 will comprise the assets and liabilities of Peel only (after adjustment for the disposal) and the investment in Skin which is valued as follows:

Fair value as at 1 March 2011	€X
Plus	
40% of the profits of Skin from 1 March 2011 to 31 August 2011	€X

Scenario 4: Partial disposal of investment in Skin Ltd
On 1 March 2011 Peel sells 700,000 of its shares in Skin. **Control is lost** as Peel now only owns 10% of the share capital of Skin. Skin is a subsidiary for half the reporting year and a trade/simple investment for the remainder. In the consolidated SoCI for the year ended 31 August 2011 full consolidation is applied to Skin for six months to 28 February 2011 and only dividends received/receivable from then until the reporting date are accounted for. The SoFP as at 31 August 2011 will comprise the assets and liabilities of Peel only (after adjusting for disposal), including the remaining investment in Skin which is valued as follows:

Fair value as at 1 March 2011	€X

The following example (**12.2**) incorporates:

Scenario 1 a parent selling its entire investment in a subsidiary;
Scenario 2 a parent selling part of its investment in a subsidiary but maintaining control over that entity;
Scenario 3 a parent selling part of its investment in a subsidiary whose status changes to an associate;
Scenario 4 a parent selling part of its investment in a subsidiary which subsequently becomes a trade investment.

Example 12.2: Different Levels of Disposal

The following draft financial statements of Pulp Plc and Shred Ltd for the year ended 31 August 2011 will be used to illustrate the accounting treatment for each of four levels of disposal of shares in a subsidiary by its parent.

Statement of Comprehensive Income

	Pulp Plc	**Shred Ltd**
	€	**€**
Revenue	1,015,000	492,000
Cost of sales	(609,000)	(295,000)
Gross profit	406,000	197,000
Distribution costs	(126,000)	(58,000)
Administrative expenses	(180,000)	(81,000)
Finance costs	(40,000)	(18,000)
Profit before tax	60,000	40,000
Income tax expense	(24,000)	(16,000)
Profit for the year	36,000	24,000
Other comprehensive income	nil	nil
Total comprehensive income for the year	36,000	24,000

Statement of Financial Position

	Pulp Plc	Shred Ltd
	€	€
Investment in Shred	75,000	–
Sundry net assets	265,000	100,000
	340,000	100,000
Ordinary €1 shares	200,000	60,000
Retained earnings	140,000	40,000
	340,000	100,000

Additional information:

1. Pulp Plc acquired 75% of the ordinary shares of Shred Ltd on 1 September 2009 when the retained earnings of Shred Ltd were €10,000.
2. Goodwill impairment for the year ended 31 August 2010 was €4,500.
3. NCI at the date of acquisition was measured using the proportion of net assets method.

SCENARIO 1: Pulp Plc sells its entire investment for €125,000 on 31 August 2011.

***Key point:* Loss of control but Shred Ltd is a subsidiary for the entire reporting year.**

Solution Notes

1. After the disposal, Shred Ltd is no longer a subsidiary of Pulp Plc.
2. The results of Shred Ltd must be included in the consolidated SoCI for the entire year to 31 August 2011 as the investment was sold on the reporting date.
3. The statement of financial position at 31 August 2011 will be that of Pulp Plc only.

IAS 27 states that, if a parent loses control over a subsidiary, the parent should:

- derecognise the assets (including any goodwill) and liabilities of the former subsidiary at the date when control is lost;
- derecognise the carrying amount of any non-controlling interests at the same date;
- recognise the fair value of any consideration received;
- recognise any investment retained in the former subsidiary at its fair value when control is lost;
- recognise the difference associated with the loss of control attributable to the parent in profit or loss.

Gain on disposal

In the consolidated SoCI:	€
Sale proceeds	125,000
Less	
Net assets at disposal date × group's share	
(€100,000 × 75%)	(75,000)
Less	
Goodwill (net of impairment)	(18,000)
Profit on disposal of investment	32,000

Goodwill	€	€
Cost of investment		75,000
Shred at acquisition date		
Ordinary shares	60,000	
Retained earnings	10,000	
	70,000	
Group's share 75%		(52,500)
Goodwill		22,500
Impairment y/e 31 August 2010		(4,500)
Balance before disposal		18,000

Consolidated Statement of Comprehensive Income
for year ending 31 August 2011

	€
Revenue	1,507,000
Cost of sales	(904,000)
Gross profit	603,000
Distribution costs	(184,000)
Administrative expenses	(261,000)
Finance costs	(58,000)
Profit on disposal of subsidiary	32,000
Profit before tax	132,000
Income tax expense	(40,000)
Profit for the year	92,000
Other comprehensive income	nil
Total comprehensive income for the year	92,000
Profit for the year attributable to:	
Owners of the parent	86,000
Non-controlling interest (25% × 24,000)	6,000
	92,000
Total comprehensive income for the year attributable to:	
Owners of the parent	86,000
Non-controlling interests	6,000
	92,000

Journal Entry Re Disposal

	€	€
Dr. Sundry net assets (cash)	125,000	
Dr. Non-controlling interests (25% × 100,000)	25,000	
Cr. Sundry net assets (Shred)		100,000
Cr. Goodwill		18,000
Cr. Retained earnings (profit)		32,000

Workings (T account method)

Investment in Shred

Debit		Credit	
Pulp	75,000	Cost of control	75,000

Sundry Net Assets

Debit		Credit	
Pulp	265,000		
Shred	100,000	Journal	100,000
Journal	125,000	SoFP	390,000
	490,000		490,000

Ordinary Shares

Debit		Credit	
Cost of control (75%)	45,000	Pulp	200,000
NCI (25%)	15,000	Shred	60,000
SoFP	200,000		
	260,000		260,000

Retained Earnings

Debit		Credit	
Cost of control (75% × 10,000)	7,500	Pulp	140,000
NCI (25% × 40,000)	10,000	Shred	40,000
Goodwill impairment	4,500	Journal	32,000
SoFP	190,000		
	212,000		212,000

Cost of Control

Debit		Credit	
Investment in Shred	75,000	Ordinary shares	45,000
		Retained earnings	7,500
		Impairment	4,500
		Journal	18,000
	75,000		75,000

Non-controlling Interests

Debit		Credit	
		Ordinary shares	15,000
Journal	25,000	Retained earnings	10,000
	25,000		25,000

WORKINGS (Columnar Method)

	Pulp €	Shred €	Adjustments €	Consol. SoFP €
Investment in Shred	75,000		(75,000)	
Sundry net assets	265,000	100,000	125,000	390,000
			(100,000)	
Goodwill (*W1*)				nil
Total assets	**340,000**	**100,000**	**(50,000)**	**390,000**
Ordinary shares	200,000	60,000	(60,000)	200,000
Retained earnings (*W2*)	140,000	40,000	10,000	190,000
Non-controlling interest (*W3*)				nil
Total equity & liabilities	**340,000**	**100,000**	**(50,000)**	**390,000**

(W1) Goodwill

Cost of investment		75,000
Shred at acquisition date		
Ordinary shares	60,000	
Retained earnings	10,000	
	70,000	
Group's share 75%		52,500
Goodwill		22,500
Impairment at 31/8/10		(4,500)
Journal re disposal		(18,000)
Balance		nil

(W2) Retained earnings

Pulp at reporting date	140,000
Share of post-acq. of Shred 75% (40 – 10)	22,500
Impairment of goodwill	(4,500)
Journal – profit on disposal	32,000
	190,000

(W3) Non-controlling interests

Shred at reporting date		
Ordinary shares	60,000	
Retained earnings	40,000	
	100,000	
NCI × 25%		25,000
Journal re disposal		(25,000)
		nil

Pulp Plc
Statement of Financial Position
as at 31 August 2011

	€
Sundry net assets	390,000
Ordinary shares	200,000
Retained earnings	190,000
	390,000

Statement of Changes in Equity
for the year ended 31 August 2011

	Ord. shares	**Ret. Earnings**	**NCI**
	€	**€**	**€**
Balance at 1 September 2010	200,000	104,000 *(W4)*	19,000 *(W5)*
TCI for the year		86,000	6,000
Disposal of subsidiary			(25,000)
Balance at 31 August 2011	**200,000**	**190,000**	**nil**

(W4) Retained Earnings at 1 September 2010

Pulp (140 – 36)	104,000
Goodwill impairment	(4,500)
Shred 75% (40 – 24 – 10)	4,500
	104,000

(W5) Non-controlling Interests

Net assets of Shred at 1/9/10 (100 – 24)	76,000	[net assets = capital + reserves]
× 25%	19,000	

Note: The opening retained earnings €104,000 will be the same under all four assumptions as all adjustments affect earnings after that date.

SCENARIO 2: Pulp Plc sold 12,000 of its shares in Shred Ltd on 31 August 2011 for €44,000. Pulp now owns 33,000 shares.

***Key point:* Sale of shares in a subsidiary but subsidiary status retained. No loss of control. Shred is a subsidiary for the full year.**

Solution Notes

1. Shred Ltd is a subsidiary for the entire reporting year.
2. Pulp Plc retains control, now owning 55% of Shred Ltd.
3. No profit is recognised on the disposal.

IAS 27: Changes in a parent's ownership in a subsidiary that do not result in a parent losing control of the subsidiary are equity transactions, i.e. transactions with owners in their capacity as owners.

- The carrying amounts of the controlling and non-controlling interests shall be adjusted to reflect the changes in their relative interests in the subsidiary.
- Any difference between the amount by which the non-controlling interests are adjusted and the fair value of the consideration paid or received is recognised directly in equity and attributed to the owners of the parent.

Journal Entry for Disposal	€	€
Dr. Sundry net assets (cash)	44,000	
Cr. Non-controlling interests (*W1*)		20,000
Cr. Adj. to parent's equity in SoCE		24,000

(W1) Non-controlling Interests

Non-controlling interests are credited with an additional 20% of the net assets of Shred Ltd at 31 August 2011 i.e. 20% × €100,000 = €20,000.

Consolidated Statement of Comprehensive Income
for the year ended 31 August 2011

	€
Revenue	1,507,000
Cost of sales	(904,000)
Gross profit	603,000
Distribution costs	(184,000)
Administrative expenses	(261,000)
Finance costs	(58,000)
Profit before tax	100,000
Income tax expense	(40,000)
Profit for the year	60,000
Other comprehensive income	nil
Total comprehensive income for the year	60,000
Profit for the year attributed to:	
Owners of the parent	54,000
Non-controlling interest (25% × 24,000)	6,000
	60,000
Total comprehensive income for the year attributed to:	
Owners of the parent	54,000
Non-controlling interest	6,000
	60,000

Workings (T account method)

Investment in Shred

Debit		**Credit**	
Pulp	75,000	Cost of control	75,000

Sundry Net Assets

Debit		Credit	
Pulp	265,000		
Shred	100,000		
Journal (cash)	44,000	SoFP	409,000
	409,000		409,000

Ordinary Shares

Debit		Credit	
Cost of control (75%)	45,000	Pulp	200,000
NCI (25%)	15,000	Shred	60,000
SoFP	200,000		----------
	260,000		260,000

Retained Earnings

Debit		Credit	
Cost of control (75% × 10,000)	7,500	Pulp	140,000
NCI (25% × 40,000)	10,000	Shred	40,000
Goodwill impairment	4,500		
SoFP	182,000	Journal	24,000
	204,000		204,000

Cost of Control

Debit		Credit	
Investment in Shred	75,000	Ordinary shares	45,000
		Retained earnings	7,500
		Impairment of g/will	4,500
		SoFP	18,000
	75,000		75,000

Non-controlling Interests

Debit		Credit	
		Ordinary shares	15,000
		Retained earnings	10,000
SoFP	45,000	Journal	20,000
	45,000		45,000

NCI is now 45% of the closing net assets of Shred, i.e. 45% × €100,000.

Workings (Columnar Method)

	Pulp €	Shred €	Adjustments €	Consol. SoFP. €
Investment in Shred	75,000		(75,000)	
Sundry net assets	265,000	100,000	44,000	409,000

Goodwill *(W1)*			18,000	18,000
Total assets	**340,000**	**100,000**	**(13,000)**	**427,000**
Ordinary shares	200,000	60,000	(60,000)	200,000
Retained earnings *(W2)*	140,000	40,000	2,000	182,000
Non-controlling int. *(W3)*			45,000	45,000
Total Equity & Liabilities	**340,000**	**100,000**	**(13,000)**	**427,000**

(W1) Goodwill

	€	€
Investment in Shred		75,000
Shred at acquisition date		
Ordinary shares	60,000	
Retained earnings	10,000	
	70,000	
Group's share 75%		52,500
Goodwill		22,500
Less impairment		(4,500)
SoFP.		18,000

(W2) Retained earnings

	€	€
Pulp at reporting date		140,000
Journal		24,000
Goodwill impairment		(4,500)
Shred at reporting date	40,000	
at acquisition date	10,000	
post-acquisition	30,000	
Group's share 75%		22,500
SoFP		182,000

(W3) Non-controlling interests

Shred at reporting date		
Ordinary shares	60,000	
Retained earnings	40,000	
	100,000	
× 25% before disposal		25,000
Journal (increasing to 45%)		20,000
SoFP		45,000

Consolidated Statement of Financial Position
as at 31 August 2011

	€
Goodwill	18,000
Sundry net assets	409,000
	427,000

Ordinary shares	200,000
Retained earnings	182,000
Total shareholders' equity	382,000
Non-controlling interests	45,000
	427,000

Consolidated Statement of Changes in Equity
for the year ended 31 August 2011

	Ordinary Shares €	**Retained Earnings €**	**NCI €**
Balance at 1 Sept 2010	200,000	104,000 (*W4*)	19,000 (*W5*)
TCI for the year		54,000	6,000
Disposal of shares in Shred		24,000	20,000
Balance at 31 August 2011		**182,000**	**45,000**

(W4) Retained earnings 1/9/10 as in Scenario 1

Pulp (140,000 – 36,000)	104,000
Shred 75% (16,000 – 10,000)	4,500
Goodwill impairment	(4,500)
	104,000

(W5) Non-controlling interest at 1/9/10 as in Scenario 1

Shred at 1 September 2010		
Ordinary shares	60,000	
Retained earnings (40–24)	16,000	
	76,000 × 25%	19,000

SCENARIO 3: Pulp Plc sold 24,000 of its shares in Shred Ltd on 31 August 2011 for €80,000. The fair value of the remaining investment in the former subsidiary is €45,000. Pulp now owns 21,000 shares.

Key point: **Sale of shares in subsidiary – loss of control – an associate exists subsequently.**

Solution Notes

1. Shred is a subsidiary for the full year under review, therefore, the consolidated SoCI will include the results of Shred for the full 12 months.
2. The SoFP as at 31 August 2011 is of an investing company and an associate.
3. The remaining investment after the disposal is valued at fair value €45,000 (carrying value €35,000) with the surplus going to the consolidated SoCI.

IAS 27 states that, if a parent loses control over a subsidiary, the parent should:

- derecognise the assets (including any goodwill) and liabilities of the former subsidiary at the date when control is lost;

- derecognise the carrying amount of any non-controlling interests at the same date;
- recognise the fair value of any consideration received;
- recognise any investment retained in the former subsidiary at its fair value when control is lost; and
- recognise the gain or loss associated with the loss of control attributable to the parent.

Gain on disposal in the individual SoCI of Pulp

	€
Proceeds	80,000
Less: Cost of shares sold 75,000 × 24,000/45,000	40,000
	40,000

Gain on disposal in consolidated SoCI

Proceeds	80,000
Fair value of 35% retained	45,000
	125,000
Less: net assets disposed, including goodwill (100 × 75% + 18)	93,000
	32,000

Note: Revaluation of the remaining investment:

Original cost of investment in Shred	75,000
Cost of shares sold	(40,000)
Remaining cost	35,000
Fair value attributed	45,000
Excess to profit and loss	10,000

Consolidated Statement of Comprehensive Income
for the year ended 31 August 2011

	€
Revenue	1,507,000
Cost of sales	(904,000)
Gross profit	603,000
Distribution costs	(184,000)
Administrative expenses	(261,000)
Finance costs	(58,000)
Profit on disposal of subsidiary	32,000
Profit before tax	132,000
Income tax expense	(40,000)
Profit for the year	92,000
Other comprehensive income	nil
Total comprehensive income for the year	92,000

	€
Profit for the year attributable to:	
Owners of the parent	86,000
Non-controlling interest (25% × 24,000)	6,000
	92,000
Total comprehensive income for the year attributable to:	
Owners of the parent	86,000
Non-controlling interests	6,000
	92,000

Statement of Changes in Equity
for the year ended 31 August 2011

	Ord. Shares €	**Ret. earnings €**	**NCI €**
Balance at 1 September 2010	200,000	104,000 (*W1*)	19,000 (*W2*)
TCI for the year		86,000	6,000
Disposal of subsidiary			(25,000)
Balance at 31 August 2011	200,000	190,000	nil

(W1) Retained earnings 1/9/10 as before

Pulp (140,000 – 36,000)	104,000
Shred 75% (16,000 – 10,000)	4,500
Goodwill impairment	(4,500)
	104,000

(W2) Non-controlling interest at 1/9/10 as before

Shred at 1 September 2010		
Ordinary shares	60,000	
Retained earnings (40–24)	16,000	
	76,000 × 25%	19,000

Note: The statement of financial position as at 31 August 2011 consists of Pulp Plc (adjusted by the sale of the investment) **plus** an investment in **an associate**. The value of the investment is the **fair value** attributed of €45,000 on the reporting date i.e. there were **no post-acquisition profits** of the associate at 31 August 2011.

Pulp Plc
Statement of Financial Position
as at 31 August 2011

	€
Investment in associate	45,000
Sundry net assets (265 + 80) (*W3*)	345,000
	390,000

Ordinary shares	200,000
Retained earnings (*W4*)	190,000
	390,000

(W3) Sundry Net Assets

	€
Per Pulp SoFP 31 August 2011	265,000
Cash proceeds on sale of investment	80,000
	345,000

(W4) Retained Earnings

Retained earnings per Pulp SoFP 31/8/11	140,000
Gain on disposal per individual SoCI	40,000
Increase in fair value of investment	10,000
	190,000

SCENARIO 4: Pulp Plc sold 40,500 of its shares in Shred Ltd on 31 May 2011 for €115,000. The fair value of the remaining investment in the former subsidiary is €15,000.

Key Point: **Loss of control. Shred is a subsidiary for nine months. The remaining investment after the disposal is 7.5% – a trade or simple investment.**

Gain on disposal

	€
(a) In the consolidated SoCI	
Sale proceeds	115,000
Fair value of remaining 7.5%	15,000
	130,000
Less	
Net assets at disposal date × group's share	
€94,000 × 75% *(W1)*	(70,500)
Less	
Goodwill	(18,000)
Profit on disposal	41,500
(b) In the individual SoCI of Pulp	
Sale proceeds	115,000
Cost of shares sold €75,000 × 40,500/45,000	67,500
	47,500

(W1) Net Assets of Shred at disposal date	€
Net assets at 31 August 2011	100,000
Less profit y/e 31 August 2011 × 3/12	
24,000 × 3/12	(6,000)
Net assets at 31 May 2011	94,000

Note: Consolidated SoCE:

1. The results of Shred can only be consolidated for 9 months as it ceased to be a subsidiary on 31 May 2011. The figures for revenue, cost of sales, distribution costs, administrative expenses, finance costs and income tax expense include 12 months for Pulp and 9 months for Shred.
2. Non-controlling interest in the profits of Shred will be calculated as follows: Profit after tax of Shred × 9/12 ×25%,
   24,000 × 9/12 × 25% = €4,500

CONSOLIDATED STATEMENT OF COMPREHENSIVE INCOME
for year ending 31 August 2011

	€
Revenue (1,015 + (492 × 9/12))	1,384,000
Cost of sales (609 + (295 × 9/12))	(830,250)
Gross profit	553,750
Distribution costs (126 + (58 × 9/12))	(169,500)
Administrative expenses (180 + (81 × 9/12))	(240,750)
Finance costs (40 + (18 × 9/12))	(53,500)
Profit on disposal of subsidiary	41,500
Profit before tax	131,500
Income tax expense (24 +(16 × 9/12))	(36,000)
Profit for the year	95,500
Other comprehensive income	nil
Total comprehensive income for the year	95,500
Profit for the year attributable to:	
Owners of the parent	91,000
Non-controlling interest (see Note 2 above)	4,500
	95,500
Total comprehensive income for the year attributable to:	
Owners of the parent	91,000
Non-controlling interests	4,500
	95,500

Note for SoFP:

The SoFP at 31 August 2011 comprises:
The original SoFP of Pulp as at the same date adjusted by Journals 1 and 2.

JOURNALS

1. Adjustment for the sale of the investment.

Dr. Cash	115,000	
Cr. Investment in Shred		67,500
Cr. Retained earnings		47,500

With sale of 90% of its holding.

2. Adjustment for remaining investment 7,500 to be increased to fair value 15,000.

Dr. Investment in Shred	7,500	
Cr. SoCI		7,500

STATEMENT OF FINANCIAL POSITION
as at 31 August 2011

	€
Sundry net assets *(W2)*	380,000
Available for sale financial asset	15,000
	395,000
Ordinary shares	200,000
Retained earnings *(W3)*	195,000
	395,000

(W2) Sundry Net Assets

	€
Per original SoFP	265,000
Cash from disposal (Jnl 1)	115,000
	380,000

(W3) Retained Earnings

Per original SoFP	140,000
Profit on disposal (Jnl 1)	47,500
Increase in investment fair value	7,500
	195,000

CONSOLIDATED STATEMENT OF CHANGES IN EQUITY
for the year ended 31 August 2011

	Ordinary Shares €	**Retained Earnings** €	**NCI** €
Balance at 1 Sept 2010	200,000	104,000 *(W4)*	19,000 *(W5)*
TCI for the year		91,000	4,500
Disposal of Shred			(23,500)
Balance at 31 August 2011	200,000	195,000	nil

(W4) Retained earnings 1/9/10 as before

Pulp (140,000 – 36,000)	104,000
Shred 75% (16,000 – 10,000)	4,500
Goodwill impairment	(4,500)
	104,000

(W5) Non controlling interest at 1/9/10 as before

Shred at 1 September 2010		
Ordinary shares	60,000	
Retained earnings (40 – 24)	16,000	
	76,000 × 25%	19,000

Conclusion

This text has taken you on a step-by-step journey from basic principles to:

- preparing and presenting consolidated financial statements (SoFP and SoCI/SoCE) to include a subsidiary, an associate, a joint venture and a trade investment;
- accounting and calculating goodwill as well as valuing the component parts of the calculation;
- recognising and treating goodwill attributable to non-controlling interests;
- the treatment of a foreign operation in group financial statements;
- preparing and presenting consolidated statements of cash flows; and
- accounting for various levels of disposal of shares in a subsidiary.

'Consolidation' has tended to be a difficult area of accounting for students. I hope that this text has made your journey less daunting and that you will face examination of this topic with confidence.

Recommended Reading

As stated throughout this text, you are encouraged to read alternative texts, as the opinions and methods of others can only help to develop a greater understanding of all topics. To this end, and in the context of this chapter, it is recommended that you also read Chapter 32, "Disposal of Subsidiaries", of *International Financial Accounting and Reporting* (3rd Edition) by Ciaran Connolly.

Summary

1. When a parent sells its entire holding in a subsidiary and loses control over that entity, the results of the former subsidiary should be included in the consolidated SoCI until the date on which control is lost. The profit/loss on sale will also be accounted for in the consolidated SoCI.
2. When a parent sells part of its holding in a subsidiary but does not lose control over that entity, the transaction should be treated as one between owners in their capacity as owners. No profit/loss is recognised in the consolidated SoCI.
3. A parent can sell part of its holding in a subsidiary which results in:
   (a) loss of control over the former subsidiary and
   (b) the status of the former subsidiary changing to an associate.

If this event occurs during a reporting year, it will result in full consolidation being used in the consolidated SoCI up to the date of sale and equity accounting for the remainder of the year.

4. A parent can sell part of its holding in a subsidiary which results in:
   (a) loss of control over the former subsidiary and
   (b) the status of the former subsidiary changing to a trade/simple investment.

   If this event occurs during a reporting year it will result in full consolidation being used in the consolidated SoCI up to the date of sale and only accounting for dividends received/receivable for the remainder of the year.

5. Any remaining investment after disposal would be accounted for under IAS 39/ IFRS 9.

QUESTIONS

Question 12.1

Port Ltd (Port) acquired 90% of the ordinary shares of Storm Ltd (Storm) on 1 April 2008. The reporting date for the group is 30 September annually.

Requirement For each of the following disposals of shares in Storm outline the accounting and related effects on the financial statements of the Port group for the year ended 30 September 2011:

(a) Port sells one-half of its holding in Storm on 30 April 2011;
(b) Port sells one-third of its holding in Storm on 31 July 2011;
(c) Port sells its entire holding in Storm on 30 September 2011;
(d) Port sells 90% of its holding in Storm on 31 August 2011.

Solution

(a) The first consequence of the disposal is that Port has **lost control** over the financial and operating policies of Storm on 30 April 2011. The results of Storm must be fully consolidated until that date (seven months). On 1 May 2011 the former subsidiary changes status to an associate. The results of Storm from 1 May 2011 to the reporting date 30 September will be accounted for using the equity method. In the statement of financial position as at 30 September 2011 Port will include its investment in Storm at a valuation which would be arrived at as follows:

Fair value of investment at 1 May 2011	€X
Plus	
45% of the profits of Storm 1 May 2011 to 30 September 2011	€X
	€X

(b) **There is no loss of control** over Storm as Port still holds a majority (60%) of the voting rights of Storm after the disposal. The disposal **is accounted for as an equity**

transaction and no profit or loss is recorded in the consolidated statement of comprehensive income for the year ended 30 September 2011. Storm is a subsidiary for the entire reporting year so all its results are fully consolidated. The non-controlling interest in the profits of Storm changes from 10% up to 31 July to 40% for the final two months.

(c) **There is loss of control** over Storm as Port has no interest in Storm after 30 September 2011. The disposal **is not accounted for as an equity transaction** and the profit or loss is recorded in the consolidated statement of comprehensive income for the year ended 30 September 2011. The results of Storm must be fully consolidated for the entire reporting year as the shares were sold on 30 September 2011. The statement of financial position as at 30 September 2011 will comprise the net assets of Port only after adjusting for the sale of the investment.

(d) **There is loss of control** over Storm, as Port has only a 9% interest in Storm after 31 August 2011. The disposal **is not accounted for as an equity transaction** and any profit or loss is recorded in the consolidated statement of comprehensive income for the year ended 30 September 2011. The consolidated statement of comprehensive income for the year ended 30 September 2011 will include the fully consolidated results of Storm for 11 months. The remaining investment in Storm (9%) is revalued to fair value on 1 September 2011. The statement of financial position as at 30 September 2011 comprises:

(i) the net assets of Port;
(ii) the adjustment for the disposal of 81% of the shares in Storm;
(iii) the remaining investment in Storm now at fair value.

Note: Question 12.2 is a longer, review-type question. The question deals with two subsidiaries, one of which becomes an associate after a disposal of shares six months into the reporting year. The solution consists of:
1. Journal adjustments
2. The T account method workings
3. The columnar method workings
4. The consolidated SoFP, SoCI and SoCE.

Question 12.2

The following are the statements of financial position of Tom Ltd, Dick Ltd and Harry Ltd as at 31 August 2011:

	Tom Ltd	Dick Ltd	Harry Ltd
	€000	**€000**	**€000**
Assets			
Non-current assets			
Property, plant and equipment	12,440	8,510	6,380
Investment in Dick Ltd	4,700	–	–

Investment in Harry Ltd	2,500	–	–
	19,640	8,510	6,380
Current assets	4,670	3,730	2,800
Total assets	**24,310**	**12,240**	**9,180**
Equity and liabilities			
Equity			
Ordinary shares €1	10,000	4,000	2,000
Retained earnings	10,110	4,890	4,660
Total equity	20,110	8,890	6,660
Current liabilities	4,200	3,350	2,520
Total equity and liabilities	**24,310**	**12,240**	**9,180**

Statements of Comprehensive Income
for the year ended 31 August 2011

	Tom Ltd €000	**Dick Ltd €000**	**Harry Ltd €000**
Revenue	9,340	6,600	5,200
Cost of sales	(2,300)	(1,650)	(1,300)
Gross profit	7,040	4,950	3,900
Operating expenses	(4,720)	(3,730)	(2,700)
Profit before tax	2,320	1,220	1,200
Income tax expense	(460)	(240)	(200)
Profit for the year	1,860	980	1,000

1. Tom Ltd acquired 80% of the ordinary shares in Dick Ltd on 1 January 2009 when the retained earnings of Dick Ltd were €1,500,000.
2. Tom Ltd acquired 1,200,000 shares in Harry Ltd on 1 December 2009 when the retained earnings of Harry Ltd were €1,800,000.
3. Tom Ltd sold half of its investment in Harry Ltd on 28 February 2011 for cash proceeds of €4,500,000. The fair value of the remaining investment in the former subsidiary was €1,500,000 at that date.
4. NCI at acquisition date is measured using the proportion of net assets method.

Requirement Prepare for the Tom Ltd group for the year ended 31 August 2011:

(a) The consolidated statement of comprehensive income;
(b) The consolidated statement of financial position;
(c) The consolidated statement of changes in equity.

Solution to Question 12.2

IAS 27 states that, if a parent loses control over a subsidiary, the parent should:

- derecognise the assets (including any goodwill) and liabilities of the former subsidiary at the date when control is lost;

- derecognise the carrying amount of any non-controlling interests at the same date;
- recognise the fair value of any consideration received;
- recognise any investment retained in the former subsidiary at its fair value when control is lost;
- recognise the gain or loss associated with the loss of control attributable to the parent in profit or loss.

Solution Notes

1. Dick Ltd is a subsidiary for the full year under review.
2. Harry Ltd
   (a) is a subsidiary for the first 6 months of the year – non-controlling interests 40%
   (b) is an associate (30%) for the second 6 months.
3. The assets, liabilities and non-controlling interests of Harry Ltd must be derecognised as of the disposal date.

Net assets of Harry at disposal date

	€000
Net assets at 31/8/2011	6,660
Profit y/e 31/8/2011 × 6/12 (1,000 × 6/12)	(500)
Net assets at 28 February 2011	6,160
4. Non-controlling interests in Harry at disposal date	
Net assets as in (Note 3) 6,160 × 40%	2,464
5. Goodwill on acquisition of Harry	
Cost of Investment	2,500
Acquired 60% (2,000+1,800)	2,280
Goodwill	220

Journal Entries

Individual Accounts of Tom	€000	€000
1. Dr. Current assets (cash)	4,500	
Cr. Investment in Harry		1,250
Cr. Retained earnings (profit)		3,250
Sale of 50% of investment in Harry		
2. Dr. Investment in Harry	250	
Cr. SoCI		250
Increase in remaining investment in Harry to fair value (1,500 – 1,250)		
3. Dr. Investment in Harry	150	
Cr. Retained earnings		150
Group's share of post-acq. profits of Harry, i.e. associate share 30% × 1,000 × 6 months		

Gain on disposal in consolidated SoCI

	€000
Proceeds	4,500
Fair value of 30% retained	1,500
	6,000

Less net assets disposed, including goodwill (6,160 × 60% + 220)	3,916
	2,084

The figures for revenue, cost of sales, operating expenses and income tax expense relating to Harry are time-apportioned by 6/12.

CONSOLIDATED STATEMENT OF COMPREHENSIVE INCOME
for the year ended 31 August 2011

	€000
Revenue	18,540
Cost of sales	(4,600)
Gross profit	13,940
Operating expenses	(9,800)
Profit on disposal of subsidiary	2,084
Share of profit of associate (Journal 3)	150
Profit before tax	6,374
Income tax expense	(800)
Profit for the year	5,574
Other comprehensive income	nil
Total comprehensive income for the year	5,574
Profit for the year attributable to:	
Owners of the parent	5,178
Non-controlling interests *(W2)*	396
	5,574
Total comprehensive income for the year attributable to:	
Owners of the parent	5,178
Non-controlling interests *(W2)*	396
	5,574

(W1) Share of profit of Associate	**€000**
Harry – profit for the year	1,000
Group share – 6 months @ 30%	150
(W2) Non-controlling interests	
Profit after tax Dick 980 × 20% =	196
Profit after tax Harry 1,000 × 6 months × 40% =	200
	396

SOFP WORKINGS (T account method)

Property, Plant and Equipment

Debit		**Credit**	
Tom	12,440		
Dick	8,510	SoFP	20,950
	20,950		20,950

Investment in Dick Ltd

Debit		Credit	
Tom	4,700	Cost of control	4,700

Investment in Harry Ltd

Debit		Credit	
Tom	2,500		
Journal 2	250	Journal 1	1,250
Journal 3	150	SoFP	1,650
	2,900		2,900

Current Assets

Debit		Credit	
Tom	4,670		
Dick	3,730		
Journal 1	4,500	SoFP	12.900
	12,900		12,900

Ordinary Shares

Debit		Credit	
Cost of control (80%)	3,200	Tom	10,000
NCI (20%)	800	Dick	4,000
SoFP	10,000		
	14,000		14,000

Current Liabilities

Debit		Credit	
		Tom	4,200
SoFP	7,550	Dick	3,350
	7,550		7,550

Retained Earnings

Debit		Credit	
Cost of control		Tom	10,110
(80% × 1,500)	1,200	Dick	4,890
NCI (20% × 4,890)	978	Journal 1	3,250
SoFP	16,472	Journal 2	250
		Journal 3	150
	18,650		18,650

Cost of Control

Debit		Credit	
Investment in Dick	4,700	Ord. shares	3,200
		Ret. Earnings	1,200
		Goodwill	300
	4,700		4,700

Non-controlling Interests

Debit		**Credit**	
		Ord. shares	800
SoFP	1,778	Ret. Earn.	978
	1,778		1,778

Workings (Columnar Method)

	Tom €000	Dick €000	Adjustments €000	Consol. SoFP €000
PPE	12,440	8,510		20,950
Investment in Dick	4,700		(4,700)	-
Investment in Harry *(W3)*	2,500		(1,250) 250 150	1,650
Goodwill *(W4)*			300	300
Current assets	4,670	3,730	4,500	12,900
Total Assets	**24,310**	**12,240**	**(750)**	**35,800**
Ordinary shares	10,000	4,000	(4,000)	10,000
Retained earnings *(W5)*	10,110	4,890	1,472	16,472
Non-controlling interests *(W6)*			1,778	1,778
Current liabilities	4,200	3,350		7,550
Total Equity & Liabilities	**24,310**	**12,240**	**(750)**	**35,800**

(W3) Investment in Harry (now an associate)

	€000	**€000**
Original cost of investment		2,500
Disposal 50%		(1,250)
Increase to fair value (1,500 − 1,250)		250
Share of post-acquisition profit (1,000 × 6/12 × 30%)		150
SoFP		1,650

(W4) Goodwill

	€000	**€000**
Cost of investment in Dick		4,700
Dick at acquisition date		
Ordinary shares	4,000	
Retained earnings	1,500	
	5,500	
Group's share 80%		4,400
SoFP		300

(W5) Retained earnings

	€000	€000
Tom at reporting date		10,110
Profit on sale of shares in Harry (Journal 1)		3,250
Share of post-acq. of Harry (Journal 3)		150
Revaluation of investment		250
Dick at reporting date	4,890	
at acquisition date	1,500	
Post-acquisition	3,390	
Group's share 80%		2,712
SoFP		16,472

(W6) Non-controlling interests

	€000	€000
Dick Ltd at reporting date		
Ordinary shares	4,000	
Retained earnings	4,890	
	8,890	
NCI × 20%		1,778

CONSOLIDATED STATEMENT OF FINANCIAL POSITION
as at 31 August 2011

	€000
Assets	
Non-current assets	
Property, plant and equipment	20,950
Goodwill	300
Investment in associate	1,650
Current assets	12,900
Total Assets	**35,800**
Equity and Liabilities	
Equity	
Ordinary shares	10,000
Retained earnings	16,472
Total shareholders' equity	26,472
Non-controlling interests	1,778
Total equity	28,250
Current liabilities	7,550
Total Equity and Liabilities	**35,800**

STATEMENT OF CHANGES IN EQUITY
for the year ended 31 August 2011

	Ord. Shares €000	Ret. Earnings €000	NCI €000
Balance at 1 September 2010	10,000	11,294 *(W7)*	3,846 *(W8)*
TCI for the year		5,178	396
Disposal of subsidiary			(2,464) *(W9)*
Balance at 31 August 2011	10,000	16,472	1,778

(W7) Retained earnings 1/9/10

	€000
Tom (10,110 − 1,860)	8,250
Dick (4,890 − 980−1,500) × 80%	1,928
Harry (4,660 − 1,000 − 1,800) × 60%	1,116
	11,294

(W8) Non-controlling Interests at 1/9/10

	€000
Net assets of Dick (8,890 – 980) × 20%	1,582
Net assets of Harry (6,660 – 1,000) × 40%	2,264
	3,846

(W9) Disposal of subsidiary (NCI share)

	€000
Net assets of Harry at disposal date 6,660 − (1,000 × 6/12)	6,160
× 40%	2,464

Appendix 1

Exam-style Questions and Solutions

The revision questions that follow are designed to revise the principles outlined in Chapters 3–9 inclusive and to gain experience in answering questions from examination papers of professional accountancy institutes.

OUTLINE OF QUESTIONS

An outline of the questions is as follows:

Question A

Sumo Plc *(Chartered Accountants Ireland, CAP 2, Summer 2010 Question 2)*
Requirements The preparation and presentation of a consolidated:
(a) Statement of financial position;
(b) Statement of changes in equity;
(c) Statement of comprehensive income;
of a parent, a subsidiary and an associate with 'complications'.

Note: The retained earnings of the subsidiary are not given in the question; they must be calculated.

Question B

Pink Plc
Requirement The preparation and presentation of a consolidated statement of financial position of a parent and two directly owned subsidiaries and including 'complications'.

Question C

Clock Plc *(Institute of Certified Public Accountants in Ireland (CPA), Professional 1 Stage 1 Corporate Reporting Examination (August 2010))*
Requirements:
(a) The calculation of goodwill on consolidation when valuing the non-controlling interests at fair value at the date of acquisition.
(b) The preparation and presentation of a statement of comprehensive income for the Clock Plc group which involves numerous adjustments.

Question D

Patch Plc
Requirements The preparation and presentation of a consolidated:
(a) Statement of financial position;

(b) Statement of comprehensive income;
(c) Statement of changes in equity;
of a parent and subsidiary **where the subsidiary is purchased with the intention of resale.**

Question A

(Chartered Accountants Ireland, P3 Summer 2010, Question 2)

SUMO Plc ("SUMO"), an Irish company that prepares its financial statements to 31 December each year, is involved in the manufacture of kit cars. On 1 January 2009, SUMO purchased 800,000 of the €/£ 1 ordinary shares in COBRA Ltd ("COBRA") for cash, a company that specialises in the manufacture of chassis. The fair value of COBRA's net assets was the same as their book value except for plant and equipment that was understated by €/£400,000. COBRA has not reflected this in its financial statements at 31 December 2009.

On 1 July 2009, SUMO purchased 300,000 of the €/£1 ordinary shares in VIPER Ltd ("VIPER") for cash, a company that manufactures customised exhaust systems. On this date, the fair value of VIPER's net assets was the same as their book value.

Statement of Comprehensive Income
for the year ended 31 December 2009

	SUMO €/£000	COBRA €/£000	VIPER €/£000
Revenue	15,000	2,500	1,000
Cost of sales	(9,000)	(1,250)	(350)
Gross profit	6,000	1,250	650
Operating expenses	(2,200)	(250)	(150)
Operating profit	3,800	1,000	500
Investment income	160	-	-
Profit before tax	3,960	1,000	500
Income tax expense	(1,200)	(300)	(120)
Profit after tax	2,760	700	380

Statement of Financial Position
as at 31 December 2009

	SUMO €/£000	COBRA €/£000	VIPER €/£000
ASSETS			
Non-current Assets			
Plant and equipment	12,000	2,500	2,000
Investment in COBRA	2,250	-	-
Investment in VIPER	750	-	-
Current Assets			
Inventory	1,800	250	100
Receivables	1,200	150	60
Bank and cash	200	50	30
	18,200	2,950	2,190

EQUITY AND LIABILITIES			
Equity Attributable to Owners			
€/£1 ordinary shares	10,000	1,000	1,000
Share premium	1,000	200	100
Retained earnings	5,200	1,460	980
Current Liabilities			
Trade payables	1,100	50	60
Dividends payable	500	200	–
Other payables	400	40	50
	18,200	2,950	2,190

Additional information:

1. In October 2009, COBRA sold goods to SUMO with an invoice value of €/£400,000 on which COBRA made a mark up of 25%. One half of these goods remained in SUMO's inventory at 31 December 2009. There was no other trading between SUMO, COBRA and VIPER during 2009.
2. None of the three companies has issued or cancelled shares since incorporation. Each of the companies depreciates plant and equipment on a straight-line basis at 25% per annum, with depreciation being reflected in operating expenses.
3. With respect to the measurement of non-controlling interests at the date of acquisition of COBRA, the proportionate share method equates to the fair value method. The directors of SUMO are confident that any goodwill arising on the acquisition of COBRA and VIPER had not been impaired at 31 December 2009.
4. The shareholders of SUMO and COBRA approved the proposed dividends in December 2009. These were paid in 2010.
5. The activities and profits of the three companies accrue evenly throughout the year.

Requirement Prepare the consolidated statements of comprehensive income and changes in equity for the year ended 31 December 2009 of SUMO and the consolidated statement of financial position as at that date.

Question B

The following are the statements of financial position of Pink Plc, Saffron Ltd and Scarlet Ltd as at 30 June 2011:

	Pink Plc	Saffron Ltd	Scarlet Ltd
	€000	€000	€000
Assets			
Non-current assets			
Property, plant and equipment	11,140	8,510	6,380
Investment in Saffron Ltd	4,700	–	–
Investment in Scarlet Ltd	3,800	–	
	19,640	8,510	6,380
Current assets	4,670	3,730	2,800
Total assets	**24,310**	**12,240**	**9,180**

Equity and liabilities			
Equity			
Ordinary shares €1	10,000	4,000	2,000
Retained earnings	10,110	4,890	4,660
Total equity	20,110	8,890	6,660
Current liabilities	4,200	3,350	2,520
Total equity and liabilities	**24,310**	**12,240**	**9,180**

Additional information:

1. Pink Plc acquired 80% of the ordinary shares of Saffron Ltd on 1 September 2009 when the retained earnings of Saffron Ltd were €2 million.
2. Pink Plc acquired 60% of the ordinary shares of Scarlet Ltd on 1 January 2011.
3. The profit of Scarlet Ltd for the year ended 30 June 2011 amounted to €1,800,000.
4. At 30 June 2011 the receivables of Pink Plc include an amount of €60,000 due from Scarlet Ltd while the corresponding payable in the SoFP of Scarlet Ltd was €40,000. Pink Plc despatched goods at invoice value €20,000 on the reporting date on which it gained a mark-up of $33^1/_3$%. Scarlet Ltd did not receive the goods until 4 July 2011.

Requirement Prepare the consolidated statement of financial position at 30 June 2011.

Question C

(Institute of Certified Public Accountants in Ireland, Autumn 2010)

Clock Plc prepares its financial statements to 30 June each year. On 1 July 2008, Clock Plc purchased 75% of the issued share capital of Mouse Ltd by issuing two shares in Clock PLC for every four shares in Mouse Ltd. The market value of Clock Plc's shares at 1 July 2008 was €4 per share. At the date of acquisition, Mouse Ltd had 10 million €1 ordinary shares and retained earnings of €9 million.

On 1 January 2009, Clock Plc acquired 30% of the shares of Tick Ltd for €3 each. Tick Ltd's issued share capital at 1 January 2009 was 4 million €1 ordinary shares.

The draft Statements of Comprehensive Income for the three companies for the year ended 30 June 2009 are as follows:

	Clock Plc	**Mouse Ltd**	**Tick Ltd**
	€000	**€000**	**€000**
Revenue	32,600	18,200	6,000
Cost of sales	(18,400)	(11,400)	(2,800)
Gross profit	14,200	6,800	3,200
Other income	3,100	1,800	200
Operating expenses	(6,400)	(2,100)	(1,400)
Operating profit	10,900	6,500	2,000
Interest payable and similar charges	(1,800)	(1,400)	(600)
Profit before tax	9,100	5,100	1,400
Taxation	(2,100)	(1,800)	(300)
Profit for the year	7,000	3,300	1,100

Additional information:

1. The fair value of the net assets of Mouse Ltd at the date of acquisition was equal to their carrying value with the exception of land. The land had a fair value of €1m below its carrying value and this has not changed since the date of acquisition.
2. At 30 June 2009, the fair value of Mouse Ltd's specialist plant and equipment was €600,000 in excess of its carrying value. The remaining useful life of these assets is four years and Mouse Ltd has not reflected this fair value in its financial statements.
3. Sales by Clock Plc to Mouse Ltd, in the year to 30 June 2009, amounted to €3.2 million. Clock Plc made a profit of cost plus a third on all sales. Mouse Ltd's year-end inventory includes €1.2 million in relation to purchases from Clock Plc.
4. Included in Mouse Ltd's operating expenses is an amount of €500,000 in respect of management charges invoiced and included in revenue by Clock Plc.
5. Clock Plc's policy is to value the non-controlling interest at fair value at the date of acquisition. At the date of acquisition, the goodwill attributable to the non-controlling interest was €200,000.
6. All profits and losses are deemed to accrue evenly throughout the year.

Requirements

(a) Calculate the goodwill arising on the acquisition of Mouse Ltd.

(b) Prepare a consolidated Statement of Comprehensive Income for the Clock group for the year ended 30 June 2009.

Question D

Patch Plc (Patch) acquired 80% of the ordinary share capital of Stitch Ltd (Stitch) for €160,000 on 1 August 2010, with the intention of resale. There have been no changes in the issued share capital of Stitch since that date. The following balances are extracted from the books of the two companies at 31 July 2011:

	Patch	**Stitch**
	€000	**€000**
Assets		
Non-current Assets		
Property, plant and equipment	218	160
Investment in Stitch	160	–
	378	160
Current Assets		
Inventories	111	65
Trade receivables	30	15
Cash	19	2
	160	82
Total assets	**538**	**242**
Equity and liabilities		
Equity		
Ordinary shares (€1)	300	100
Share premium	20	10

General reserve	68	15
Retained earnings	50	55
	438	180
Current Liabilities		
Trade payables	50	32
Taxation	50	30
	100	62
Total equity and liabilities	**538**	**242**

Additional information:

1. At 1 August 2010 the balances on the reserves of Stitch were as follows:

	€000
Share premium	10
General reserve	20
Retained profits	30

2. At the date of acquisition of Stitch the fair values of the net assets were the same as their carrying values with the exception of Property, plant and equipment:

	€000
Carrying value	140
Fair value (less cost to sell)	120

3. At 30/07/11 the carrying value of the inventory of Stitch exceeded the fair value (less cost to sell) by €10,000.
4. Statements of comprehensive income year ended 31 July 2011

	Patch €000	Stitch €000
Revenue	600	500
Cost of sales	(420)	(350)
Gross profit	180	150
Operating expenses	(90)	(80)
Profit before tax	90	70
Income tax expense	(60)	(45)
Profit for the year	30	25
Other comprehensive income	nil	nil
Total comprehensive income for the year	30	25

SOLUTIONS

Solution to Question A

Group structure

		Cobra		Viper
Group	800/1,000	80%	300/1,000	30%
Non-controlling interests		20%		

Journal adjustments

	€000	€000
1. Dr. Plant & equipment	400	
Cr. Cost of control (80%)		320
Cr. Non-controlling interests (20%)		80
Recognising fair value at acquisition date		
2. Dr. Retained earnings (Cobra)	100	
Cr. Plant & equipment		100
Depreciation on surplus for 1 year		
3. Dr. Retained earnings (Cobra)	40	
Cr. Inventory		40
Unrealised profit 400 × $^1/_5$ × $^1/_2$.		
4. Dr. Dividends payable	160	
Cr. Receivables		160
Cancellation of intragroup dividend		
5 Dr. Investment in Viper	57	
Cr. Retained earnings (Sumo)		57
Share of post-acquisition profit of Viper		
380 × $^6/_{12}$ × 30%		

Workings (T account method)

Plant and Equipment

S	12,000	Journal 2	100
C	2,500		
Journal 1	400	SoFP	14,800
	14,900		14,900

Investment in Cobra

S	2,250	Cost of control	2,250

Investment in Viper

S	750		
Journal 5	57	SoFP	807
	807		807

Inventories

S	1,800	Journal 3	40
C	250	SoFP	2,010
	2,050		2,050

Receivables

S	1,200	Journal 4	160
C	150	SoFP	1,190
	1,350		1,350

Bank and Cash

S	200		
C	50	SoFP	250
	250		250

Ordinary Shares

Cost of control 80%	800	S	10,000
NCI 20%	200	C	1,000
SoFP	10,000		
	11,000		11,000

Share Premium

Cost of control 80% × 200	160	S	1,000
NCI 20% × 200	40	C	200
SoFP	1,000		
	1,200		1,200

Retained Earnings

Journal 2 Cobra	100	S	5,200
Journal 3 Cobra	40	C	1,460
Cost of control *(W1)*	768		
NCI *(W2)*	264	Journal 5 Sumo	57
SoFP	5,545		
	6,717		6,717

(Wa)

	€000
Retained earnings Cobra at year end	1,460
Retained earnings for year (700 − 200)	500
Retained earnings at acquisition date	960
Group's share 80%	768

(Wb)

	€000
Retained earnings Cobra at year end	1,460
Journal 2: additional depreciation	(100)
Journal 3: unrealised profit	(40)
	1,320 × 20% = 264

Trade Payables

		S	1,100
SoFP	1,150	C	50
	1,150		1,150

Dividends Payable

Journal 4	160	S	500
SoFP – non-controlling interest	40	C	200
SoFP – owners of parent	500		
	700		700

Other Payables

		S	400
SoFP	440	C	40
	440		440

Cost of Control

Investment in C	2,250	Journal 1	320
		Ord. shares	800
		Share premium	160
		Retained earnings	768
		SoFP – goodwill	202
	2,250		2,250

Non-controlling Interests

		Journal 1	80
		Ord. shares	200
		Share premium	40
SoFP	584	Retained earnings	264
	584		584

Workings (Columnar Method)

	Sumo €000	Cobra €000	Adjustments €000	Consol. SoFP €000
Plant and equipment	12,000	2,500	400 (100)	14,800
Investment in Cobra	2,250		(2,250)	
Goodwill *(W1)*			202	202
Investment in Viper	750		57	807
Inventory	1,800	250	(40)	2,010
Receivables	1,200	150	(160)	1,190
Bank and cash	200	50		250
Total Assets	**18,200**	**2,950**	**(1,891)**	**19,259**
Ordinary shares	10,000	1,000	(1,000)	10,000
Share premium *(W2)*	1,000	200	(200)	1,000
Retained earnings *(W3)*	5,200	1,460	(1,115)	5,545
Non-controlling interests *(W4)*			584	584
Trade payables	1,100	50		1,150
Dividends payable	500	200	(160)	540
Other payables	400	40		440
Total Equity and Liabilities	**18,200**	**2,950**	**(1,891)**	**19,259**

(W1)
Goodwill

	€000	€000
Cost of investment in Cobra		2,250
Cobra at acquisition date		
Ordinary shares	1,000	
Share premium	200	
Retained earnings *(Wa)*	960	
Revaluation surplus	400	
	2,560	
Group's share 80%		2,048
SoFP		202

(W2)
Share premium

	€000	€000
Sumo at reporting date		1,000
Cobra at reporting date	200	
acquisition date	200	
post-acquisition	nil	
Group's share 80%		nil
SoFP		1,000

(W3)
Retained earnings

	€000	€000
Sumo at reporting date		5,200
Journal 5 – share of Viper post-acq.		57
Cobra at reporting date	1,460	
Journal 2-additional depreciation	(100)	
Journal 3-unrealised inventory profit	(40)	
	1,320	
Cobra at acquisition date *(Wa)*	960	
Post-acquisition	360	
Group's share 80%		288
SoFP		5,545

(W4)
NCI

	€000	€000
Revaluation surplus Journal 1		80
Cobra at reporting date		
Ordinary shares	1,000	
Share premium	200	
Retained earnings as per *(W3)*	1,320	
	2,520	
× 20%		504
SoFP		584

Sumo Plc
CONSOLIDATED STATEMENT OF FINANCIAL POSITION
as at 31 December 2009

	€000
Assets	
Non-current assets	
Plant and equipment	14,800
Goodwill	202
Investment in associate	807
	15,809

	€000
Current assets	
Inventory	2,010
Receivables	1,190
Bank and cash	250
	3,450
Total assets	**19,259**
Equity and liabilities	
Equity	
Ordinary share capital	10,000
Share premium	1,000
Retained earnings	5,545
Total shareholders' equity	16,545
Non-controlling interests	584
Total equity	17,129
Current liabilities	
Trade payables	1,150
Dividends payable	540
Other payables	440
	2,130
Total equity and liabilities	**19,259**

SoCI Workings

	Sumo	**Cobra**	**Adjustments**	**Consol. SoCI**
	€000	**€000**	**€000**	**€000**
Revenue	15,000	2,500	(400)	17,100
Cost of sales	9,000	1,250	(400) 40	(9,890)
Gross profit	6,000	1,250	(40)	7,210
Operating expenses	(2,200)	(250)	(100)	(2,550)
Share of profit of associate			57	57
Profit before tax	3,800	1,000	(83)	4,717
Income tax expense	1,200	300		(1,500)
Profit for the year	2,600	700	(83)	3,217

Sumo Plc

Consolidated Statement of Comprehensive Income
for the year ended 31 December 2009

	€000
Revenue	17,100
Cost of sales	(9,890)
Gross profit	7,210
Operating expenses	(2,550)
Share of profit of associate	57
Profit before tax	4,717
Income tax expense	(1,500)

Profit for the year	3,217
Other comprehensive income	nil
Total comprehensive income for the year	3,217
Profit for the year attributable to:	
Owners of the parent	3,105
Non-controlling interests *(W5)*	112
	3,217
Total comprehensive income for the year attributable to:	
Owners of the parent	3,105
Non-controlling interests *(W5)*	112
	3,217

(W5) Non-controlling interests

	€000
Cobra–profit after tax	700
Additional depreciation	(100)
Unrealised profit	(40)
	560 × 20% = 112

Sumo Plc
CONSOLIDATED STATEMENT OF CHANGES IN EQUITY
for the year ended 31 December 2009

	Ord. Shares €000	Share Premium €000	Retained Earnings' €000	NCI €000	Total €000
Balance at 1 January 2009	10,000	1,000	2,940 *(W6)*	–	13,940
Acquisitions				472	472
Proposed dividend			(500)		(500)
TCI for the year			3,105	112	3,217
Balance at 31 December 2009	10,000	1,000	5,545	584	17,129

(W6) Retained earnings 1/1/2009

	€000	€000
Sumo (5,200 − 2,260)	2,940	
Cobra	nil	
Viper	nil	2,940

Cobra and Viper cannot be included in the group retained earnings at the start of the year as both were acquired during the reporting year.

Solution to Question B

SOLUTION NOTES

1. Even though Pink Plc has two subsidiaries:
   - Use **one** cost of control account
   - Use **one** non-controlling interest account

2. The investments by Pink Plc in Saffron Ltd and Scarlet Ltd are both direct investments, therefore, they are debited in full to cost of control when calculating goodwill or a gain from a bargain purchase.
3. Scarlet Ltd was acquired during the year under review, therefore its retained earnings at the date of acquisition are not given – this is a frequent issue in examination questions. The figure must be calculated as follows:

	€000
Retained earnings at 30 June 2011	4,660
Less profit for year × 6/12	900
Retained earnings at 1 January 2011	3,760

Group structure:

	Saffron	Scarlet
Group	80%	60%
NCI	20%	40%

Journal Entries

	€000	€000
1. Dr. Inventory (cost price)	15	
Dr. Retained earnings (profit)	5	
Cr. Receivables		20
2. Dr. Payables	40	
Cr. Receivables		40

Workings (T account Method)

Property, Plant and Equipment

Pink	11,140		
Safron	8,510		
Scarlet	6,380	SoFP	26,030
	26,030		26,030

Investment in Saffron

Pink	4,700	Cost of control	4,700

Investment in Scarlet

Pink	3,800	Cost of control	3,800

Current Assets

Pink	4,670		
Saffron	3,730	Journal 1	20
Scarlet	2,800	Journal 2	40
Journal 1	15	SoFP	11,155
	11,215		11,215

Ordinary Shares

Cost of control (80%)	3,200	Pink	10,000
NCI (20%)	800	Saffron	4,000
Cost of control (60%)	1,200	Scarlet	2,000
NCI (40%)	800		
SoFP	10,000		
	16,000		16,000

Current Liabilities

Journal 2	40	Pink	4,200
		Saffron	3,350
SoFP	10,030	Scarlet	2,520
	10,070		10,070

Retained Earnings

Journal 1 (Pink)	5		
Cost of Control (Saffron) (80% × 2000)	1,600	Pink	10,110
		Saffron	4,890
Cost of Control (Scarlet) (60% × 3760)	2,256	Scarlet	4,660
		Gain from bargain purchase	100
NCI Saffron (20% × 4890)	978		
NCI Scarlet (40% × 4660)	1,864		
SoFP	13,057		
	19,760		19,760

Cost of Control

Inv. in Saffron	4,700	Ord.shares – Saffron	3,200
Inv. in Scarlet	3,800	– Scarlet	1,200
Gain from bargain purchase	100	Ret. earnings – Saffron	1,600
		– Scarlet	2,256
		SoFP Goodwill	344
	8,600		8,600

Non-controlling Interests

		Ord. shares – Saffron	800
		– Scarlet	800
		Ret. earnings – Saffron	978
SoFP	4,442	– Scarlet	1,864
	4,442		4,442

Workings (Columnar method)

	Pink	Saffron	Scarlet	Adjs.	Consol. SoFP
	€000	**€000**	**€000**	**€000**	**€000**
Property, plant & equip.	11,140	8,510	6,380		26,030
Investment in Saffron	4,700			(4700)	–
Investment in Scarlet	3,800			(3800)	–
Goodwill *(W1)*				344	344
Current assets	4,670	3,730	2,800	15 (20) (40)	11,155
Total assets	**24,310**	**12,240**	**9,180**	**(8201)**	**37,529**
Ordinary share capital	10,000	4,000	2,000	(6,000)	10,000
Retained earnings *(W2)*	10,110	4,890	4,660	(6,603)	13,057
Non-controlling int. *(W3)*				4,442	4,442
Current liabilities	4,200	3,350	2,520	(40)	10,030
Total equity and liabilities	**24,310**	**12,240**	**9,180**	**(8201)**	**37,529**

(W1) Goodwill

	€000	**€000**
Cost of investment in Saffron		4,700
Saffron at acquisition date		
Ordinary shares	4,000	
Retained earnings	2,000	
	6,000	
Group's share 80%		4,800
Gain from bargain purchase transferred to retained earnings Pink		100
Investment in Scarlet		3,800
Scarlet at acquisition date		
Ordinary shares	2,000	
Retained earnings	3,760	
	5,760	
Group's share 60%		3,456
SoFP		344

(W2) Retained earnings

		€000		€000
Pink at reporting date				10,110
Less profit on goods in transit				(5)
Gain from bargain purchase of Saffron				100
Saffron	at reporting date	4,890		
	at acquisition date	2,000		
	post-acquisition	2,890	× 80%	2,312
Scarlet	at reporting date	4,660		
	at acquisition date	3,760		
	post-acquisition	900	× 60%	540
SoFP				13,057

(W3) Non-controlling interests

	€000	€000
Saffron at reporting date		
Ordinary shares	4,000	
Retained earnings	4,890	
	8,890 × 20%	1,778
Scarlet at reporting date		
Ordinary shares	2,000	
Retained earnings	4,660	
	6,660 × 40%	2,664
SoFP		4,442

Pink Plc
CONSOLIDATED STATEMENT OF FINANCIAL POSITION
as at 30 June 2011

	€000
Assets	
Non current assets	
Property, plant and equipment	26,030
Goodwill	344
	26,374
Current assets	11,155
Total assets	**37,529**
Equity and liabilities	
Equity	
Ordinary shares	10,000
Retained earnings	13,057
Total shareholders equity	23,057
Non-controlling interests	4,442
Total equity	27,499
Current liabilities	10,030
Total equity and liabilities	**37,529**

Solution to Question C

SOLUTION NOTES

1. Mouse Ltd is a 75% owned subsidiary of Clock Plc which was acquired on the opening day of the reporting year. The results of Mouse for the full year can be consolidated.
2. Tick Ltd is a 30% owned associate which was acquired half way through the reporting year. The amount to be consolidated using the equity method is:
   Profit after tax €1,100,000 × $^{6}/_{12}$ × 30% = €165,000
3. Cost of investment in Mouse
   10,000,000 × $^{2}/_{4}$ × 75% × €4 = €15,000,000

(a) Calculate the goodwill on acquisition of Mouse Ltd:
Journal Entries

	€000	€000
(i) Dr. Cost of control	750	
Dr. Non-controlling interest	250	
Cr. PPE		1,000
With reduction to fair value of land		
(ii) Dr. Goodwill	200	
Cr. Non-controlling interests		200
Goodwill attributable to NCI at acquisition date		

WORKINGS (T account method)

Cost of Control

Investment in M	15,000	Ord. shares (75% × 10,000)	7,500
Journal 1	750	Ret. Earnings (75% × 9,000)	6,750
		Transfer goodwill	1,500
	15,750		15,750

Goodwill

Cost of control	1,500		
NCI	200	SoFP	1,700
	1,700		1,700

WORKINGS (Columnar method)

	€000	€000
Cost of investment		15,000
Mouse at acquisition date		
Ordinary shares	10,000	
Retained earnings	9,000	
Revaluation of land to fair value	(1,000)	
	18,000	
Group's share 75%		13,500
Goodwill attributable to parent		1,500
Goodwill attributable to NCI		200
Total goodwill		1,700

(b) Adjustments for consolidated SoCE:

1. Land revaluation: no adjustment is necessary as land is not depreciated.
2. Other comprehensive income of €600,000 must be shown in the consolidated SoCI of which 25% (€150,000) is attributable to the non-controlling interests.
3. Reduce Revenue and Cost of Sales by intragroup sales €3,200,000.
   Increase Clock's Cost of Sales by unrealised inventory profit €1,200,000 × $^1/_4$ = €300,000.
4. Reduce Revenue (Clock) and Operating Expenses (Mouse) by management fees €500,000.

CONSOLIDATED SoCI WORKINGS

	Clock €000	Mouse €000	Adjustments €000	Consol. SoCI €000
Revenue	32,600	18,200	(3,200) (500)	47,100
Cost of sales	18,400	11,400	(3,200) 300	(26,900)
Gross profit	14,200	6,800	(800)	20,200
Other income	3,100	1,800		4,900
Operating expenses	(6,400)	(2,100)	500	(8,000)
Finance costs	(1,800)	(1,400)		(3,200)
Share of profit of associate			165	165
Profit before tax	9,100	5,100	(135)	14,065
Income tax expense	(2,100)	(1,800)		(3,900)
Profit for the year	7,000	3,300	(135)	10,165

CONSOLIDATED STATEMENT OF COMPREHENSIVE INCOME
for the year ended 30 June 2009

	€000
Revenue	47,100
Cost of sales	(26,900)
Gross profit	20,200
Other income	4,900
Operating expenses	(8,000)
Finance costs	(3,200)
Share of profit of associate	165
Profit before tax	14,065
Income tax expense	(3,900)
Profit for the year	10,165
Other comprehensive income	
Revaluation gain on property, plant and equipment	600
Total comprehensive income for the year	10,765
Profit for the year attributable to:	
Owners of the parent	9,340
Non-controlling interests *(W1)*	825
	10,165
Total comprehensive income for the year attributable to:	
Owners of the parent	9,790
Non-controlling interests *(W2)*	975
	10,765

(W1)

	€000	€000
Profit after tax Mouse	3300 × 25%	825

(W2)

As per (W1)	825
Revaluation gain (600 × 25%)	150
	975

Solution to Question D

Solution Notes

When a subsidiary is acquired with the intention of resale the consolidation procedures are the same as usual but the presentation in the consolidated financial statements is significantly different in accordance with IFRS 5 *Non-current Assets Held for Sale and Discontinued Operations* thus:

1. In the consolidated SoCI the results of the subsidiary are shown as a single line item as follows:
   Profit/Loss on discontinued operation €X
2. In the consolidated SoFP the total assets and liabilities of the subsidiary are each reported as a single line item as follows:
   Assets held for sale €X
   Liabilities held for sale (€X)

Journal Entries:

		€000	€000
1.	Dr. Cost of control	16	
	Dr. NCI	4	
	Cr. Property, plant and equipment		20
	With revaluation at acquisition date		
2.	Dr. Retained earnings – S	10	
	Cr. Inventory		10
	With revaluation at reporting date		

Workings (T account method)

Property, Plant and Equipment

P	218	Journal 1	20
S	160	SoFP	218
		SoFP held for sale	140
	378		378

Investment in Stitch

P	160	Cost of control	160

Inventories

P	111	Journal 2	10
S	65	SoFP	111
		SoFP held for sale	55
	176		176

Receivables

P	30	SoFP	30
S	15	SoFP held for sale	15
	45		45

Cash

P	19	SoFP	19
S	2	SoFP held for sale	2
	21		21

Ordinary Shares

Cost of control 80%	80	P	300
NCI 20%.	20	S	100
SoFP	300		
	400		400

Share Premium

Cost of control	8	P	20
NCI	2	S	10
SoFP	20		
	30		30

General Reseves

CoC (80% × 20)	16	P	68
NCI (20% × 15).	3	S	15
SoFP	64		
	83		83

Retained Earnings

Journal 2 (S)	10	P	50
Cost of control (80% × 30)	24	S	55
NCI 20% (55 - 10)	9		
SoFP	62		
	105		105

Cost of Control

Investment in S.	160	Ord. shares	80
Journal 1	16	Sh. premium	8
		Gen. reserves	16
		Ret.earnings	24
		SoFP goodwill	48
	176		176

Non-controlling Interests

Journal 1	4	Ord. shares	20
		Sh. premium	2
SoFP	30	Gen. reserves	3
		Ret. earnings	9
	34		34

Payables

SoFP	50	P	50
SoFP held for sale	32	S	32
	82		82

Taxation

SoFP	50	P	50
SoFP held for sale	30	S	30
	80		80

Workings (Columnar method)

	Patch	Stitch	Adjustments	Consol. SoFP	Consol. SoFP Held for sale
	€000	**€000**	**€000**	**€000**	**€000**
PPE	218	160	(20)	218	140
Investment in S	160		(160)		
Goodwill *(W1)*			48	48	
Inventories	111	65	(10)	111	55
Receivables	30	15		30	15
Cash	19	2		19	2
Total assets	**538**	**242**	**(142)**	**426**	**212**
Ordinary shares	300	100	(100)	300	
Share premium *(W2)*	20	10	(10)	20	
General reserve *(W3)*	68	15	(19)	64	
Retained earnings *(W4)*	50	55	(43)	62	
Non-controlling interests *(W4)*			30	30	
Payables	50	32		50	32
Taxation	50	30		50	30
Total equity and liabilities	**538**	**242**	**(142)**	**576**	**62**

(W1) Goodwill

	€000	€000
Cost of investment		160
Stitch at acquisition date:		
Ordinary shares	100	
Share premium	10	
General reserve	20	
Retained earnings	30	
Revaluation deficit on PPE	(20)	
	140	
Group's share 80%		112
SoFP		48

(W2) Share premium

	€000	€000
Patch at reporting date		20
Stitch at reporting date	10	
at acquisition date	10	
post-acquisition	nil × 80%	nil
SoFP		20

(W3) General reserve

	€000	€000
Patch at reporting date		68
Stitch at reporting date	15	
at acquisition date	20	
post-acquisition	(5) × 80%	(4)
SoFP		64

(W4) Retained earnings

Patch at reporting date		50
Revaluation deficit on inventory × 80%		(8)
Stitch at reporting date	55	
at acquisition date	30	
post-acquisition	25 × 80%	20
SoFP		62

(W5) NCI

	€000	€000
Stitch at reporting date		
Ordinary shares	100	
Share premium	10	
General reserve	15	
Retained earnings	55	
Revaluation deficit on inventory	(10)	
	170 × 20%	34
Share of PPE deficit at acquisition date		(4)
SoFP		30

Consolidated Statement of Financial Position
as at 31 July 2011

Assets	**€000**
Non-Current Assets	
Property, plant and equipment	218
	218
Current Assets	
Inventory	111
Receivables	30
Cash	19
	160
Assets held for sale	260
Total assets	**638**
Equity and liabilities	
Equity	
Ordinary share capital	300
Share premium	20
General reserve	64
Retained earnings	62
Total shareholders' equity	446
Non-controlling interests	30
Total equity	476
Current liabilities	100
Liabilities held for sale	62
Total equity and liabilities	**638**

Consolidated Statement of Comprehensive Income
for the year ended 31 July 2011

	€000
Revenue	600
Cost of sales	(420)
Gross profit	180
Operating expenses	(90)
Profit before tax	90
Income tax expense	(60)
Profit after tax	30
Profit on discontinued operation (25 – 10)	15
Profit for the year	45
Other comprehensive income	nil
Total comprehensive income for the year	45

Profit for the year attributable to	
Owners of the parent – from continuing operations	30
– from discontinued operations	12
Non-controlling interests – from continuing operations	–
– from discontinued operations	3
	45

Total comprehensive income for the year attributable to	
Owners of the parent – from continuing operations	30
– from discontinued operations	12
Non-controlling interests – from continuing operations	–
– from discontinued operations	3
	45

Consolidated Statement of Changes in Equity
for the year ended 31 July 2011

	Share Capital €000	Share Premium €000	General Reserve €000	Retained Earnings €000	NCI €000
Balance at 1 August 2010				20*	–
Acquisition	300	20	64		27
TCI for the year				42	3

(*Stitch was acquired during the reporting period, therefore there were no post-acquisition profits at 1 August 2010. Stitch can not be included in the opening retained earnings.)